W9-AMU-067

4/18/09

CHURCH

ADMINISTRATION

HANDBOOK

CHURCH
ADMINISTRATION
HANDBOOK

Third Edition · Revised and Updated

BRUCE P. POWERS

EDITOR

NASHVILLE, TENNESSEE

Copyright © 2008
by Bruce P. Powers
All rights reserved
Printed in the United States of America

978-0-8054-4490-2

Published by B&H Publishing Group
Nashville, Tennessee

Dewey Decimal Classification: 254
Subject Heading: CHURCH ADMINISTRATION

Scripture quotations are marked as follows: KJV, the King James Version of the Bible; NASB, the New American Standard Bible, © the Lockman Foundation, 1960, 1962, 1963, 1968, 1971, 1972, 1973, 1975, 1977, used by permission; NEB, The New English Bible, © The Delegates of the Oxford University Press and the Syndics of the Cambridge University Press, 1961, 1970, reprinted with permission; NRSV, New Revised Standard Version of the Bible, copyright © 1989 by the Division of Christian Education of the National Council of Churches of Christ in the United States of America, used by permission, all rights reserved. Phillips, reprinted with permission of Macmillan Publishing Co., Inc., from J. B. Phillips: The New Testament in Modern English, revised edition, © J. B. Phillips 1958, 1960, 1972; and the RSV, Revised Standard Version of the Bible, copyrighted 1946, 1952, © 1971, 1973.

1 2 3 4 5 6 7 8 9 10 11 12 • 16 15 14 13 12 11 10 09 08 07
LB

*Dedicated to the memory of three servant leaders who
represented the best in congregational leadership and church renewal*

*Theodore F. Adams
C. Roy Angell
Findley B. Edge*

MEET THE AUTHORS

WILLIAM G. CALDWELL

Dr. Caldwell is retired distinguished professor of administration, Southwestern Baptist Theological Seminary, Fort Worth, Texas, and trainer for the National Association of Church Business Administrators.

ROBERT D. DALE

Dr. Dale is director of the Leadership Center and retired assistant executive leader of the Baptist General Association of Virginia, Richmond, Virginia.

BOB I. JOHNSON

Dr. Johnson is an intentional interim pastor who served many years as a pastor, as a seminary professor of pastoral ministry, and as dean at Boyce Bible School, Louisville, Kentucky.

BRUCE P. POWERS

Dr. Powers is Langston professor of Christian education and former associate dean for graduate programs, Campbell University Divinity School, Buies Creek, North Carolina.

JAMES T. ROBERSON JR.

Dr. Roberson is dean and professor, Shaw University Divinity School, Raleigh, North Carolina.

JUDY J. STAMEY

Dr. Stamey is associate director of the Church Business Administration Certification Center, Fort Worth, Texas, and trainer for the National Association of Church Business Administrators.

CONTENTS

Section One
How a Minister Relates to Organizations and to People

Section Two
How a Minister Performs Administrative Responsibilities

Section Three
How a Minister Develops Leadership and Ministry Skills

LIST OF FIGURES

PREFACE

Preparation for ministry has been gradually changing for more than thirty years. The first shifts came as churches began to insist that their ministers be prepared not only to know and preach the Bible but also to work effectively in the areas of leadership, administration, and education. Change was slow, but many divinity schools and seminaries embraced the disciplines of pastoral care, evangelism, church administration, and discipleship development. Others resisted and insisted that traditional biblical and theological studies were sufficient.

The curriculum in most theological schools today provides a balance between the classical studies that focus on *knowing* the gospel and practical studies that focus on *doing* the gospel. However, the needs of people and of churches have continued to change, with questions now being raised about the quality of congregational life, the nature of leadership, and responsibility for ministry among *all* believers.

Consequently, effective theological education for the future must have an added dimension—preparing congregational leaders who can help disciples live in and engage a culture that is more diverse and demanding than at any previous time in modern history.

The third edition of this book, therefore, has been refocused. It deals more specifically with leading and transforming those within the congregation as well as those who live in or participate in the life of the community or parish. As we have prepared this edition, we have sought to address five primary needs:

1. leadership skills and administrative tools that can be adapted for use in varied contexts from traditional to contemporary, from rural to urban, and from unicultural to multicultural;
2. spiritual formation that relates to all of life (from birth to death);
3. mission consciousness (in the community, regionally, nationally, and globally);
4. ministry of all believers (particularly calling out and equipping vocational, bivocational, and lay ministers); and

5. leadership competence (the ability to inspire, motivate, and equip the saints for the work of ministry).

The material compiled in this volume is our best effort to guide church leaders and students preparing for ministry into a commitment to the mission of the church in every facet of life and to equip them with theological understanding and administrative skills to develop a *Christ-centered, Bible-based,* and *ministry-focused* congregation.

The content moves sequentially through three broad categories crucial to administrative leadership: (1) how a minister relates to organizations and to people; (2) how a minister performs administrative functions; and (3) how a minister develops leadership and ministry skills. Each chapter provides basic information, then gives guidelines and procedures related to the topic. At the end of the book is a list of resources for further information.

You can study the material systematically from beginning to end, or you can consult chapters topically, as in a reference book. You will find a survey of foundational information and procedures in all major areas. The contents are not intended to be exhaustive but to give sufficient guidance for administrators who then, if specialized assistance is necessary, can go or refer others to the resources listed.

The authors of this volume are well suited to prepare an administrative handbook for church leaders and a textbook for ministerial students. They have served in churches, in denominational administrative positions, and as teachers in theological schools. They are highly respected writers, speakers, and practitioners who believe that administration must support the church through positive, servant leadership among God's people.

I would like to express appreciation to the authors, especially for their common vision of a biblically based, servant-oriented style of leadership that they are sharing at every opportunity; to our colleagues and students who have helped us refine the concepts, values, and skills presented; and to the many denominational and church leaders who reacted to outlines, previewed this material in conferences, and encouraged the publication of this material for others.

I would like to express personal gratitude to Dr. John Landers of B&H Publishing Group, who shepherded this project; to my wife, Jean Clark Powers, who assisted with the technical preparation of the manuscript; and to my colleagues and students who have supported, encouraged, and assisted me during the preparation of the manuscript.

Bruce P. Powers
Campbell University Divinity School
Buies Creek, North Carolina

▣ SECTION ONE ▣

HOW A MINISTER RELATES
TO ORGANIZATIONS
AND TO PEOPLE

Chapter 1

TRANSFORMATIONAL LEADERSHIP IN A TECHNOLOGICAL AGE

Bruce P. Powers and James T. Roberson Jr.

I t is surprising, and sometimes puzzling to church leaders, that the New Testament nowhere provides a definitive description of the church. Rather, the Bible speaks profusely on the nature and mission of the church but always in models and illustrations, never in straightforward definitions. The clearest understanding can be gained from three primary images that have informed church leaders over the centuries.

Understanding the Nature and Purpose of the Church*

The Church as the People of God

The church is sometimes pictured as *the people of God*. This concept has its roots in the Old Testament. God made a covenant with the people of Israel, and they became God's own people (Gen 12:1–3; 17:1–8). Israel understood God's expectations of them but had trouble abiding by them, just as Christians sometimes have difficulty living faithfully by the teachings of Christ.

Upon the faithfulness of Jesus, early Christians declared, God made a new covenant in fulfillment of that foretold by Jeremiah (Rom 11:27) and Joel (Acts 2:16–21). God had not called a new people but transacted a new covenant with his people. They were to be no longer Israel "after the flesh" but Israel "after the spirit" (Rom 9:6–13). Thus the followers of Jesus Christ, like Israel of the Old Testament, became the people of God—a people charged with the responsibility of sharing the Word that can restore the broken relationship between sinful humanity and a just, loving God.

3

e Church as the Body of Christ

Another image of the church, frequently employed in Paul's letters, is *body of Christ*. This image or model of the church portrays Christ as the head and individual believers, grafted into the body through the redemptive love of Christ, as other parts of the body. As members of the body, different persons are given different gifts, abilities, and functions. Together the members accomplish the work of the body under the direction of Christ, the head. Though the body is characterized by diversity of function, it is unified in purpose and mission.

The Church as the New Humanity

Sometimes the image of the church as the *body of Christ* is combined with the image of the church as the *new humanity*. Both images are frequently found in the writings of Paul, and *new humanity* is especially present in Ephesians and Galatians. God has brought the new humanity into being through the redemptive mission of Jesus Christ. The old humanity consisted of persons who were dead in their trespasses and sins (Eph 2:1). But Christ has raised them up and made them alive. "For we are what he made us, created in Christ Jesus for good works, which God prepared beforehand to be our way of life" (Eph 2:10 NRSV).

As the *new humanity*, the church is the evidence of God's continuing creative activity. It consists of people who have been made new and gifted with the ability to do what the old humanity could not accomplish. Whereas the old humanity was self-centered and rooted in law and judgment, *new humanity* would be God-centered and focused on grace and reconciliation. *New humanity* is God's new creation, made capable of righteousness and love through Jesus Christ.

These images clearly emerge from the New Testament. But take care not to overinterpret them. For example, the *body of Christ* (the church) does not always do the will of the divine head, and it would be inaccurate for some to think that whatever the church did was clearly the same action that Christ himself would undertake if he were present in person.

Similarly, the church as the new humanity does not always show love and righteousness, and it would be disastrous to think of some of the acts of church people as God's will. Sometimes the actions of the *new humanity* are nothing more than sin expressed in its most sinister form—the garb of piety. So each of us must be careful to seek faithfully to follow Christ and to serve one another in love. We must also be quick to recognize our shortcomings with one another and seek forgiveness and reconciliation.

Although the church seldom lives up to everything each image suggests, these models clearly suggest what God intended when the church was brought into being. Once we understand what the church is to be, then we must agree on the purpose of the church and what it is to do.

The Purpose of the Church

Before dealing with the practical issues of congregational leadership, it is important to clarify the purpose of the church. Without clarity in biblical and theological foundations for ministry, techniques and methods can become detached from the very vision that birthed them. A church can drift away from its reason for existence and become a religious country club.

The church is to be a community of persons who are wholeheartedly committed to doing what God wants to be accomplished on earth. This most certainly includes the great commandments, loving God supremely and loving our neighbor as ourselves (Matt 22:37–39). If the church accomplishes its purpose, the result will be more love for God and for humanity. Love of God should result in prayer, devotion, commitment, a sense of piety, and growth in one's spiritual life. Love of neighbor should result in caring, giving, confronting, admonishing, seeking justice, and working for the common good.

Jesus added another commandment at the Last Supper, asking followers to love one another in order to be a positive witness to unbelievers (John 13:34–35). Put together, these commandments suggest that the purpose of the church is to engage in activities consistently described in Scripture that increase the love of God, neighbor, and brothers and sisters in Christ. These activities are often referred to as the functions, or tasks, of the church: *worship, proclamation, education, ministry,* and *fellowship.*

The church brings individuals into community where they contribute to the common good and give encouragement, support, and discipline to one another. This is the *koinonia,* the spiritual fellowship that inspires and enables believers to perform the functions of the church, thereby giving witness to the world. Through and with the help of this community, the church, we share with the world our belief in Jesus Christ, our trust of Scripture, and our best interpretation of how we have experienced and must serve God. It is this message—what we know, believe, and do—that becomes the dominant force as we seek to nurture believers, minister to those in need, and evangelize those who need a Savior.

Each function, or task, of the church is crucial, and none is superior to the others. A church that does mostly worship is no more what God intended than the church that does mostly evangelism. The church that engages in worship and evangelism but does not take seriously the community of fellowship is only doing part of what God intended. All tasks are necessary for the church to fulfill its purpose and claim its identity as the *people of God,* the *new humanity,* and the *body of Christ.*

The Mission of the Church

The *mission* of the church is to achieve the *purpose* of the church—*to be, do, and tell the gospel.* From a biblical viewpoint there generally are two dimensions for evaluating our effectiveness: how individuals respond and how the church responds.

Individual Response

Our effectiveness in relating to individuals must focus on the mandate (1) that belief in Jesus is the only way to God and (2) that believers will keep Christ's commandments. According to John 14:6–17, Jesus described individual responsibility as the essence of faith and practice. One way to evaluate our effectiveness is to look at how those under our influence are responding individually.

This raises two questions: *Are persons expressing belief in Jesus? Is their living consistent with Jesus' teachings?* The degree to which you and the congregation can respond positively to *both* these questions illustrates your or my effectiveness in influencing individuals.

Church Response

Individuals who have responded to the call of God in Christ must then focus on an added dimension to the Christian life: that those who profess Jesus as Lord unite themselves in a body—the church—to carry out God's will. The New Testament knows nothing of a Lone Ranger approach to Christianity. Where the gospel is preached and the lost come to Jesus, it is always as a part of the life and ministry of the church.

Individuals usually profess Christ as Savior after hearing the gospel message and becoming acquainted with believers in a local church. It is in this environment that we relate to others and through which they come to know us. We are saved and come to understand church in this relationship with believers, and we become a part of the church so that we might share personally in its life and work.

But what is the life and work of the church? It is the same as God's call to all Christians: *to be his people and to continue the earthly ministry of Jesus.* The church must be the means through which the eternal purpose of God is declared.

You can evaluate your effectiveness in this area by determining the extent to which those under your influence become involved in the life and work of the church.

What Are the Results?

Our influence, then, cannot be evaluated apart from tangible results—as individuals respond to God and as they involve themselves in a church. Naturally, we would all want to interpret the specific meaning given to the type and quality of tangible results. But the fact remains, as we seek to influence the faith of others, there *is* a response. And that response must be judged by criteria such as those described above.

The question now comes back: *How successful are we in fulfilling the purpose and mission of the church?*

Evaluating Your Witness

How do you and the congregation evaluate your influence as Christian witnesses? If your response is typical, there are some ways in which you have been effective, but there also are areas of shortcoming or, perhaps, areas that had not previously been considered.

The important thing is to recognize the discrepancies that exist between the witness we *want* to share and the witness we *are* sharing with the world. Ideally, these are the same. If they are not, the points of difference represent areas in which the minister(s) and the congregation need to discuss expectations and clarify hopes and dreams for the church's future.

What are we trying to do to people? The bottom line is that we want people to come to faith, grow in faith, serve in faith, and live in faith—just as Jesus taught. The primary job of ministers and of the congregation is to (1) *bring people to Jesus Christ*, and (2) *help them grow in his likeness.* As described in Eph 4:11–13, the task of church leaders is to equip, or prepare, God's people for the work of Christian service. It is the duty of every believer to seek to understand, develop, and use in Christian service the gifts God has provided. It is the job of the church to perform the functions that will enable believers to have a positive witness to the world. *Reaching, teaching,* and *developing* are the key words for what we are trying to do. The *purpose* of the church, ultimately, is to make disciples and lead them to live and serve under the lordship of Christ (v. 15).

Working Together in the Church

One of the primary expectations for ministerial and lay leaders is to provide leadership. This requires being clear about the biblical nature and mission of the church as well as the vision and direction for the life of your congregation. A church's ministerial leadership team and the lay leaders of the church share responsibility for (1) maintaining clarity of purpose and vision for the church and (2) interpreting and assisting the congregation in understanding and supporting the church's purpose and vision.

Developing Productive Partnerships

For ministers and congregations to have long and productive partnerships, there must be consensus about the approach to and style of leadership. This requires ministers and congregational leaders to clarify their commitments during the call and start-up phases as new ministers begin their work and continue to monitor faithfulness among all key leaders to the agreed-upon leadership principles that are central to the life and ministry of the church.

This chapter provides principles on which ministers and congregations must agree. Discussions should be held and covenants made concerning these principles, and these will become the guidelines for working together. Applying the principles will then be entrusted to the ministers and various lay leaders as they work through the church's organizational structure.

Church members have every right to expect that ministers and lay leaders will agree on the purpose, vision, and principles by which their congregation will be led. The leaders also have a corresponding right to expect trust and support as they carry out day-to-day duties and develop and recommend policies and programs to fulfill God's plan for the church. Being clear and together on theological principles—especially purpose, vision, and leadership style—keeps church ministry under the lordship of Christ; being clear also frees ministers and lay leaders to fulfill their duties without reprisal as long as their actions are strongly rooted in the agreed-upon theological principles.

The definition of leadership implies that we are seeking to develop unity in the pursuit of common goals. Ministers and lay leaders usually agree on the church's overall purpose but sometimes disagree on the principals that guide their day-to-day decisions. To avoid conflict and keep a congregation focused on its mission, it is important for leaders to clarify and monitor their faithfulness to agreed-upon doctrine and theological principles for leadership.

Determining the Nonnegotiables

The doctrine and theological principles for Christian leadership presented in this book are the *who* and *why* issues of faith. They are not negotiable and must inform leadership style and strategy in all of church life. Agreement and support on these issues among staff members, lay leaders, and the congregation can be an extremely positive influence in keeping a congregation healthy and happy.

Review the principles in the following section,[1] relating them to the biblical and theological foundations presented above. Decide to what degree you can freely pledge to use each as a guideline for your life and to what degree each principle should be at the heart of the life and ministry of your church. Then, in discussions with the church staff and with lay leaders in the church, jointly share your perceptions and agree on the principles that should guide the life and ministry in your congregation.

Principles for Life and Ministry

1. Principle of Responsible Freedom

We must live and act within the framework of our basic commitments. We are created in the likeness of God to be God's people and to do God's work. Within the guidelines God has given, we are free to develop structures—the means, the ways, the how-tos—for being his people and passing on these basic commitments.

2. Principle of Servant Leadership

Christians are called to grow continually toward the likeness of Christ. This requires understanding and practicing a style of leadership consistent with the teachings of Jesus, caring for and serving others. A major responsibility is involving others in the process of discovering, developing, and using their spiritual gifts in Christian service.

3. Principle of Renewal

Just as in human life, there are cycles in organizations. There are periods of birth, development, peak strength, plateau, and decline. In this process the shift in priority moves inevitably from creating what could be to protecting what is—a subtle change in primary focus from the mission of the church to maintaining its structures. Although the life-cycle phases are sequential, decline and death are not inevitable. With appropriate leadership and God's blessing, a church can be renewed and persons can be redeemed.

4. Principle of Paradox

Mature faith requires that Christians be able to transcend rational thinking, to accept paradoxes. The simplest paradoxes are easy to understand: a child may also be a parent, water may also be ice or vapor, and one who is old may be young. But it takes great faith to accept other paradoxes: last *and* first; sinner *and* saint; judge *and* redeemer; sinfulness *and* goodness; God *and* Jesus; divine *and* human; Father *and* Son; God *is* love; God *is* truth; and the most unlikely possibility—you and I are the body of Christ! The ability to trust beyond human reason is the gift that allows us to have personal contact with God, to experience the mystery and wholeness of the Holy Other.

5. Principle of Acceptance

How we view ourselves and others influences how we seek to lead. Christ gave us the example of accepting ourselves, others, and institutions

9

as imperfect yet potentially good and useful in God's plan. All have potential for redemption.

6. Principle of Discrepancy

Discrepancy is the energizing force that enables us to solve problems and achieve dreams. Motivation and learning function best when people identify for themselves the differences between where they are and where they would like to be, between what is and what might be, between reality and the ideal that Christ has for us. Leading people to recognize discrepancies and act to resolve them is a basic strategy of life-giving leaders.

7. Principle of Authority and Responsibility

In the local church God has delegated authority and responsibility to the body, the church. Biblical teachings about spiritual gifts tell how members of the body are to work together under the lordship of Christ: as the church has affirmed *my* gifts, I am to take initiative and you are to assist. As the church has affirmed *your* gifts, I am to provide support. As we give to and receive from one another, we carry on the life and work for which we have been commissioned.

8. Principle of Unity and Diversity

We find our unity in Christ, his message, and the basic commitments to ministry, mission, and relationship. These are the *ends*, the goals for which the Christian body exists. We find diversity in the *means*, the ways by which we seek to live and pass on our faith. The *ends* of our faith are not negotiable, and people must choose to accept or not. However, the *means* usually are negotiable in order to find the best expression of God's will for a particular congregation. The body of Christ functions effectively when all parts accept their diversity in function yet work together on God's mission.

9. Principle of Inclusiveness

A necessary dimension of our life together requires interdependence among believers. All parts of the body are valuable, contributing to the life and mission of the church: young and old, male and female, doctor and grocery clerk, deacon and nursery worker, ordained and unordained, brown and white and black and yellow. There is no greater or lesser in the sight of God.

10. Principle of Faith, Hope, and Love

This is the underlying principle that holds the other nine together. The qualities of faith, hope, and love must guide application of the other nine principles and permeate the lives of those who seek to be life-givers with Christ.

- *Faith*—the Christian term for knowing the unknowable, seeing the unseeable, touching the untouchable, experiencing the impossible, incarnating the Alpha and Omega—the Beginning and the End.
- *Hope*—the underlying conviction that all can be redeemed, forgiven, made right, work together for good for those who love the Lord.
- *Love*—the glue that binds hearts, minds, and souls—all creation—together in a timeless and spaceless demonstration of Immanuel, God with us!

All Are Necessary

No principle stands alone, nor can it be emphasized to the neglect of others. All ten are the checks and balances for determining leadership strategy and teaching ministry in a local church.

Paradigm Shifts

Apart from major shifts in doctrinal interpretations, denominational alignments, and worship styles that dominated the paradigm shifts during the last century, the church in North America is now being transformed by lesser shifts but ones that hold significant promise for renewal of the church as a missional body. Simply put, the church is on the brink of becoming more like the New Testament image of the body of Christ and the Old Testament image of the people of God.

As illustrated in figure 1.1, the paradigm shifts answer four questions about the twenty-first-century church.

Where Does the Church Do Its Work?

For most of the last century, the church became increasingly centralized. Part of this was the growth in wealth among Christians, and part was the development of programs and ministries designed to operate in particular types of facilities, such as sanctuaries, fellowship halls, recreation centers, and Sunday school classrooms. The church building boom of the last half of the twentieth century created the most visible example of the church being a *place*. This paradigm shift toward missional ministry suggests that, increasingly, congregations and individual Christians are reverting to the concept that the church is *people*, not a place.

The church can be gathered in one place, or it can be scattered in a variety of locations; but it is still the church. Similarly, programs and ministries, once located almost exclusively in the church's facilities, now are located in a variety of facilities and locations, many without direct ownership or control by church authorities. Even so, the church is present because members are dispersed throughout the community providing education, worship, pastoral care, social services, and other church-related programs and ministries on behalf of the home congregation.

Members come and go—gathering with the larger community of faith for corporate worship, training, and fellowship—but returning to their fields of service for evangelism and ministry.

Where does the church do its work? At home *and* in the community.

Who Is Responsible for Leadership in a Church?

Until the first part of the last century, multiple ministers working with a single congregation was rare. The first staff ministers other than pastors were drawn largely from talented lay members, particularly Sunday school leaders.

Although many lay leaders contributed significantly to church life, ordained ministers held primary responsibility for religious leadership in the church and parish/community. Shifts became apparent, however, as the Sunday school movement and other lay-led organizations became more popular and were incorporated into the ministry structure of most churches.

Following World War II, a great recovery of congregational life resulted in growth of churches, development of many new programs and ministries, and a building boom—new churches and new educational facilities.

To meet the need for leaders, many of those who had been lay leaders began serving as staff ministers; they cared for various programs and ministries, provided leadership for age-group ministries, and handled the business and administrative functions of the church. In addition, theological schools began providing degree programs for those desiring to serve in staff positions; students in pastoral ministry and those preparing for a variety of other church and related ministries studied together and earned theological degrees. Thus, those who formerly were called *directors* gradually became associates to the pastor, or ministers of _____ .

Increasingly, churches have *multiple* ministers (including full- and part-time) and many lay leaders. Whereas for the last century churches had a pastor and staff who were responsible for leadership, today there is a major shift toward multiple ministers and lay leaders working together in a *shared ministry* as ministry teams under the guidance of a staff minister. This transition has largely been the result of an emphasis on discipleship training, a growing lay ministry movement, and a conviction that all believers are called to ministry.[2]

Who is responsible for leadership in a church? Ministers *and* teams.

How Is a Church Organized?

Traditionally, the church has been organized in a hierarchy. In fact, during the Middle Ages, this was called a "ladder of perfection." Ordained church leaders were closer to the top, and the common people were at the bottom. In some ways that tradition has influenced modern corporations, businesses, and even churches and denominations. However, Christian theology since the Reformation has focused on the equality of all believers; as disciples, they have the right and responsibility to worship, commune, petition, and serve God directly without any mediator except the Lord Jesus Christ. The hierarchy that we inherited has been crumbling. Today, with the ministry of every believer, organization has been reduced to only the structures and layers necessary to fulfill the mission of the local church. And in denominations and other church-related organizations, the hierarchy of ownership and control that has traditionally governed relationships is for many shifting to affiliations and partnerships.

How is a church organized? It is flat rather than hierarchical with only the organization necessary to fulfill its purpose.

How Does a Church Measure Success?

Depending on denominational and cultural heritage, churches have traditionally measured success by a combination of factors such as baptisms, community influence, buildings, attendance, financial stability, faithfulness of members, and mission support. Essentially for the last fifty years most congregations have been happy when they have had a growing church and good programs.

A growing church is defined as increasing membership, attendance, and contributions. So, when churches are declining rather than growing, ministers and congregations are unhappy.

Good programs attract people, provide a meaningful experience, and bond them to the church. When a program is not functioning well, people don't attend, and the purpose of the program or ministry is thwarted. When programs are dying, the church is dying, and ministers and congregations are unhappy.

Today churches still measure success by whether the church is growing. But the theological understanding of church has added additional criteria beyond membership and giving, such as spiritual growth, growth in service, and growth in understanding and application of biblical principles. Yes, today's ministers and congregations still want a growing church. But rather than being satisfied just with having good programs, they look for the *results* of those programs. Are lives being changed? Are members practicing their faith at church and also in the community? Are they becoming missional, living and serving as Jesus did?

How does a church measure success? A church is successful when members of the congregation are growing in faith as the body of Christ, in all ways unto him, and disciples are discovering, developing, and using their gifts in Christian service within the body, in the community, and in partnership with other believers around the world.

A Vision for the Future

Transformational leadership appears to be the necessary ingredient to help congregations renew their visions and commitments to be the people of God and the body of Christ in a new world. Shifting paradigms related to leadership patterns, worship styles, program and ministry structures, and institutional affiliations point to the need for revisiting and renewing our core theological, organizational, educational, and missional understandings.

Our biblical principles do not change, for they are eternal. But the methods we use to share the gospel and cast a kingdom vision for a technologically oriented society do change. So ministers and other church leaders need to make a choice: do we resist the future and try to maintain the status quo, or do we seek to be *life-changing* leaders, assisting congregations and individual believers to be all that they can be, in the likeness of their Lord?

It is the conviction of the authors of this book that ministers must revisit their call to ministry, renew their commitment to servant leadership, and, together with their congregations, redream their visions of the kingdom and what it means to be a community of faith, a church, in the twenty-first century. That is our mission for this new age.

Transformational Leadership in the Church

To move toward transformational leadership requires that ministers *and* congregations be willing to create dynamic, active, developing organizations within the church that are responsive to the complex needs of its members, the community served by the church, and the regional and global mission fields. In addition, as leaders of the church, we ourselves must engage in our own process of transformation.

Before we can talk about transformational leadership, we must define what we mean. To do this, we will first grapple with the concept of transformative learning and transformation. Then we will consider organizational structure and leadership in the church. Finally, we will focus on transformational leadership in the church and suggest approaches to using the information in this book to enrich the lives of church leaders and the effectiveness of congregations in fulfilling the purpose for which they exist—to be the people of God and the body of Christ.

Transformative Learning and Transformation

Learning is a necessary ingredient for transformation. Among those experienced with professional development, there are three primary pillars: *self-directed learning, critical reflection,* and *transformative learning*.[3] Self-directed learning is viewed as the foundation of transformative learning, and critical reflection is the central process.[4] Transformative learning occurs when an individual has reflected on assumptions or expectations, has found them to be inadequate or faulty, and chooses to revise them whether related to one's personal and professional life or to broader social and cultural issues.

Figure 1.1

PARADIGM SHIFTS

The Church		
Traditional		*Missional*
Centralized	Location of programs and ministries	Dispersed
Pastor and staff	Leadership	Ministers and teams
Hierarchy	Organization	Flat
A growing church and good programs	What makes you happy?	A growing church and people on mission

People work out of meaning perspectives, frames of reference that serve as a (usually tacit) belief system for interpreting and evaluating the meaning of experience.[5] These perspectives are paradigms, which refer to our ways of seeing, method of inquiry, belief, ideas, values, and attitudes. They shape our perceptions of ourselves, others, and our surroundings. Patricia Cranton notes that our perspectives of meaning are formed through experiences and that one's past shapes the way in which each of us responds to and assimilates new experiences.[6]

There are two dimensions to transformative learning in the individual: the transformation of meaning schemes and the transformation of meaning perspectives.[7] The transformation of *meaning schemes* (the particular knowledge, beliefs, value judgments, and feelings that make up our interpretations of experience) goes with reflection and does not necessitate a major change in our lives. Persons experiencing this kind of transformation will correct their interpretation schemes, which makes for minor adjustments. Persons engaging in a praxis model of education will continuously experience a transformation of meaning scheme.

Transformation of *meaning perspectives* is quite different. Only when we are forced to assess or reassess the basic premises we have taken for granted and find them unjustified does transformation of meaning perspectives happen. Normally such transformation is accompanied by major life change and leads to emancipatory knowledge.[8]

With *meaning perspective* transformation, we become critically aware of how our assumptions have come to constrain the way we perceive, understand, and feel about the world. Changing these basic assumptions opens us up to new possibilities, and hence we experience a transformation. Some researchers place this kind of transformation in the process of adult development rather than adult learning.[9] We are looking for this kind of meaning perspective transformation in transformational leaders. This transformation allows individuals to discard old assumptions based on outdated facts, and it can lead them to a self-awareness that is crucial to *transformational leadership.*

In addition, *meaning perspective* transformations can occur not only in individuals but also in mass, or a collective transformation. If we are part of a group, it is possible for the transformation to occur in several persons in the group and eventually affect the entire group. Persons who have undergone a meaning perspective transformation can be catalysts in a social movement. A meaning perspective transformation may begin with one individual and spread through an entire organization, indeed, throughout society. This would make it possible for an individual to transform an entire organization or society.[10]

Organizational Structure

Organizations are complex groups of people who function as an organism. They are structures of interdependent and subordinate elements or units whose relations and properties are largely determined by their function in the whole. Most organizations are defined with a specific purpose in mind. The organization is generally structured to accomplish that specific purpose.

In a widely used textbook on organizational renewal, leaders are advised to view their organizations through four frames:[11]

1. The *structural* frame, which describes the basic issues that managers need to consider in designing structural forms that fit the organization's goals, tasks, and context.
2. The *human resource* frame, which looks at the relationship between organizations and human nature.
3. The *political* frame, which focuses on the power of political dynamics in making organizational decisions.
4. The *symbolic* frame, which demonstrates the power of symbol and culture in organizations. This frame spells out the basic symbolic elements in organizations such as myths, metaphors, stories, humor, play, rituals, and ceremonies.

In each organization a common thread speaks to the mission or purpose of the organization and how the organization is structured to accomplish that mission.

The units within most organizations are divided along *functional* lines. Each unit owns the responsibility for getting the organization to its goal. Each unit has a manager or leader whose responsibility is to ensure that the unit makes its required contribution to the overall mission of the organization. The functional unit may itself be further structured into smaller units that have the responsibility of seeing to it that the unit reaches its goals.

The collection of functional managers or leaders is normally considered the leadership team of the organization. As long as the organization is running smoothly and the goals are being met, there is little issue with leadership. Most would probably agree that the organization is being successful and fulfilling its purpose.

Organizational Leadership

The leadership of the organization is that person or team of persons who have the responsibility of ensuring that the organization is organized to reach its goals. A normal leadership team would consist of the functional unit leaders and the overall leader of the organization. The measure of success of a leader is determined by whether the organization has reached its projected goals.

Most organizations are structured to run with minimal intervention on the part of the leader. However, in transitional periods, organizational goals and structures are required to change if the stated goals are to be met. When the environment changes, there must be change within the organization. Either the goals must be modified, or the structure of the organization must be modified. Leadership is about managing change and not about managing the status quo. A leader's effectiveness has to do with how well he or she can manage change, whether it is external or internal to the organization. Such change requires a clear understanding of why the organization exists and what the goals of the organization are.

The Church

The church is the living body of Jesus Christ. It is to have functional parts as any other organization. We can envision the leaders of the church as those who have identified with the principles of Jesus Christ—the head of the church. As discussed earlier, the leaders in a church have traditionally been the pastor and staff, but now many congregations are being led by ministry teams under the overall leadership of a senior pastor.

Leaders must be prepared to cope with some unique characteristics, the most significant of which is that people serve the church not for monetary reward but because of a sense of duty or calling. For this reason transactional leadership sometimes is difficult. People in the church can be extremely positive if they are committed to the stated goals, mission, or vision of the church. On the other hand, if their commitment is *against* the stated, or unstated, goals, their response will reduce the church's overall ability to accomplish its mission. Such reaction can lead to fragmentation and serious conflict in the life of a church.

Transformational Leadership

The idea of transformational leadership has been around for some time. Researchers have developed differing but complementary definitions of the term. James McGregor Burns, in his seminal work *Leadership*,[12] refers to it as the process of pursuing collective goals through the mutual tapping of leaders' and followers' motives based toward the achievement of the intended change. Others suggest that transformational leadership occurs when all stakeholders converge on a compelling vision and seek to work in a cohesive body to accomplish a common purpose. In the church transformational leaders are those who share the vision, embrace the purpose, and give their lives to building up the body in the image of Christ. Consider this definition as a way to understand and explain transformational leadership:

> Transformational leaders create an appealing and compelling organizational vision that often necessitates a metamorphosis in cultural values to reflect greater institutional inventiveness. To achieve the vision, leaders attempt to secure greater effort and commitment from members by bonding individual and collective interests. The Transformational Leader is also thoroughly aware of conditions outside the organization and works collaboratively with leaders of other organizations to ensure the goals of the whole community rather than merely the organizational goals.[13]

The most significant characteristics of transformational leadership include

- Appropriating a shared vision
- Communicating that vision
- Motivating others to own the vision
- Addressing real problems within the organization
- Encouraging others to put forth their personal best

The Transformational Leader

One of the fundamental traits of a transformational leader is a clear sense of self-identity and worth. The transformational leader has enjoyed the emancipatory knowledge that has caused him or her to challenge old assumptions and view the world through a new set of lenses. Having been transformed, the transformational leader is open to risk-taking and improving what he or she does. This person is not stuck in a paradigm that has lost its functional meaning and is not afraid to seek renewal, whether related to personal, church, or community issues. In addition to having been transformed, the transformational leader has the ability to inspire others to take on a challenge.

The trademarks of transformational leaders are empowerment, collaboration, creative problem solving, and shared decision making. As leaders, we are required to rethink relationships of power within our setting. This rethinking involves moving away from top-down, hierarchical modes of functioning and moving toward shared decision making, teamwork, and community building. We are about connecting people, connecting with people, and then inviting them and challenging them to live up to their strengths.

The Church as a Transformistic Organization

As church leaders and as transformational leaders, our task is to make the church a transformistic organization. We are to transform individuals within the church, thereby transforming the church itself. Our task is to further use the influence of the church, empowered by the Holy Spirit, to transform society. We manage an organization whose objective is to provide for more abundant life.

The Invitation

Renewal requires analysis and then a strategy for change. Leaders must be able to engage the church in a dialogue whereby the congregation, particularly the leadership team, must decide what the problems and/or opportunities are and then decide on how to address them. Any attempt to dictate problems and solutions to the church will probably meet with serious resistance.

Most church members will want to follow their own hermeneutical understanding of Jesus and the Scriptures. It may be necessary, therefore, to do some biblical teaching before a transformation can take place. If and when the church can come to a common understanding of the church's major problems and opportunities, then and only then can strategies be developed and significant change occur. The congregation must choose. *The role of leaders is to proclaim the gospel and to invite response.*

Strategies for change and guidelines for leaders are presented throughout this book, particularly in chapters 4, 8, and 21.

Chapter 2

MANAGING CHURCHES AND
NOT-FOR-PROFIT ORGANIZATIONS

Robert D. Dale

C hurch administration is ministry, not methods. It's people, not paperwork. It's human processes, not inhumane policies. It's management, not manipulation.

Administration and management refer to an organization's "people processes" and help institutions use their resources well. In the church and other Christian institutions, administration is growing people, not simply doing things. Administration is vital if a church is to reach its mission. But "administrivia" is to be avoided if morale for the mission is to remain high.

Administration: Science, Art, Gift

Church administration or management is a science, an art, and a gift. As a science, church management involves procedures that can be learned by study and practice. As an art, administration calls for relational sensitivity, intuition, and timing. These artistic people skills are largely natural talents but can be enhanced to some degree by experience and training.

Additionally, the apostle Paul names administration as a spiritual gift (1 Cor 12:28). Different translations of the New Testament refer to this gift by using a variety of terms such as "governments" (KJV), "forms of leadership" (NRSV), "workers of spiritual power" (Phillips), and the "power to guide" (NEB). The Greek term for administration in this passage translates to "helmsman." In the same manner that pilots steer their ships through the rocks and shallows safely to their destinations, ministers guide their congregations toward their missions. Two important observations about steersmen apply also to Christian managers.

- Helmsmen are members of the ship's larger crew. Steering is only one vital function in the operation of a ship or an institution. Likewise ministers serve a congregation's overall needs.
- Helmsmen take orders from the captain. No minister stands above Christ in the management of Christian ministry.

Recent management approaches have reversed a key perspective and practice. Administrators used to lead by *managing*. Now we manage by *leading*.

Overview: Choosing, Creating, Catalyzing, and Coordinating

Secular business management has become a highly technical field. Since congregations are volunteer, not-for-profit organizations, and since ministers generally see themselves as paraprofessional managers, the model which follows is streamlined. Four actions—one personal and three congregational—describe church administration.

Fundamentally, church management calls for choosing, creating, catalyzing, and coordinating personal and institutional resources. The following model describes basic processes in congregational management and specifies "what" (a definition of the process), "why" (a theological perspective), "who" (initiators of the processes), and "how" (applications of the process).

Choosing: Self-Management Actions

Ministers who manage congregations or other Christian institutions make three crucial choices: they choose an ad-ministry style, choose start-up strategy, and choose a closure approach. These choices reflect the minister's freedom to choose among options or alternatives.

1. You Can Choose Your Ad-ministry Style

What? Ad-ministry style describes the process of selecting and using a management pattern consistently. Choosing a personal approach or pattern of managing a congregation's or other Christian institution's resources boils down to how ministers structure their personal time. Self-management is, after all, largely a matter of stewardship of time and life.

Why? Theologically, administrators can affirm several statements about style and the stewardship of time.

21

- God is the God of time and history. God has done redemptive work through persons and amid history, through the exodus, the exile, the incarnation, and the empty tomb. God's use of time for redemption makes the use of our personal time precious.
- The Bible speaks of two kinds of time: *chronos* and *kairos*. *Chronos* is the measured, durative time typical of clocks and calendars. All *chronos* belongs to God. *Kairos* is more like timing and refers to time becoming ripe, full, and overflowing with opportunity (Mark 1:15; Luke 4:21; Matt 16:3; Luke 12:56). Ministers must use *chronos* well in order to be ready to use *kairos* at all.
- Jesus had time enough to do God's will. Think of the scope of Jesus' task and the relatively short time he had to accomplish it in. Yet he managed both the task and the timeframe without apparent frustration. Jesus knew that persons are given adequate time to accomplish God's purpose in their lives.
- Grace frees Christians from yesterday's sin and guilt as well as tomorrow's fears and challenges.

Who? Ministers have numerous resources for selecting a consistent administry style. Friends and advisers offer feedback. Studying the great biblical leaders provides behavioral models of effective ministry. Biographies of Luther, Wesley, famous evangelists and missionaries, and other denominational and institutional leaders yield insights into management styles. Taking into account that past leaders and current mentors minister in settings that differ from our personal circumstances, only individual ministers make the final choice about their own styles.

How? The basic management challenge for ministers is self-management. Ministers set their own schedules and do eternal work that's always difficult to measure and evaluate. Time use, then, provides the proof of effective style stewardship. Some principles guide ministers in time management.

- Find out how you're using your time now. Keep a time diary of your actual work activities for a week. What do you notice about your stewardship of your professional energies?
- Plan to use your time on priorities. Most effective ministers work from a prioritized to-do list of daily tasks. They also use a "quiet hour," an uninterrupted time for concentrating on crucial projects. They reserve the times when their biological clocks are at their best for working on their most challenging tasks. They plan before they attempt to complete their work.
- Work on a weekly and daily schedule. Regular structure improves productivity.
- Handle a piece of work once. Use a three-step cycle of action: start, work, stop.

- Delegate to team members. Free yourself for crucial tasks and give others a chance to participate and grow.
- Refresh yourself. Move from intense involvement to "sabbath" refreshment.
- Group similar tasks together. For example, think "communication" and write a thank-you note while you're waiting on someone to come to the phone.
- Plan to grow personally and professionally.
- Live one day at a time.
- When uncertain or frustrated, ask yourself the basic time-stewardship question: "What's the best use of my time right now?"

2. You Can Choose Your Ministry Start-up Strategy

What? Ministry start-up generally refers to the first twelve to eighteen months of establishing ministry in a new post. Given average tenures, from 30 to 50 percent of a minister's total professional life is spent in start-up transitions and processes.

Why? Theologically speaking, the Christian view of history provides a foundation for ministry start-up work.

- Christianity is a historical religion. The Bible is a book of history. For Christians, history really is "his-story."
- Christians believe history has a purpose. History has beginnings, middles, and ends—just as ministry has personal and organizational chapters. In God's plan, history's theme is redemption.
- Christ is the apex or pivot point of history. Christ stands at the center of all history. Ministers must guard against an attitude of self-importance, especially at the beginning of a ministry, when members tend to overestimate abilities.

Who? Personnel committees and pastor selection committees are increasingly serving temporarily as support groups for ministers. They, or other support networks, provide encouragement, information about congregational or institutional reactions, advise on relationships and the progress of programs, give feedback, and help evaluate ministries.

How? Start-up is usually conceived as a three-step process: understanding and using the dynamics of the interim period, knowing what to expect in a new ministry setting, and developing a general strategy for establishing yourself in ministry relationships in a new post are key issues.[1]

Understanding and using the dynamics of the interim period. The interim period between ministers actually blends into the next minister's work. How the time between the former minister's resignation, firing, or death has been used determines the beginning point and shapes the climate of ministry start-up. Ordinarily, four issues arise during interim periods.

- The emotions of grief—loss, anger, and guilt—should be recognized and resolved.
- The period creates a management vacuum in which the internal leadership circle shifts as old leaders fade and new leaders emerge.
- Relationships to denominational resources are examined.
- Most importantly, the interim period allows the basic mission and identity of the church or institution to be evaluated and, if needed, redefined.

Knowing what to expect in a new ministry setting. A checklist of things to be alert to during start-up is an important tool.[2] In random order, here are several predictable issues surrounding start-up:

- Most congregations tend to feel the minister is settled in after the moving van is gone and several casseroles have been delivered. More attention is usually paid to physical concerns than to emotional or spiritual issues.
- Generally, the denominational structures expect the new minister "to make things happen."
- The history of a congregation includes more than the statistical and sociological information ordinarily given a new or prospective minister. The congregation's beginnings, heroes, "golden years," conflicts, building programs, and sense of vision shape its present and its future.
- When the self-confidence of the minister or the congregation has eroded during the interim, two perils may develop: the congregation may become overly dependent on the minister as a rescuer, or the minister may feel the pressure for a "quick win" and fall back on programs that were successful elsewhere.
- First impressions are built on intuitive responses to two questions: Are you genuine? and, Do you care?
- Watch what surprises you during start-up. Surprises indicate a difference between what you expected and what happened. If a pattern of surprises emerges, step back and try to understand what's happening.
- The "honeymoon" is a time when the new minister is given extra leeway. This momentum is precious and should be patiently invested in priority ministries.
- Early in start-up, change only what is needed, wanted, and supported.
- It's easier to follow effective ministers and build on the trust they've accumulated than to inherit the ill will assigned to ministers who have been disappointments.
- Expect to be tested.

- The end to the honeymoon is frightening and calls for clarifying and renegotiating expectations.
- Members with views like the new minister's will tend to move into the centers of power in the church or institution.
- The first conflict in a new ministry helps "set the rules" for future disagreements.
- When the new minister's leadership style exerts more initiative than the congregation expects, overlaps in responsibility occur, and conflict is apt to surface. When the new minister's leadership style takes less initiative than the congregation expects, vacuums in responsibility develop, and frustration results. The new minister is usually more able to sense the differences and adjust levels of leader initiative appropriately than the congregation-at-large.

Developing a general strategy for establishing yourself in ministry relationships in a new post. Broad strategy for start-up lends a structure for establishing ministry.[3] While numerous approaches are available, some guidelines clarify ministry priorities:

- Begin with people and build relationships for ministry and for personal encouragement.
- Help the congregation or institution define its basic purpose or dream.
- Build ministry on mainstream needs.
- Cultivate healthy organizational habits that will facilitate Christian growth.

3. You Can Choose How to Close Out a Ministry

What? Closure means saying good-bye to a church or institution at the conclusion of a tenure of ministry. Official documents like constitutions and bylaws may specify the mechanics of how the minister terminates, but the minister decides the manner of exiting. Closure flavors ministry and tends to make the minister's impact and reputation better or worse.

Why? Eschatology provides a theological perspective for closure.

- Christians believe that God will draw history to a close in a purposeful, redemptive, and decisive manner.
- Human history, like all processes, has an end, and that conclusion is in God's hands.

Who? The minister works with appropriate committees, councils, and task forces to ensure an orderly and productive transition. Official documents may spell out formal procedures for an interim period or tradition may suggest informal approaches.

How? The process of saying good-bye is largely a relational one. While proclamation (evangelism, preaching, teaching, and worship) and pastoral care (counseling, family ministry, grief work, and officiating special events) enter into closure strategies, management is the focus here. Closure involves several attitudes and actions.

- After resigning, ministers immediately become lame ducks and quickly lose their change agent's influence.
- How members of the congregation or institution react to the minister's resignation is an indication of the minister's overall administry style. If ministers have encouraged or allowed the congregation to become dependent, the members may feel betrayed and panic. If ministers have developed and expanded the leadership base of the church and if administrative processes have been clearly identified and consistently used, the congregation will face interims with more confidence.
- Lame duck leaders should wrap up unfinished projects rather than attempt to launch new ministries.
- An exit interview may be offered by the minister. The experience of working with an overall responsibility for a congregation's ministry can lend insights into the potentials, problems, and characteristics of the total group that can serve well the search for a new minister.
- A transition packet containing administrative documents and listing of community and denominational resources is a thoughtful gesture. These materials may assist the next minister's start-up.

Creating: Innovative Congregational Actions

Some management actions are administratively creative: creative dreaming, creative evaluating, creative planning. These administrative initiatives focus on originating and producing new ministries and programs.

1. You Can Help Your Congregation Define Its Dream

What? Dreaming is the process of clarifying, taking ownership of, and communicating forcefully the congregation or institution's redemptive vision.[4]

Why? Jesus' vision of the kingdom of God formed his core teaching.

- Over eighty times in the Gospels, Jesus spoke of the kingdom he came to introduce and embody. He mentioned the kingdom of God or kingdom of heaven more than any other theme.
- Most of Jesus' parables, the center of his teachings, describe "what the kingdom is like."
- The kingdom of God calls persons and their institutions to submit to God's rule and provides Christians with the clue to Jesus' dream.

Who? Since every congregation has its own personality and since the kingdom has a virtually endless variety of local embodiments, the membership at large should shape the congregation's dream of ministry. All leaders in the ministries of the church guide the process of dreaming.

How? Numerous steps can be used in guiding a congregation or institution to focus on its dream.

- Congregations move through a "health cycle" from vigor to disease (see figure 2.1). The health cycle model can be used to "read" the church, to discover the organization's stage of vitality or illness, and to find ways to renew the congregation.

- Broadly stated, healthy congregations build on and are renewed by their dreams, plan proactively, and minister to others. Unhealthy churches doubt themselves into decline (and occasionally death), reactively solve problems, and demand to be ministered to themselves.

- Preaching and teaching Jesus' parables can provide a consciousness-raising experience for a congregation to use when beginning to dream together about what God wants from them here and now.

- One important clue to a congregation's current vision is the dream of the founding group. Not all dreams are of equal value, of course. Negative and narrow visions tend to yield more rigid and ideological congregations. Mission- and service-oriented beginnings develop into churches with more positive climates for ministry.

Figure 2.1

HEALTH CYCLE

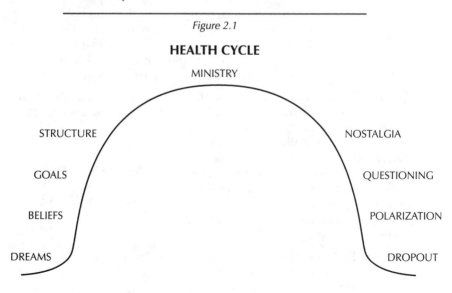

MINISTRY

STRUCTURE   NOSTALGIA

GOALS   QUESTIONING

BELIEFS   POLARIZATION

DREAMS   DROPOUT

- A balance between leader vision and initiative and broad congregational consensus yields two crucial elements for the dreaming process: sharp focus and general ownership of the vision.

2. You Can Help Your Congregation Evaluate Its Ministry Programs

What? Evaluating is the process of discovering and duplicating the congregation or institution's successes while discovering and eliminating the organization's failures. Evaluation provides an appraisal, feedback, and control mechanism.

Why? Theologically, judgment provides a doctrinal framework for the administrative process of evaluation. Several affirmations apply.

- Although judgment is built into the fabric of human experience, God is the final judge. Both the New Testament and the creeds of Christian history declare that at the end of history Christ will return gloriously to judge the living and the dead.
- Mere humans lack the objectivity to make valid judgments on others' lives. Christ reminds us of our limited perspectives when he observed we may be critical of the specks in others' eyes while we overlook the logs in our own eyes (Matt 7:3–4).
- Self-evaluation is an ongoing discipline for every Christian (1 Cor 9:24–27; 11:28).
- In congregational settings we measure a volunteer worker's service by the goals set earlier by the congregation at large. This approach is a type of self-evaluation too. If the original goal-setting process involved the total congregation, then this volunteer has made two commitments to goals—one during the development of the congregation's original goals and another when he or she agreed to serve in the ministry programs of the church. Actions taken toward these goals can be observed and evaluated.

Who? Every group in a congregation with responsibility for ministry actions or for resource management should evaluate its work regularly. Most congregations use a representative church council to appraise the total program of the congregation. The evaluation process of monitoring, reviewing, and correcting intends to turn trial and error into trial and success (figure 2.2).

How? Evaluation involves five critical elements.

- Evaluating calls us to measure performance against purpose. Good evaluation demands that

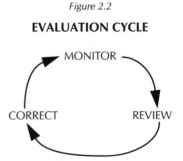

Figure 2.2

EVALUATION CYCLE

MONITOR

REVIEW

CORRECT

standards of effectiveness or success be established beforehand. Goals always precede evaluations.

- Evaluating uses both quantitative and qualitative information. More objective information—like statistics, attendance reports, and budget summaries—need to be considered. Additionally, more subjective materials—opinions and other clues to the morale levels of the congregation—need to be included to balance and blend feelings into the factual picture.
- Evaluating uses a range of persons and a variety of methods. Both planners and implementers, along with persons involved in a program *and* those not involved, should be included in the evaluative process. Statistical records, interviews, questionnaires, continua, and pretests and posttests provide a variety of data. Involve as many members as possible and gather only information that will be used. When information is requested, members assume it will be used and are disillusioned if it isn't. Expect persons with negative perspectives to speak up early and loudly; take their opinions seriously without overreacting.

Figure 2.3

EVALUATION MODEL

PAST Positive (+) "In the past, I am proud that our church has . . ."	PAST Negative (-) "In the past, I am disappointed that our church has . . ."
FUTURE Positive (+) "In the future, I hope that our church will . . ."	FUTURE Negative (-) "In the future, I fear that our church will . . ."

- A model for evaluation should invite both positive and negative perspectives and consider both past and future time frames (figure 2.3).
- Evaluation is a continuing cycle. Preevaluation provides status checks before a ministry is launched. Midevaluation double-checks progress either to assure that the project is on course or to make midcourse corrections. Postevaluation includes both an immediate debriefing after a project is completed and more seasoned reflections later on.

3. You Can Help Your Congregation Plan Effective Ministry Programs

What? Planning is the process of creating your organizational future before it happens. Planning attempts to write history in advance.

Why? Hope provides a theological foundation for planning.

- God modeled orderliness and planning in creation and redemption.
- The future is God's possession. Only God knows the future; only God holds the future. Planning, then, becomes an act of faith that the God who gave us today will also provide a meaningful tomorrow.
- Ultimately, the Christian's hope is Christ.
- Christians live between the times. Our planning efforts strive to move our institutions from where we are to where God wants us to be.

Who? The leader team for church planning includes the pastor and other church staff ministers as facilitators and resource persons as well as a specific planning group, like a church council. Remember that people support what they help plan. The participation guideline for planning, then, is: *everyone who will be expected to implement the plan should be involved in planning.*

How? Planning provides congregations and institutions with reasonable targets for fulfilling their dream. Planning processes usually involve several considerations.

- All planning is an abstraction. Project planning, involving concrete acts of ministry, is the least abstract and simplest type of planning. Project planning appeals to smaller organizations and members with more concrete styles of thinking.
- Churches practice two types of planning: operational and directional. Operational planning is usually referred to as annual planning and implements the shorter-range tactical planning. Directional planning forecasts the future needs and wants of your congregation, sets directions, and usually builds on a three- to five-year strategic framework. Numerous computerized planning models are available for church use.

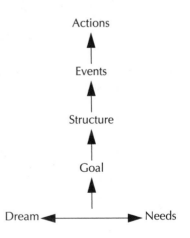

Figure 2.4

PLANNING SEQUENCE

Actions

↑

Events

↑

Structure

↑

Goal

↑

Dream ◄————————► Needs

- Ordinarily, a planning sequence begins with the dream or purpose of the congregation or the needs of the church and community and develops goals. Budgeting, then, builds on the goals. New or different organizational structures extend out of budgeted goals. Ministry events and, finally, detailed actions are projected (see figure 2.4).
- Plan from *ends* to *means* and implement your plans from *means* to *ends*.
- Set high but possible congregational goals.

Catalyzing: Responsive Congregational Actions

Catalysts in chemistry cause reactions and speed changes. They are change agents: budgeting is catalytic; motivating is catalytic; advertising is catalytic. These processes are catalytic management activities for churches.

1. You Can Change Your Congregation through Your Church Budget

What? Budgeting is the process of allocating resources toward goals by expressing the church's dream in dollars. An institution's budget is a theological document because it's an expression of the congregation's redemptive dream.

Why? Stewardship to the individual Christian and budgeting to the congregation reflect our response to God as Creator.

- God calls believers to become partners and trustees in creation. Jesus followed this pattern when he made the good steward a key figure in the parables.
- Our response to God's order of creation demands that Christians use things responsibly, love persons responsibly, and worship God responsibly.
- The challenge of Christian stewardship is to use things, love persons, and worship God without mixing the verbs and objects. To mismatch the verbs and objects is to sin.

Who? In some smaller churches, an informal group may suggest a budget structure. But most congregations choose a committee or team (variously called stewardship, budget, or finance) to examine ministry plans, gather information on giving and spending, propose a basic budget structure, and implement an ongoing program of stewardship education.

How? Budgeting is resource management. The budget of an institution provides a stackpole for the coordinated use of the church's four primary resources:

- *Money*—through an adopted, unified budget

- *Time*—via the church's calendar
- *Facilities*—by developing and maintaining buildings and properties; and, most importantly
- *People*—through a plan of evangelism, member development, and leader enlistment and training

The steps in budgeting vary with the philosophy being used. Ministry-action budgeting is the approach outlined here.[5]

- Analyze the congregation's current ministries.
- Request ministry groups to propose ministry actions for the coming year.
- Evaluate the proposals.
- Prepare a budget for congregational discussion.
- Present the revised budget for congregational adoption.
- Educate the congregation about the budget and attempt to subscribe it completely.
- Keep the congregation informed throughout the church year about progress toward the ministry actions and the funds involved.
- Begin the review and evaluation process for the next year's budgeting procedures.

2. You Can Help Your Congregation Improve Its Motivational Climate

What? Motivating is the process of helping members discover, take ownership of, and use their reservoirs of spiritual energy.

Why? Theologically, the Holy Spirit is the Christian's motivator.

- The Holy Spirit lives within the Christian (John 14:17). This biblical insight favors the internal theories of motivation ("persons are always motivated on their own to do something") over the external approaches ("I cause others to act"). Manipulative "carrot on a stick" approaches to motivating others are inconsistent with a reliance on the Spirit of Christ. Motivation in congregational settings, then, becomes largely a matter of setting a motivational climate and helping members channel their energies.
- The Holy Spirit energizes Christians by encouraging and guiding us (John 14:18; Matt 28:20).
- The Holy Spirit ministers actively to our needs (John 14:25–31). The Spirit's internal ministry to our personal concerns is the model of motivational leadership for us to follow.

Who? The leader team for improving the motivational climate includes all organizational directors and leaders. Persons who have other members under their supervision must work to uplift the morale level of their portion of the overall institution.

How? Setting a motivational climate and helping members channel their energies toward the congregation's dream are the challenges of church leaders. Several management actions yield big dividends.

- Create a motivational climate by helping members meet their legitimate needs. People enjoy participating in an organization they can both give to and get from. Legitimate personal needs include our hunger for recognition, structure, and intimacy. Legitimate interpersonal needs involve belonging with others in a meaningful group, influencing our group's life, and being loved by important others.

- Create a motivational climate by building a ministry team. Administrators know that churches thrive on an atmosphere of "we did it" teamwork rather than a self-glorifying "I did it" attitude. Recently I heard a pastor brag, "I raised three million dollars in a week. I deserve to tell them what to do!" I wonder who that pastor thinks contributed the three million? A "we" atmosphere builds a team for long-term, constructive ministry.

- Create a motivational climate by reaching clear agreements with your ministry team. People are motivated by knowing what's expected of them, by negotiating some issues, and by agreeing on their privileges and responsibilities. Groups are held together by promises their members make to one another. These promises or contracts keep us from the demotivating tyranny of undefined expectations. Leaders must build and maintain their credibility if they are to create a motivational climate.

3. You Can Help Your Church Advertise Its Ministries

What? Advertising is the process of communicating Christ's message and the congregation's image to its community by means of people, print, and other media.

Why? The concept of revelation provides a theological foundation for advertising the congregation's vision.

- A revelation is an unveiling. For Christians, revelation refers almost exclusively to God's redemptive actions.
- God takes the initiative to establish a personal relationship with us. Then believers become a basic channel for revealing God's kingdom and work.
- God's revelation is concrete, direct, intense, and awesome. Christ's incarnation is the highest and most concrete revelation of God's nature and intent.
- Revelation is dialogic. God is revealed to us through Christ; we praise and witness to God's mighty acts.

33

Who? The pastor and church staff usually coordinate communications about the congregation's ministry. Some churches elect a public relations committee to assist the overall congregation and to help ministry groups tell the stories of their processes and events.

How? Just as a variety of approaches were used to communicate God's mighty acts (Heb 1:1–2), congregations must work strategically to publicize their work. The management of an advertising process incorporates several steps.

- Advertising requires focus. That is, the answers to some questions keep advertising efforts on target. Which message? To whom? For what response? When? Through which media?
- Advertising means putting yourself into the other person's shoes and telling others how your ministry benefits them.
- Advertising uses power words to trigger a positive emotional response to your church and its ministries. Power words are graphic communication tools that make your church attractive and credible.
- Advertising uses images as well as words. A logo, pictures, and Web sites identify your church and its work.
- Advertising shows quality. Attractive material has impact. It sets a mood, creates images, and builds expectations.
- Advertising conveys a clear message. One theme is presented to one audience. The action you hope your reader/hearer will take is specified.

Coordinating: Balancing Congregational Actions

Coordination calls on the church manager to relate the varied elements and activities properly in order that ministry functions harmoniously: coordinating by organizing, coordinating by staffing, coordinating by team building. These processes draw the people and administrative processes together for ministry.

1. You Can Organize Your Congregation's Ministry

What? Organizing is the process of developing a structure and work plan that help persons become meaningfully involved in the goals of the congregation.

Why? The product of God's creation provides a theological perspective for the organizing process.

- God is ultimately responsible for the being of the world. He made it out of nothing. Now creation depends on God to sustain it.
- God's creation is good. This view argues against religious leaders who claim any organization is bad.

- Man is a responsible steward of God's creation. Organizational structuring is one congregational application of creation.

Who? The pastor, church staff, church council, program organizational leaders, and finally the entire congregation are responsible for creating new ministry units and pruning away old ones.

How? Organizing the congregation for action is a basic management practice.

- How much organization is necessary? A congregation is underorganized if portions of its dream have no structured work units to implement them. A congregation is overorganized if structured work units exist with no direct connection with the dream. The implicit warning in these two statements is simple: Don't create unnecessary organizational units since new units have to be maintained after they are set up.
- Form follows function: that's the *master principle* of organization. The product you want determines the organization you need.
- Most organizing efforts move through a fairly predictable cycle.

  (1) Define the congregation's dream.
  (2) Define the ministry program you need to organize.
  (3) Divide the ministry into manageable units.
  (4) Relate the various units of ministry into a workable arrangement.
  (5) Enlist workers.
  (6) Clarify workers' tasks and train them to do the job.
  (7) Empower workers to do their ministries by delegating authority to them that's equal to their responsibility.
  (8) Evaluate the program of ministry in case some reorganization is needed.

2. You Can Coordinate Staffing Your Congregation's Organizations

What? Staffing is the process of finding, enlisting, training, and encouraging the congregation's volunteer and paid leaders.

Why? Spiritual gifts provide the basis for staffing the church's organization.

- Every Christian is gifted for service. More than thirty different spiritual gifts are mentioned in the five New Testament listings (1 Cor 12:4–10, 28–30; Eph 4–11; Rom 12:6–8; 1 Pet 4:10–11). All of these gifts are God given and are closely tied to the Christian virtue of love (1 Cor 13).

- All of the spiritual gifts are significant and are designed to advance the gospel.
- God provides every congregation with the human resources to implement its kingdom dream. Members are the most valuable resource in any congregation.

Who? Most churches use a nominating committee or a spiritual gifts discovery team to find, enlist, and offer preservice training to workers. Computerized talent searches simplify this committee's work.

How? Several issues are crucial to staffing church organizations.

- The ideal staffing system relates three persons to each job—one person training for the future, one doing the job now, and one experienced worker coaching the other two.
- Persons who are responsible for enlisting workers need to be clear about the motivations, rewards, and morale levels of volunteer workers (and how these factors differ from those of employees).
- Forecast the church's leadership needs.
- Identify future leaders.
- Enlist needed leaders. Link their personal gifts with organizational goals.
- Provide a listing of tasks and expectations and agree on what work will be done.
- Provide training opportunities for the new volunteer leaders.
- Provide supervisory-skills training for directors who will guide the volunteer staff.[6]

3. You Can Build Your Church's Ministry Team

What? Team building is the process of turning diversity toward unity. Team-building efforts are needed anytime two or more persons depend on one another and work together.

Why? Paul's "body of Christ" image of the church (Rom 12 and 1 Cor 12) lends theological substance to the management challenge of team building.

- The body of Christ has diverse parts. Leadership in team building and coordination are required if congregations are to remain robust (Rom 12:4,6).
- All of the diversity is necessary for Christ's body to function well (1 Cor 12:14–26).
- Christ is the unifier of the diversity (1 Cor 12:12–13).

Who? The pastor, church staff, and church council provide the primary resources for team building.

How? Team building holds two congregational concerns in balanced tension: creating a family atmosphere and getting ministry done. (See chapter 4, "Working with People.")

Implications: Act Now

The administrative model of choosing, creating, catalyzing, and coordinating provides church leaders three advantages by:

- Providing a platform for confident actions
- Relating practice and theology
- Helping ministers discover the broad administrative area(s) and/or specific skills they need to develop by further research and education

These three advantages call for simple actions: *think, believe, grow.* The helm of the ship is in your hands. Act now as a Christian administrator.

Chapter 3

ORGANIZING FOR MISSION AND MINISTRY

Bruce P. Powers

O
rganization in a church is structure designed to enable a congregation to make disciples, help members grow, and develop spiritual
power in their lives. Organization is a way to help people find a
place and direction in their spiritual journey; it is the design for relating to
one another effectively in order to do the Lord's work.

Organization begins with the nature and mission of the church, for it
is biblical foundations that should always determine programs and ministries. There are five distinguishing characteristics of the New Testament
church: worship, proclamation, education, ministry, and fellowship. It is
these traits that we define as the primary functions of a local church and
around which all organization develops.

To support these five functions, we add a sixth that is implicit in Scripture
and very much needed in today's church—leadership. Administrative leadership is the glue, or support, that enables the five primary functions to operate
together as the body of Christ. Thus, when a congregation is organized and
functioning correctly, all efforts are focused on fulfilling the purpose of the
church under the lordship of Jesus Christ. (See Eph 4:1–16 and Rom 12.)

Based on the functions of a church, programs and organizations are
developed. These are *means*, or *ways*, for achieving the mission or purpose
of the church; they are not *ends* in themselves. Each program or organization exists to achieve a specific purpose or portion of a church's ministry.
And each, theoretically, should be the most effective structure to achieve
the purpose for which it exists.

Organizational Distinctives

Because of common objectives among evangelical churches—making
disciples, enabling members to grow and mature, and developing spiri-

tual awareness and power in the lives of believers—similar structures have evolved among denominations to enable churches to do their work. For example, most churches have various types of worship and fellowship opportunities as well as organizations to facilitate Bible study, discipleship development, mission activities, and Christian living. Although names of these may vary, such as Sunday school, Bible school, and church school, the functions and general organizational principles are remarkably similar from denomination to denomination.

Basic Church Programs

These structures or organizations are the primary channels for the ongoing ministries provided by a congregation. Activities are usually designed according to the ability and/or need level of participants. Basic church programs are designed to help a church achieve its objectives and, also, to meet the general needs of people in the congregation.

The basic programs, or organizations, that exist in some form in most evangelical and Protestant churches will be covered in this chapter. Each program has a cluster of tasks that are essential, continuing, and important to the work of a church (see figure 3.1).

Other organizations are necessary to provide effective ministry in a church but are not considered basic programs for all members of the congregation. These are primarily service-oriented (like media or recreation ministries) or specialized programs for subgroups in the congregation (like a club for senior adults).

Figure 3.1

BASIC CHURCH PROGRAMS

There are six established church programs, each with a cluster of tasks that are basic, continuing, and of primary importance to the life of a church. Each program develops organization and seeks to involve the congregation in its work. Because these organizations form the foundation of church structure, they are called basic church programs. Listed below are the tasks that each program assumes in the life of the church.

Bible Teaching
1. Reach persons for Bible study.
2. Teach the Bible.
3. Witness to persons about Christ and lead them into church membership.
4. Minister to persons in need.
5. Lead members to worship.

Discipleship Training
1. Reach persons for discipleship training.

2. Orient new church members for discipleship and personal ministry.
3. Equip church members for discipleship and personal ministry.
4. Teach theology, doctrine, ethics, history, and church polity.
5. Train church leaders for their tasks.

Music Ministry

1. Provide musical experiences in congregational services.
2. Provide church music education.
3. Lead the church to witness and minister through music.
4. Assist the church programs in using music and in training related to music.

Men's Mission Program

1. Engage in missions activities.
2. Teach missions.
3. Pray for and give to missions.
4. Develop personal ministry.

Women's Mission Program

1. Teach missions.
2. Engage in mission action and personal witnessing.
3. Support missions.

Pastoral Ministries

1. Lead the church in accomplishing its mission.
2. Proclaim the gospel to believers and nonbelievers.
3. Care for the church's members and other persons in the community.

All programs interpret and undergird the work of the local church and the denominational groups with which the congregation cooperates in mission and ministry efforts.

Determining Organizational Structure

The essential elements in deciding how to organize include:

1. *Identifying the specific purpose of the organization.* Ask questions such as: Why does (should) it exist? What is its unique contribution to the church? What would happen if we did not have this organization?

2. *Finding the best way to achieve the stated purpose.* Ask questions such as: What resources (leaders, facilities, denominational assistance, financial support, and such) are available? What are the priorities within and among the various organizations? What structures will provide efficient and effective teamwork among leaders and also contribute toward fulfilling the church's objectives?

3. *Defining clear areas of responsibility and decision making in the overall administration of the church and in each component.* Ask questions such as: What is the distinct responsibility for each position? What decisions should the person in each position be able to make without consultation? What are the positions that link each level (or unit) with the larger body

for purposes of planning, evaluation, communication, and such? Do all leaders have someone to whom they are responsible?

General Coordination

An effective organizational structure includes a church council or other administrative group that would be charged with planning, coordinating, and evaluating the church's programs and ministries. (Information about a church council is given in figure 3.2.)

Figure 3.2

CHURCH COUNCIL

The church council serves as a forum for a church's leaders to guide planning, coordination, conducting, and evaluation of the total work of the church. The council depends on the various church organizations to implement the church's program according to their assigned tasks. As chair of the church council, the pastor is able to lead in developing a unified program that gives major attention to priority needs.

Principle Function: To assist the church in determining its course, and to coordinate and evaluate its work.

Method of Election: Church leaders become members of the church council as a result of election to designated church leadership positions.

Term of Office: Corresponds to term of office in church-elected position.

Members: Pastor (chair), church staff members, program directors, deacon chair, stewardship committee chair, missions committee chair, and other committee chairs as needed.

Duties

- Help the church understand its mission and define its priorities.
- Coordinate studies of church and community needs.
- Recommend to the church coordinated plans for evangelism, missions, Christian development, worship, stewardship, and ministry.
- Coordinate the church's schedule of activities, special events, and use of facilities.
- Evaluate progress and the priority use of church resources. In most churches this group would be chaired by the pastor and would include:
  - √ church staff members
  - √ leaders of all church programs and ministry organizations
  - √ leader of the deacons (or church board)
  - √ chairpersons of key committees (those closely related to the work of church programs and ministries, such as missions, stewardship, and nominating committees)

In larger churches with several full-time ministers, activities might need to be planned, coordinated, and evaluated through a separate, specialized council or committee in each major area of work. Members would include church staff personnel who have an assignment for that program or ministry, leaders representing the various components, and age-group coordinators (if used) as illustrated for educational ministry in figure 3.3.

Similarly, each program organization would have an administrative council or staff to guide the work for which it is responsible, as shown in figure 3.4. (Information about a program council/staff is given in figure 3.5.)

Figure 3.3

ORGANIZATION FOR EDUCATIONAL ADMINISTRATION

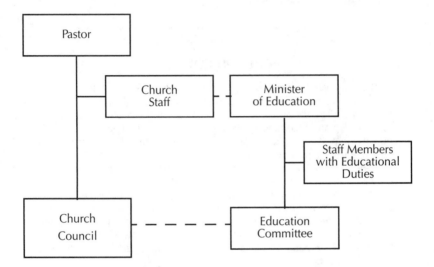

Figure 3.4

ORGANIZATION FOR CHURCH PROGRAM ADMINISTRATION

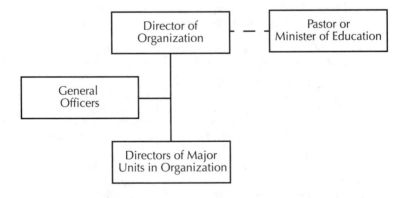

Figure 3.5

PROGRAM COUNCIL AND/OR STAFF

Principal Functions: To assist the program to determine its course, to coordinate program efforts, and to relate to the church council for overall coordination.

Membership and Method of Election: Directors of major units/age divisions in the program become members of the program council as a result of election by the church to program leadership positions. If there are no age division directors, the leader of each department represents his or her group.

Term of Office: Corresponds to term of office in church-elected position.

Report: As a program, to the church; director serves on church council or other general coordinating body.

Duties

- Help the program understand its mission and define its priorities in light of church priorities.
- Conduct studies of church and community needs related to program tasks.
- Coordinate the program's activities and schedules.
- Evaluate progress, effectiveness, and priority use of church resources.

Age-Division Coordination

Because most administration is handled within programs, those who work with similar age groups in different organizations often need to link up to coordinate work and support one another. This can be achieved through age-level coordination.

The simplest approach is for leaders of a particular age division to meet periodically to coordinate their work and their use of space, equipment, and supplies. This is most effective for small churches and age divisions with few workers.

Another approach is to schedule periodic conferences for age-division coordination, the purpose being to deal with issues of common concern among leaders within each age group. Persons in each group could elect a convener to facilitate meetings and channel messages.

In large churches age-group coordinators often will be necessary. (Some churches use directors or ministers in this role.) Their principle function is to facilitate the work of all programs within the age division throughout the church. Coordinators should serve on the education committee, or church council. (Descriptive information concerning age-division coordination is given in figure 3.6.)

Figure 3.6

AGE-DIVISION COORDINATION

Age-division coordination may be accomplished in three ways: self-coordination, age-division conferences, or age-division coordinators/directors. The approach used by a church is determined by the complexity of the organization within the age division.

Self-Coordination

Self-coordination exists when organization leaders of an age division voluntarily coordinate their work and their use of space, equipment, and supplies. This is the simplest and most effective way. It is particularly suited for small churches and age divisions with few workers.

Age-Division Coordination Conferences

Principal Function: To serve as a counseling, advisory, and coordinating group when self-coordination is inadequate.

Members: Leaders of departments, choirs, and other organizational units of a particular age division.

Convener: One of the members of the group elected by the group.

Age-Division Coordinators/Directors

Principal Function: To counsel age-division leaders and coordinate the work of units within the age division as assigned.

Age-division coordinators are elected by the church and responsible to the pastor or minister of education as designated by the church. The pastor leads in developing procedures for providing consultative and advisory services to the minister of music and other staff members as needed.

Duties

- Consult with department leaders to resolve philosophical, procedural, and scheduling problems.
- Give assistance in classifying and enrolling new members.
- Consult with department leaders to coordinate the use of program materials, supplies, equipment, and space.
- Give individual guidance to department directors and workers.
- Work with church program leaders to provide training opportunities for department leaders and workers.
- Work with director of recreation to provide appropriate services.
- Give assistance as needed to department directors in discovering and enlisting department workers.
- Coordinate age-division visitation.
- Encourage and provide assistance to leaders in planning and evaluating their work.
- Serve as ex officio members of program council.

Grouping People

There are three general approaches to dividing congregations into manageable groups for educational or other purposes: age, compatibility, and interest. To a lesser extent some churches choose to create additional sub-groupings by using distinctives such as gender and marital status.

Age

Age grouping, or grading, is used most often when trying to match developmental needs of individuals with the educational experiences provided. This is the approach usually recommended by denominational program leaders to facilitate an ongoing, systematic study of curriculum materials by all ages.

Under this plan organizational groupings follow a general pattern but often are adjusted when subgrouping to allow for compatibility and/or interest groups. For example, the "Organization Planning Chart," figure 3.7, lists the major divisions, suggested maximum enrollment per unit, and worker-pupil ratio for preschool and children's departments. By completing the chart, you can figure out the number of classes/groups/departments needed and the approximate number of workers.

In a small church try to have a nursery plus at least two departments for preschoolers (up through age two and ages three–five) and two for children (grades one–three and four–six). Only if space is not available should all preschoolers, or grades one through six, be together.

If space and leaders are available, set up three groups for preschoolers (up to age one, ages two and three, and ages four and five). Also, provide three groups for children (grades one and two, grades three and four, and grades five and six).

Provide at least two classes for youth if space and leadership are available and there are sufficient participants for each group (six or more enrolled). Divide older and younger youth, possibly using the same grading system as your local public school—junior high/middle school and high school.

If possible, provide a class for each group of twenty-five adults enrolled. Begin by dividing younger and older (using some midpoint age) or by having a class for women and a class for men. Additional classes might be graded as shown in the Organization Planning Chart or formed according to compatibility or interest.

Larger churches would add more classes/groups/departments for each of the age groups according to enrollment and the availability of leaders and space.

Compatibility

Grouping according to compatibility is used in many churches—particularly among adults—to allow persons who have the most in common to be together. People congregate due to factors such as preferred learning style or fellowship needs, and these preferences are established as a regular part of the organizational structure.

This grouping approach typically is used in combination with age grading and may be seen, for example, in a "Fellowship Bible Class." Sometimes

Figure 3.7

ORGANIZATION PLANNING CHART

	1		2 Enrollment		3 Prospects		4 Total Possibilities		5 Suggested Maximum Enrollment	6 Departments Needed	7 Suggested Maximum Enrollment	8 Classes Needed	9 Suggested Worker / Member Ratio[a]	10 Approximate No. of Workers Needed
DIVISION	Member Classification Age (Grade)		M	F	M	F	M	F						
PRESCHOOL	Birth–1	Cradle Roll							35		x	x	1/6	
		Babies							9		x	x	1/3	
		Ones							9		x	x	1/3	
	2								12		x	x	1/4	
	3								16		x	x	1/4	
	4								16		x	x	1/4	
	5								16		x	x	1/4	
CHILDREN	Special Education								20		x	x	1/4	
	6 (Grade 1)								30		x	x	1/6	
	7 (Grade 2)								30		x	x	1/6	
	8 (Grade 3)								30		x	x	1/6	
	9 (Grade 4)								30		x	x	1/6	
	10 (Grade 5)								30		x	x	1/6	
	11 (Grade 6)								30		x	x	1/6	

ORGANIZATION PLANNING CHART (CONTINUED)

Category	Age / Grade					Enrollment	Classes	Ratio [a]
YOUTH	12 (Grade 7)					60	12	1/8
	13 (Grade 8)					60	12	1/8
	14 (Grade 9)					60	12	1/8
	15 (Grade 10)					60	12	1/8
	16 (Grade 11)					60	12	1/8
	17 (Grade 12)					60	12	1/8
ADULT	18–24 (College)					125	25	1/5
	18–24 (Single)					125	25	1/5
	25–34 (Married)					125	25	1/5
	25–34 (Single)					125	25	1/5
	35–44 (Married)					125	25	1/5
	35–44 (Single)					125	25	1/5
	45–64 (Married)					125	25	1/5
	45–64 (Single)					125	25	1/5
	65–up					125	25	1/5
	Weekday S. S. Classes					X	25	1/5
	Adults Away				x	75	5	1/5
	Homebound				x	75	5	1/5
	Outreach Bible Study Group			x		x	x	x
	New Sunday Schools					x	x	x
	Pastor/Staff/Gen. Officers	x	x	x	x	x	x	x
	Total					x	x	x

a. Adult ratio in Column 9 includes care group leaders in the classes

47

the compatibility groupings develop informally, such as in a class of persons who have chosen to remain together despite suggestions that they promote to another age-group class.

Interest

Interest grouping is used when persons are free to select the most appealing study or activity. These groups exist as long as the particular study or activity is provided; consequently, this approach is used primarily with short-term educational activities and special emphases.

In some churches all three approaches will be used; however, age-group divisions remain the foundation. Additional groups can be organized as necessary or appropriate to meet the needs of participants and to fulfill the purpose of the organization.

Church Officers and Committees

In addition to basic programs, ministries, and councils, churches also are heavily dependent on elected church officials—officers—and committees.

Officers usually include moderator, clerk, treasurer, financial secretary, and trustees. These leaders fulfill not only needed duties for the congregation but also serve in a legal capacity on behalf of the church. Persons who serve in these positions usually are recommended by a nominating committee and elected by the congregation to serve for a specified time. Information and guidelines are included at the end of the chapter, in the section on "Church Officers."

Committees exist to plan, coordinate, implement, and evaluate the work assigned to them by the church. With a small group of members who have specialized skills, a church committee can study and complete an assignment much more efficiently than can the congregation in business sessions. Materials about the work of church committees, duties of members, and sample descriptions for several committees are at the end of the chapter, in the section on "Resources for Use with Church Officers and Church Committees."

Choosing a Pattern

The amount of organizational structure needed by a church must be determined by each local congregation, depending on its size, needs, and resources. Ultimately, every church is responsible for finding how best to organize and administer its work. The guidelines and options that have been described will help you assess possibilities; but, in consultation with other church leaders, you must choose the most appropriate arrangement.

The variety and extent of church structure will vary greatly, depending on a church's size and resources. There is no standard organization, only the principle that there must be a balanced ministry in congregational life, focusing on worship, proclamation, education, ministry, and fellowship.

For possible patterns and assistance in evaluating church organization, see figure 3.8. By studying these options, you can clarify how best to proceed with any adjustments needed in your church.

Figure 3.8a

CHURCH ORGANIZATION

Organization is grouping persons in a way that enables individuals and groups to accomplish their goals. In organization:

- Activities and responsibilities are assigned to individuals and groups.
- Working relationships are established.
- Responsibility and authority are delegated to enable individuals and groups to use initiative in their work.

Organizational Patterns

Possible Organization Components: A church can design many organizational components to perform its work. Components commonly found include staff, deacons, church officers, church committees, coordinating units (councils), Sunday school, discipleship training, music ministry, mission organizations, media center/library, and recreation.

Effective Organization: Effective organization grows out of an understanding of the church's mission, resources, and traditions. No pattern is best, even for churches of a similar size. Each must develop its own organization. Objectives, priorities, tradition, availability of leaders, needs and numbers of people, space and equipment, and time considerations will influence decisions about organizational patterns in a church.

Evaluating Options

Figure 3.8b gives suggestions and describes alternatives for organization. By studying these options you could determine how best to proceed with any adjustments needed in your situation.

Guidelines for the Administrator

Here are guidelines that will enable you to give effective and strong leadership to church organizations.

1. Determine the purpose and organizational structure for each program. Prepare a chart listing every position and unit, and the

Figure 3.8b

Possibilities for Church Organization

Type of Unit Position	Churches with Fewer than 150 Members*	Churches with 150 to 399 Members	Churches with 400 to 699 Members	Churches with 700 to 1,499 Members	Churches with 1,500 or more Members
Staff	Pastor Music Director[1]	Pastor Music Director Secretary[2] Custodian[2] Pianist/Organist[1]	Pastor Minister of Music and Education Secretary Custodian Organist[1] Pianist[1]	Pastor Minister of Music Minister of Education Secretaries[3] Custodians[3] Organist[1] Pianist[1] Age-Division Ministers[3]	Pastor Associate Pastor Minister of Education Minister of Music Business Administrator Minister of Recreation Evangelism/Outreach Minister Age-division Ministers Organist-Music Assistant Family Life Minister Secretaries[3] Custodians[3] Hostess Food service personnel[3]
Deacons	Deacons (1 deacon per 15 family units; minimum of 2 deacons)	Deacons (1 deacon per 15 family units)	Deacons (1 deacon per 15 family units)	Deacons (1 deacon per 15 family units)	Deacons (1 deacon per 15 family units)

Possibilities for Church Organization (Continued)

Type of Unit Position	Churches with Fewer than 150 Members*	Churches with 150 to 399 Members	Churches with 400 to 699 Members	Churches with 700 to 1,499 Members	Churches with 1,500 or more Members
Church Officers	Moderator (Pastor) Trustees Clerk Treasurer	Moderator Trustees Clerk Treasurer	Moderator Trustees Clerk Treasurer	Moderator Trustees Clerk Treasurer	Moderator Trustees Clerk Treasurer
Church Committees	Nominating Stewardship Missions Evangelism	Nominating Property and Space Stewardship Ushers Missions Preschool[4] Evangelism	Nominating Property and Space Stewardship Personnel Missions Preschool History Ushers Weekday Education[4] Public Relations Evangelism	Nominating Property and Space Stewardship Personnel Missions Preschool Food Service History Ushers Weekday Education[4] Public Relations Evangelism	Nominating Property and Space Stewardship Personnel Missions Preschool Food Service History Ushers Weekday Education[4] Public Relations Evangelism Other committees as needed
Service Programs	Media Services Director	Media Services Director- tor (up to 3 workers) Recreation Director	Media Staff Recreation Staff	Media Staff Recreation Staff	Media Staff Recreation Staff

Possibilities for Church Organization (Continued)

Type of Unit Position	Churches with Fewer than 150 Members*	Churches with 150 to 399 Members	Churches with 400 to 699 Members	Churches with 700 to 1,499 Members	Churches with 1,500 or more Members
Special Ministries		Senior Adult Ministry	Senior Adult Ministry Singles Ministry	Senior Adult Ministry Singles Ministry	Senior Adult Ministry Singles Ministry Intergenerational Activities
Coordination	Church Council	Church Council WMU Council S. S. Council Brotherhood Council	Church Council S. S. Council C. T. Council Music Council WMU Council Brotherhood Council Division Coordination Conferences	Church Council S. S. Council C. T. Council Music Council WMU Council Brotherhood Council Division Coordination Conferences	Church Council S. S. Council C. T. Council Music Council WMU Council Brotherhood Council Media Services Council Division Coordination Conferences
Bible Teaching	General officers and organization for each age division	Departments of each age division	Multiple departments as needed	Multiple departments as needed	Multiple departments as needed
Church Training	Church Training Director Age-group leaders[4]	Member training groups and departments for each age division New Church Member Training	Member training groups and departments for each age division New Church Member Training	Member training groups and departments for each age division New Church Member Training	Member training groups and departments for each age division New Church Member Training

Possibilities for Church Organization (Continued)

Type of Unit Position	Churches with Fewer than 150 Members*	Churches with 150 to 399 Members	Churches with 400 to 699 Members	Churches with 700 to 1,499 Members	Churches with 1,500 or more Members
WMU	WMU Director Age level organizations as needed	Age level organizations as needed	Age level organizations as needed	Age level organizations as needed	Age level organizations as needed
Brotherhood	Brotherhood Director	Baptist Men Royal Ambassador groups as needed	Baptist Men Royal Ambassador groups as needed	Baptist Men Royal Ambassador groups as needed	Baptist Men Royal Ambassador groups as needed
Music Ministry	Music Director[5] Pianist Choir	Music Director[5] Organist Church Choir or Ensemble Age-division choirs when possible	Age-division choirs Instrumental groups as needed	Fully developed Music Ministry	Fully developed Music Ministry

[1]Volunteer or part-time
[2]Part-time
[3]As needed
[4]If needed
[5]Person serves as program leader and staff member

*NOTE: It is important to encourage, in any way possible, churches of 150 members or less to have choir, recreation, and other needed ministries even though directors or other leaders for that activity might not be listed in column one of this chart.

53

name of every officer and teacher. Place this information at the front of a reference notebook/folder devoted to educational administration.

2. Use, or establish, a church council or committee of key leaders to plan, coordinate, and evaluate the church's total ministry. Meet at least monthly. (Suggestions for forming such a group are included in chapter 8, "Planning and Budgeting.")

3. Prepare job descriptions for all positions. Be sure to include duties, decision-making authority, and the person to whom the worker is responsible.

4. Make annual plans for each organization. Following the enlistment of officers for a new church year, schedule a planning workshop to develop goals and make plans for the next twelve months. Before the meeting distribute the appropriate purpose and organizational statements to each leader along with suggested areas for evaluation and goal setting. Ask each organizational leader to consult with his or her coordinating group for orientation and evaluation and to develop proposed goals and plans to be considered at the planning workshop. (See figure 3.9 for a work sheet. For assistance with planning, see chapter 8.)

5. Budget for regular expenses such as curriculum materials and for all special items in the annual plan. Delegate to organizational leaders as appropriate.

6. Maintain a master calendar listing all plans, person(s) responsible, and budget provisions, if any. Use this calendar to monitor activities, record progress toward goals, as a diary of your reactions concerning various events, and as a guide in planning with the church staff.

7. Maintain a complete record system for each organization listing persons involved, contact information, officers, and attendance records. This information is needed for communication and planning.

8. Use information to keep work focused. Information gathered and the materials developed will be especially helpful when enlisting and orienting new leaders, planning for enlargement, determining organizational problems, and other similar administrative duties.

9. Evaluate programs and organizations periodically and annually. Spend time before each church council or program committee meeting assessing the effectiveness of recent work. Look at records, review your master calendar, and check any information you have received or gained from your contact

with the various programs, departments, or committees. Discuss current needs with other leaders and adjust the annual plan as necessary. Prepare annually an extensive evaluation to present to the congregation and to the planning workshop; use these in developing future goals and plans.

10. Follow the basic principles of working with, for, and through people in administering church organizations. The three I's will guide you:

Inform. Tell specifically what is happening and why. Seek a clear understanding of all plans and procedures, providing opportunities for open discussion of pertinent issues. Keep in touch with key leaders in all organizations.

Inspire. Minister to and support the persons with whom you work. Whatever you are as a leader will be the most powerful influence on those through whom you must work. Administration is not doing the work yourself but eliciting, combining, and guiding the resources of the congregation. Your leadership will be multiplied through others.

Involve. Share leadership duties widely among responsible people. This requires giving major attention to:

- Equipping leaders to do their tasks
- Delegating responsibility to them
- Supporting and encouraging them as they do their jobs
- Involving workers in making decisions that will affect them or the duties for which they are responsible

---

Figure 3.9

GOAL PLANNING WORKSHEET

Use the following when exploring and planning goals for your committee, department, organization, or church.

1. Proposed goal:
2. What we hope to accomplish by this goal is to . . .
3. This goal is related to the following objective(s):
4. What is already being done related to this goal?
5. Specific age or interest group(s) to which this goal is related:
6. We will feel we have made progress toward this goal when . . .
7. Major obstacles we see in implementing this goal:
8. Major resources needed to begin:
9. Decision regarding proposed goal:
    _____ Approved
    _____ No decision at this time
    _____ Hold for further discussion/development
    _____ Develop action plan(s)
    _____ Secure input from . . .
    _____ Other:

Name of Group: _____

Chair: _____   Date: _____

How to Relate to Organizational Leaders

Administration, as described throughout this book, focuses on working with and through people. Being administrator does not mean that you make all the decisions, attend all the meetings, or do all the work yourself. Remember that your job is to coordinate and guide many areas of work rather than to immerse yourself in the details of one or two organizations. This requires serving as *a primary leader in a few groups* and as an *adviser* to many others.

The pastor, or other designated person responsible for the church's organizational life, is the chair of the general body that plans, directs, and evaluates all activities sponsored by the congregation. All program leaders participate with the minister(s) in this central leadership council and then provide direct leadership in their respective organizations. The pastor and other staff ministers, then, would serve as advisers to the subgroups without having direct leadership responsibility.

The pastor or other designated person would have direct, administrative responsibility for one group and would serve as adviser to the members of that body as they, in turn, lead their respective organizations. This organizational arrangement is illustrated in figure 3.10.

Organizational Records and Reports

Each group, class, department, division, and program should keep records of its activities and report regularly to the next larger unit. All basic programs and organizations, such as Sunday school, discipleship training, music ministry, and missions, should report regularly to the church. Provide an update of activities in monthly or quarterly business meetings and a summary report at the end of the church year.

Records

Program and ministry leaders should determine what information they and others need to keep informed and to give adequate guidance to the work of each organization. A record system usually is in place that can be adjusted as needs for information change. Religious bookstores and publishers have a variety of record-keeping and report forms that can be used as is or adapted for your situation.

Some have found it feasible to use computer systems to serve the records needs in a church. Individuals and companies are in business to help congregations with their use of computers not only with educational records but also with financial and church membership records.

Once leaders select an appropriate record system and secure the essential supplies for its operation, there should be training to assure proper use of the system. An annual training session for those who prepare the

Figure 3.10

LINE AND STAFF RELATIONSHIPS

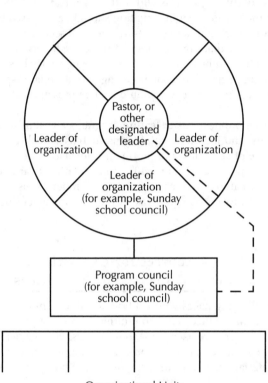

Organizational Units
(for example, age divisions, departments, and classes)

records can be a great help in getting accurate and complete information. For example, training would be useful for Sunday school group leaders, class secretaries, department secretaries, division secretaries, the general secretary, and hosts who work at welcome desks (including those who receive guests, get information from them, and help them find the appropriate group according to the church's grouping and grading plan).

Good records enable leaders to discover needs and opportunities so that appropriate and timely responses can be made. A secondary benefit concerns their historical value. Not only are records necessary when studying your heritage or dealing with legal issues, but data over the years can be studied for trends and needs that can be of significant use in determining leadership actions and planning strategy.

Reports

Each unit in an organization should report essential information to the leaders of the next larger unit of which it is a part. General leaders of a church organization need accurate and complete information about the effectiveness of the major units within the organization. Report forms that summarize the key items of information should be prepared by designated persons within each unit and sent to the general secretary.

It is important that organizations of the church periodically report on their work. This can be done in a monthly or quarterly business meeting, through a church newsletter, or by using promotional displays in major traffic areas. A summary report should also be presented at the end of the church year.

Use church publications to feature programs and ministries. Highlight special events, and include regular items such as a weekly or monthly report, schedule of activities, and pertinent information needed to keep the congregation informed. Use bulletin or information boards to report key items of information, such as attendance, number of visitors, and offerings. And, of course, make good use of the announcement period in regular services.

Resources for Use with Church Officers and Committees

On the following pages you will find additional information regarding the work of church officers and committees. This material is not intended to be exhaustive or to replace guidebooks published specifically for church officers and committees. Rather, you will find helpful reference and administrative materials that you can easily use in providing leadership for your church.

Figures 3.11 and 3.12 provide agenda outlines for church council and church business meetings. Information and job descriptions for church officers are in figures 3.13 through 3.17. Orientation materials and guidelines to train church committees are provided in figures 3.18 through 3.21. Sample committee guidelines (such as might be used to develop a church committee manual) are given for four key committees (figures 3.22 through 3.25).

Figure 3.11

CHURCH COUNCIL AGENDA

1. Call to order by chairperson.
2. Scripture/prayer/devotional by person enlisted in advance.
3. Approval of/additions to agenda (distribute tentative agenda in advance).

4. Approval of minutes of last meeting.
5. Follow-up reports from last meeting, if scheduled.
6. Review and evaluate church program events and activities conducted since the last meeting. As appropriate, receive reports from program and ministry leaders, staff ministers, and committee chairs.
6. Preview and coordinate events and activities planned for the next three months.
7. Plan and/or overview future events and activities that are more than three months away.
8. Summary of meeting and decisions by chairperson.
9. Preparation of any recommendations.
10. Assignments for follow-up by next meeting (for example, special projects and reports).
11. Brief evaluation of meeting.
12. Adjourn.

Figure 3.12

CHURCH BUSINESS MEETING AGENDA

1. Call to order by moderator
2. Prayer/devotional
3. Approval of minutes from previous meeting(s)
4. Church clerk's report

   - Request for letters
   - Letters received (for new members)
   - Deletions
   - Membership statistics

5. Church treasurer's report
6. Old business
7. Reports from committees

   - Standing committees
   - Special committees

8. Reports from directors of programs and ministries
9. Report from church council
10. Report from deacons or other councils
11. Reports from ministerial staff
12. New business (from floor)
13. Adjourn with prayer

Figure 3.13

MODERATOR

Principal Function: The chief responsibility of the moderator is to prepare for and preside at church business meetings; that is, to coordinate and facilitate productive business meetings in an orderly, efficient manner. (Many churches require that the pastor serve as moderator.)

Duties

1. Develop church business meeting agenda in cooperation with appropriate persons. Copies should be shared with church staff members, chairperson of deacons, and others included on the agenda prior to each session, if possible. (See the sample Church Business Meeting Agenda.)
2. Help members stay informed and involved in church business by promoting attendance and participation in business meetings.
3. Preside over all church business meetings.
4. Clarify matters voted on; determine action and follow up as appropriate.
5. Evaluate each business session and its activities.

Relationships

1. Work with the church clerk in preparation of agenda before business meetings and in preparation of minutes after meetings.
2. Consult with church staff members, committee chairpersons, program directors, and other responsible persons in preparation of the business meeting agenda and in evaluation of each business session and its activities.
3. Follow up after each business meeting with responsible committees, officers, individuals, and others to ensure that decisions are executed.
4. Be in touch with as many members as possible to know the spirit and mood of the congregation.
5. Serve as requested on the church council.

Tips for Moderators

1. Maintain the spirit of Christian love and fellowship while presiding by conducting meetings in an orderly manner. (The moderator must maintain a neutral position while presiding. If it is necessary to become personally involved in debate on a question under consideration, ask an assistant to preside.)
2. Be familiar with prescribed parliamentary procedure. Help members to understand parliamentary procedure without embarrassing them.
3. Insist that motions be stated and seconded before they are discussed.
4. Suggest that a member make a motion by stating: "If a motion is in order, I move . . ."
5. Call on the person who makes a motion to discuss it first.
6. Encourage full and free debate. Lead members to talk through their disagreements.
7. Execute business with dispatch, making certain that all matters are clear and concise. Avoid wasting time on trivialities. Bring people with differing views and perspectives together in the bond of love.

8. Alternate discussions so as to bring out both sides of a question. A member who has not spoken should be given preference over one who has. Be fair and courteous with all.
9. Respect the minority. The minority has a right to be heard even though the majority must prevail.
10. Always take the affirmative vote first. Take the negative vote next, and always take it.

Figure 3.14

CHURCH CLERK

Principal Function: The church clerk is responsible for recording, processing, and maintaining accurate records of all church business meeting transactions. The clerk also is responsible for all official church membership records and communications. (Some responsibilities may be assigned to church staff members.)

Duties
1. Assist in preparation of the agenda for church business meeting(s).
2. Keep an accurate record (in the form of minutes) of all business transactions made and approved in church business meetings.
3. Present the minutes of the prior meeting(s) at each business meeting for official church approval.
4. Provide clerical assistance during the invitation period of the worship services for new members, rededications, and other decisions.
5. Maintain accurate member records. This includes: (a) adding new names and pertinent information to the chronological membership roll and dropping other names as necessary through transfer, inactivity, or death; (b) correcting records for change of address or phone number; and (c) sending a memo as needed to all church personnel keeping separate records to avoid incorrect information.
6. Request letters by transfer from other churches for new members, forward letters to other churches requested by members, and notify persons when their names are removed from the church roll for any reason other than transfer of membership by letter.
7. Prepare and mail all official church correspondence.
8. Preserve records for present and future use.
9. Prepare the annual reports, submit for church approval, and send to appropriate offices.

Relationships
1. Work with the moderator in preparation of agenda before meetings and in preparation of minutes after meetings. (It may be necessary at times to consult with appropriate church staff members, program leaders, committee chairpersons, deacons, and others to be sure that the wording in the minutes is correct as given in the business meetings to avoid confusion either in the next business meeting or at later dates.)
2. Work with the church secretary in getting the minutes prepared for distribution to the members in the next business meeting. (A typed copy of

the business meeting minutes should be sent to the church staff members and moderator no later than one week following a business session.)

3. Serve as resource person to the church historian and/or history commit-tee as requested. (If the church does not have a history committee, the church clerk should be the church's designated historian.)
4. Provide statistical information on the church membership as requested.
5. Work with appropriate church staff members in handling official cor-respondence with other organizations/churches.
6. Work with the trustees in preparation of legal documents.
7. Work with various staff members, church program leaders, and commit-tee chairpersons in preparing the annual church report.
8. Give necessary information about new members to the church office, to the person in charge of new member orientation, and to program lead-ers so the new members can be enlisted in appropriate programs.

Figure 3.15

TREASURER

Principal Function: The church treasurer is responsible for the proper receipt, accounting, and disbursement of church funds within policies es-tablished by the church for adequate financial control. The treasurer's work focuses primarily on financial records and payment procedures rather than the handling of cash. (In larger churches this duty is sometimes assigned to a staff member who works with all church financial matters.)

Duties
1. Keep accurate records in appropriate financial journals of all monies received and disbursed.
2. Reconcile monthly bank statements and correct ledgers as needed.
3. Sign checks in accordance with church policies and procedures, always verifying supporting data for each check request.
4. Make monthly and annual reports to the finance committee and the church.
5. Provide for records of individual contributions to be maintained.
6. Suggest possible investment opportunities; advise about bond purchasing.
7. Keep church staff informed of any trends or changes in fiscal matters.
8. Instill and preserve high financial morale throughout the congregation.
9. Submit accurate financial records for annual audit according to church policy.

Relationships
1. Serve as ex officio member of the finance committee. Confer with this committee in:
    √ recommending and establishing policies related to receiving, ac-counting, and disbursing of church money.
    √ developing the annual church budget and coordinating the an-nual stewardship campaign.

√ preparing and presenting a monthly financial report in the church business meeting. (Also confer with moderator about presentation of report.)
√ providing a continuing program of stewardship education for the church.

2. Receive copy of deposit slip and summary of receipts record from the counting committee after each deposit.
3. Work closely with the financial secretary in maintaining records of individual contributions.
4. Confer with the church staff members and deacons to maintain communication in financial matters of the church.
5. Work with staff members, officers, and organizations in administering financial details of church projects.
6. At the request of the finance committee, serve as advisor to various requesting committees in preparing and maintaining their budgets.
7. Be available to help individual church members plan the personal and family budget.
8. Serve as requested on the church council. Advise the council and various committee chairpersons about available funds and budgeted funds.

Figure 3.16

FINANCIAL SECRETARY

Principal Function: The financial secretary is responsible for maintaining accurate records of individual member contributions.

Duties
1. Post offerings weekly to individual accounts.
2. Mail a quarterly and annual statement of contributions to each contributor.
3. Provide statistical financial data as requested by treasurer, finance committee, and/or the church staff.

Relationships
1. Receive copy of deposit slip, summary of receipts record, and individual offering envelopes from the counting committee after each deposit.
2. Work with the treasurer in the posting and reporting of member contributions.
3. Work with the church secretary in mailing member contribution reports.
4. Serve as resource person to the church staff, church program leaders, officers, and committees to provide needed statistical information about patterns of giving.
5. Maintain confidentiality about specific member contributions except with approved persons.
6. Serve as requested on the church council.

Figure 3.17

TRUSTEES

Principal Function: The trustees serve as legal representatives in all transactions related to the church. They hold legal title to the church property, and they sign all documents related to the purchase, sale, mortgaging, or rental of church property after approval by the church in regular business session.

Duties
1. Hold legal title to all church property (as required by state law) and act only as directed by the church in regular business session.
2. Sign all legal documents involving church property upon direction by the church in regular business session.
3. Maintain an up-to-date inventory of all church property, mortgage loans, and insurance on church property. (Such information should be kept in a safety deposit box with copies filed in the church office for ready reference.)

Relationships
1. Relate to appropriate civil officials in all legal matters involving the church.
2. Keep abreast of latest insurance and legal changes (innovations, programs, etc.), report such changes to the appropriate church leaders, and advise the church staff and any committees concerning legal matters.
3. Counsel with appropriate church officers and committees in matters related to church properties.
4. Maintain all church legal documents in conjunction with the church clerk.
5. If qualified, serve as resource personnel to the church staff and church families in legal matters.
6. Report on legal issues related to the church as necessary and/or requested.
7. Serve as requested on the church council.

Figure 3.18

THE WORK OF CHURCH COMMITTEES

Benefits
1. The use of committees spreads the administrative load among members of the congregation and broadens participation. This provides church staff members and deacons more freedom for ministry to the people. Through committees responsibility is delegated, and the church is helped to perform its tasks.
2. The use of committees uses skills and talents of members of the congregation and makes the church a more efficient and effective ministering body.
3. The use of committees gives opportunity for differing points of view to be presented and reconciled, thereby producing more harmony among church members.

Types of Committees

There are two kinds of work done by committees in a church. The first type of work relates to the long-term, ongoing ministries and programs that are basic to the church's life, such as the financial program. For this type of work, the church needs to have committees that are permanent. Such a committee is called a standing (or regular) committee. The stewardship committee and the property committee are examples of standing committees. The members should serve on a rotating basis, with a portion of the committee being replaced each year.

Rotation assures that there are experienced members on a committee and, also, that there are always new people with fresh ideas being involved in church life. Committee members usually serve a three-year term with one-third of the group rotating off each year. After a year off, persons may be reelected to the same committee if the church desires.

The second type of committee work in a church relates to short-term or temporary needs such as planning for a homecoming or conducting a fund-raising drive. For this type of work, a church uses committees that operate only long enough to accomplish their assigned task. This kind of committee is called a special, or ad hoc, committee. A building committee and pastor selection committee are examples. The members of a special committee do not rotate but serve as long as the committee exists.

Standing committees carry out very different functions from special committees. The work of standing committees usually revolves primarily around the needs of the church to maintain the best of what it now has. Standing committees give attention to maintaining, operating, and stabilizing already-existing ministries and programs that are ongoing.

Special committees, in contrast, usually focus their work on the needs of the church that are short-term, such as for constitutional revision or adding an addition to a building. They give attention to creating something new or to revising something old. Special committees are formed and disbanded as needed; they should not continue beyond the time needed to perform their church-assigned task.

In planning an effective committee structure for a church, balanced attention should be given to meeting the need that a church has to maintain both long-term and short-term ministries and programs. Long-term ministries and programs require standing committees. Short-term ministries and programs need special committees.

The work of all church committees should be coordinated by a central coordinating unit such as the church council. Thus, the chairpersons of all church committees should serve as ex officio members of the church council, meaning they are on call when needed.

The members of all committees (standing and special) should be recommended by the nominating committee and elected by the church. Since the church brings each committee into existence, each committee reports back to the church. There should be a regular time allocated at each church business meeting for church committees to report on work accomplished.

Most of the new committees established by a church will be special committees although it is not unusual for a new standing committee to be created. When it seems desirable to form a new committee:

1. Determine the need for a new committee.
2. Formulate its purpose and duties.

3. Prepare to allocate necessary resources.
4. Present to the church for discussion and vote.
5. Submit personnel needs to the nominating committee.
6. Present committee members, with chairperson designated, for church approval.
7. Educate new committee members.

Figure 3.19

DUTIES OF A COMMITTEE MEMBER

1. Know the purpose, duties, and members of the committee.
2. Be present and on time for meetings.
3. Participate in discussions.
4. Contribute to the planning and achievement of activities/projects.
5. Complete assignments as agreed upon.
6. Keep the committee chairperson informed about progress on assignments.
7. Report on assignments at committee meetings.

Figure 3.20

DUTIES OF A COMMITTEE CHAIRPERSON

1. Know the purpose, duties, and members of the committee.
2. Request and administer committee budgeting.
3. Serve as an ex officio member of the church council.
4. Plan the agenda for each meeting of the committee.
5. Conduct meetings.

    √ Each meeting should have a purpose.
    √ Each meeting should have an agenda.
    √ Each meeting needs resources.
    √ Each meeting should plan for follow-up.
    √ Each meeting should be reported.

6. Supervise the work of the committee secretary.
7. Assign responsibility to committee members for follow-through actions.
8. Lead the committee to:

    √ Identify and schedule some activities/projects.
    √ Develop a sequence of actions.
    √ Prepare a timetable.
    √ Determine the resources needed.
    √ Complete activities/projects.

9. Report committee action(s), as appropriate, to the church council and/or the church business meeting.
10. Collaborate as necessary with church staff members, church officers, church council, program directors, and other committees.

Figure 3.21

GUIDELINES FOR EFFECTIVE COMMITTEE WORK

1. Maintain a rotating membership for all standing committees, with one third of the members rotating off each year.
2. Maintain nonrotational membership on all special committees; that is, all members serve until the work of the committee is completed or the committee is disbanded by church action.
3. Limit committee membership to only one standing committee and, if desirable by the church, to one special committee. (Make exceptions only in unusual circumstances.)
4. Have the nominating committee recommend members for committees, standing and special, to the church. The nominating committee should staff newly created committees with at least three members, with one-third of the membership rotating off each year. Add additional members (in any quantity) as necessary but maintain rotational membership for all committees.
5. Usually a committee member should not be reelected to same standing committee for a period of one year following a three-year term. However, a year of ineligibility should not be mandatory. Need and willingness to serve should be the primary considerations.
6. Have the nominating committee designate the chairperson of each committee. (This should be done when the committee members are presented to the church for election. Chairpersons of standing committees should be designated to serve one year. Chairpersons of special committees should be designated to serve until the committee completes its work or is disbanded by church action.)
7. Assign a church staff member to each committee to act as advisor and consultant. (In a single staff church, there should be no more committees than the pastor can counsel and advise adequately. If necessary, consider asking other key leaders for assistance.)
8. Be certain each chairperson understands that he or she—not pastor or any staff member—is to lead the committee and that committee members—not the pastor or any other staff member—are to do the work.
9. Prepare a job description for every committee and provide a copy to every committee member. In preparing job descriptions:
   √ Use available material and information as a guideline (church practice, church bylaws, pamphlets, books, and resources from other churches).
   √ Write with your church's needs in mind.
   √ Secure committee approval on all parts of each description.
   √ Copy the job descriptions and present them to the church business meeting for approval.
   √ Make them a part of the bylaws or put them in a handbook to give to each church family.
   √ Update the descriptions periodically as the church situation changes.
10. Provide orientation for new chairpersons and new committee members.
11. Meet with the chairperson of each committee periodically to discuss the work of the committee and to coordinate activities.

12. Set aside one night a month (or quarter) as the committee meeting night. (For example, the second Wednesday of each month before prayer service. Do not expect committees to have unnecessary meetings. Whether the various committees meet should be left to the discretion of each chairperson. Make the chairperson responsible for seeing that members know whether the committee is to meet.)
13. Instruct committees to report directly to the congregation during a regular business meeting when necessary or upon request. (Every committee should report at least quarterly.) Reports that involve major recommendations or require major decisions by the church should be shared with the church staff/church council and deacons for review and/or response prior to the business meeting. Committee reports to the church are beneficial because they:

√ inform the church about the work of a committee,
√ develop a spirit of achievement, and
√ provide promotion for the work of a committee.

Figure 3.22

NOMINATING COMMITTEE

Principle Function: To lead the church in securing staff for all church-elected leadership positions filled by volunteers; to approve all volunteer workers before they are nominated to serve in church-elected positions.

Relationships and Responsibilities

1. Committee chairperson serves as ex officio member of the church council, contributing and receiving information related to the work of the nominating committee.

With Committees

1. Study the work responsibilities of all committees to understand the nature and scope of their work.
2. Counsel with the chairperson of each committee to determine present and/or future leadership needs.
3. Contact and enlist all nominees prior to presentation for election.

With Church Officers

1. Study the work responsibilities of all church officers to understand the scope of their work.
2. Contact and enlist all church officer nominees prior to presentation for election.
3. Chairperson of committee informs moderator of reports to be made in the church business meeting.
4. Chairperson of committee gives a copy of any reports made during the church business meeting to the church clerk for permanent record in the minutes of the church.

With Program Directors

1. Study the work responsibilities of all directors to understand the nature and scope of their work.

2. Contact and enlist all director nominees prior to presentation for election.
3. Counsel with each director to determine present and/or future leadership needs.
4. Assist directors in contacting and enlisting nominees prior to presentation for election.

Note: Program directors should serve on the nominating committee.

With Church Staff

1. Counsel with staff members to determine present and future leadership needs in the church and in developing plans to satisfy those needs.
2. Work closely with staff members in discovering potential leaders.

With Church Business Meeting

1. Make periodic reports on the work of the nominating committee.
2. Answer questions about the work of the nominating committee.
3. Recommend all members of every standing committee.
4. Recommend all members of every special committee.
5. Recommend all members of deacons or related groups.
6. Designate chairperson of each standing committee annually.
7. Designate chairperson of each special committee when committee is elected.
8. Recommend all church-elected leadership for programs such as Sunday school, discipleship training, missions, and music ministry.
9. Recommend all church officers.

Figure 3.23

PERSONNEL COMMITTEE

Principle Function: To assist the church in administrative matters related to all employed personnel.

Relationships and Responsibilities

With Councils

1. Committee chairperson serves as ex officio member of the church council.

With Committees

1. Consult with the finance committee in developing and budgeting salary schedule and benefit provisions for all church staff members annually.
2. Consult with the finance committee in budgeting for any additional church staff members.

With Church Officers

1. Committee chairperson informs moderator of reports to be made in the church business meeting.
2. Committee chairperson gives a copy of any reports made during the church business meeting to the church clerk for permanent record in the minutes of the church.

3. Committee chairperson keeps the church treasurer informed regarding budgeted salary and benefit provisions for all staff members.

With Church Staff
1. Work with all staff members to:
   √ prepare and update job descriptions annually.
   √ negotiate a salaries schedule and benefit provisions annually.
   √ develop church policies and procedures relating to church staff personnel.
   √ discuss needs for additional church staff positions.
2. Consult with appropriate staff member(s) in locating, interviewing, and recommending additional church staff personnel.
2. Assess job performance of each staff member at least annually (and be sensitive to job insecurities that may plague them).

With Church Business Meeting
1. Make periodic reports on work of the personnel committee.
2. Answer questions about the work of the personnel committee.
3. Recommend all employed personnel for every church staff position.
4. Recommend administrative policies and procedures for all employed personnel.

Figure 3.24

FINANCE COMMITTEE

Principle Function: To plan and promote stewardship education in all areas of church life and to lead the church in budget planning, promotion, subscription, and administration.

Relationships and Responsibilities

With Councils
1. Committee chairperson serves as ex officio member of the church council.
2. Develop and recommend to the church council an overall stewardship education and promotion plan.

With Committees
1. Review with chairpersons periodically the expenditures of committees to ensure correspondence with budget allocations and budget adjustments.
2. Consult with the chairperson of each committee annually to determine financial resources needed by each committee for its work during the following year.

With Church Officers
1. Committee chairperson informs moderator of reports to be made in the church business meeting.
2. Committee chairperson gives to church clerk a copy of any reports made during the church business meeting for permanent records in the minutes of the church.

3. The church treasurer serves as an ex officio member of the finance committee.

With Program Directors

1. Review with each director periodically the expenditures of the organization in terms of budget allocations and budget adjustments.
2. Consult with each director annually to determine financial resources needed by each organization for its work during the following year.

With Church Staff

1. Consult with appropriate church staff member(s) in the planning, promotion, subscription, and administration of the church budget.
2. At least one church staff minister serves as staff advisor and consultant on the finance committee.

With Church Business Meeting

1. Make periodic reports on the work of the finance committee.
2. Answer questions about the work of the finance committee.
3. Recommend financial policies and procedures to be practiced by the church.
4. Make recommendations concerning proposed expenditures not included in the current budget.
5. Recommend an annual church budget.

Figure 3.25

PROPERTY AND SPACE COMMITTEE

Principle Function: To assist the church in the care of all properties and buildings, to study and recommend the use of space and furnishings as they relate to all programs and activities, to study the need and recommend acquiring property and creating space, and to administer work assigned to it.

Relationships and Responsibilities

With Councils

1. Committee chairperson serves as ex officio member of the church council.

With Committees

1. Present an annual budget proposal to the finance committee for financial resources needed by the property and space committee to accomplish its assigned work.
2. Recommend to the personnel committee the employment, training, and supervision needs of maintenance personnel.
3. Work with the missions committee to recommend acquisition and to maintain property and space for mission purposes.
4. Work with the long-range planning committee in determining future property and space needs of the church.
5. Assist other church committees in responsibilities that may relate to the assigned work of the property and space committee.

6. Prepare recommendations to the finance committee for additional property.

With Church Officers

1. Committee chairperson informs moderator of reports to be made at the church business meeting.
2. Committee chairperson gives the church clerk a copy of any report made during the church business meeting for permanent record in the minutes of the church.
3. Committee chairperson submits purchase order to church treasurer to request finances for budgeted items.

With Program Directors

1. Conduct with each director an annual evaluation of space allocations to determine areas needing adjustment and enlargement.
2. Recommend to directors space rearrangement to secure maximum use for education, special activities, and worship.
3. Recommend to directors policies regarding the use of space, equipment, and properties.
4. Assist directors in recommending and maintaining proper and adequate furnishings for programs and activities.

With Church Staff

1. Consult with appropriate staff member(s) in conducting an annual evaluation of space allocations to determine areas needing adjustment and enlargement.
2. Consult with appropriate staff member(s) in determining space rearrangement to ensure maximum use of facilities for worship, education, and special activities.
3. Assist the church staff in arranging, equipping, and administering adequate worship space.
4. Work with the staff member responsible for supervision of the maintenance personnel in developing and recommending maintenance policies and procedures.
5. Consult with appropriate staff member(s) regarding the need and process in acquiring new space for continued growth.
6. At least one church staff minister serves as staff advisor/consultant on the property and space committee.

With Church Business Meeting

1. Make periodic reports on work of the property and space committee.
2. Answer questions about the work of the property and space committee.
3. Recommend policies and procedures regarding the use of space, equipment, and properties.
4. Recommend the appointment of a church building survey and planning committee when needed and appropriate.

Chapter 4

WORKING WITH PEOPLE: THE MINISTER AS TEAM LEADER

Robert D. Dale

S ome ministers appear to love humanity but hate people. These folks find themselves uncomfortable in local congregations because those fellowships are just people—all kinds of people.

Interpersonal relationships provide the bridges over which ministry moves. The effective church administrator learns to build one-to-one friendships. Moreover, managers must also expand their skills in relating to work groups, ministry committees, and program councils by learning to function well in one-to-several and one-to-many settings.

Working with church people well as a team leader involves a variety of administrative challenges.

- Understanding congregations as service organizations
- Ministering through committees
- Rewarding volunteers
- Building a unified team for ministry
- Solving problems
- Managing ministry meetings
- Chairing decision-making meetings
- Relating to church staffers
- Delegating ministry opportunities
- Supervising fellow church members
- Dealing with difficult people
- Shaping the organizational climate

Working with volunteers in congregations requires keen relational and management skills.

Understanding Congregations as Service Organizations

The management sciences distinguish among three kinds of organizations: the for-profits, the governmental, and the not-for-profits. Churches and other Christian institutions fit into the not-for-profit category. Management experts agree that not-for-profits are by far the most challenging organizations to administer. Since the church is both spiritual organism and human organization, congregations are doubly difficult to manage.

What are the factors that make not-for-profits and volunteer organizations so tough to manage?

- Not-for-profits exist to render a service; for-profits exist to show a profit.
- Volunteers relate to their organizations in a somewhat avocational manner.
- Not-for-profits sometimes serve the second-level goals of their members. (Churches, however, should serve ultimate goals.)
- Volunteer organizations often relate to diverse and ill-defined constituencies. Most churches are clear about their formal membership but may be unclear about the various groups of persons in the community to whom they will try to minister.
- The purpose or dream of the not-for-profit is the most serious challenge for volunteer groups. Objectives are frequently too diffuse to provide a sharp focus for management.
- Not-for-profits are judged by their members' perceptions of effectiveness. Such varied expectations and such imprecise measurements of success create virtually unmanageable work climates.
- Not-for-profits usually produce intangibles.
- The benefits to the members of volunteer organizations are often indirect and sometimes vague.
- Not-for-profits generally function within a high (but occasionally hidden) level of competition. In most communities a large number of volunteer organizations compete for the allegiance, time, and money of local residents.
- The mission of many not-for-profits is often unattainable in the short run.
- Not-for-profits customarily pay their leaders poorly and sometimes recruit their volunteers on an "anybody we can get to take the job" basis.
- Not-for-profit managers must be skilled in consensus building and other political abilities.
- Not-for-profit managers stay caught between an ongoing mission and volunteers who serve part-time or once in a while.

- Volunteer organizations and their committees often find they aren't well served by counting on their informal traditions for formal management clues.

Ministering through Committees and Teams

Churches that take the "priesthood of every believer" principle seriously take work groups seriously too. Behind most congregational ministries and services lie the efforts of a committee or committees. This imperfect method of coordinating ministry has a way of working well enough in the end to advance the mission of the congregation.

Keep these things in mind as you work with church committees.[1]

- Committees exist for the church, not vice versa. Committees have no life independent of the congregation. Committees are to help the larger body of believers implement its ministry.
- The congregation sets church policy; committees carry out established policies. Because of a committee's special knowledge of certain congregational needs, that committee may propose new policies or changes in existing policies to the church, however.
- The function of church committees is to help the congregation accomplish tasks that can't be done as well by the congregation acting as a committee of the whole.
- The congregation owes its committees a job description, orientation of its chairperson and members, and a forum for reporting their work to the church.
- Orientation sessions for committees are intended to (1) discuss how committees function in this church, (2) inform committee members of their specific duties, (3) elect any officers whom the church hasn't already specified, and (4) train the committee to complete its planning, implementing, and reporting.
- Regular meetings and special meetings called by committee chairpersons should be held to ensure the consistent service of the committee for the church.
- Any committee recommendation for congregational consideration should be accompanied by full information such as the problem being attacked, the options considered and rejected, the formal recommendation itself, sufficient time to discuss the issue, and the amount of time and/or financial support necessary.
- Some congregations designate a time in their official calendars for committees to meet and do their work.
- Periodically congregations should evaluate their committee structure in order to cover emerging needs and eliminate any gaps or overlaps in committee duties. Wasted motion is demotivating to all workers, especially volunteers who have less time to invest.

Personal Rewards for Volunteers

Rewards for volunteers? Doesn't that idea fly in the face of the definition of a volunteer as a person who serves freely by personal choice? Not really. It's true that volunteers do not receive wages, fringe benefits, or bonuses. But volunteers do receive psychic and spiritual rewards.[2]

Consider these personal rewards for volunteers:

- Contributing to a vital cause. Some persons find great satisfaction in being part of a goal-oriented organization. They join with others on the same mission and feel the exhilaration of being "on the team." These volunteers are concerned with excellence, production, problem solving, and goal achievement.
- Enjoying the fellowship of like-minded persons. These volunteers relish being with other persons in whose company they feel comfortable. They value warm and friendly relationships and enjoy listening, sharing information and feelings, and encouraging others.
- Influencing individuals and groups. These volunteers want to be heard, like to have their advice heeded, and enjoy position and prominence. They generally hold strong opinions, are outspoken and fluent, sometimes like to debate issues and win arguments, and intend to change others. Hopefully, their major concern at this point is to invest their influence in inspiring and empowering others to reach group goals.

These three categories of volunteers have been called achievers, affiliators, and power people.

- *Achievers* serve their volunteer organizations best by organizing new projects and programs, by solving challenging problems, and by brainstorming possibilities and options.
- *Affiliators* nurture and lend support by counseling, greeting, listening, and acting as hosts and hostesses.
- *Power people* are the movers and shakers who raise money, persuade others to join in, and generally keep the organizational structures moving forward in positive directions or backward in reactionary modes.

In other words, each of these types of volunteers is needed in churches and other volunteer agencies. Additionally, each of these volunteers receives personal rewards. Yes, volunteers are paid—in service, recognition, growth, challenge, results, love, and teamwork.

Building a Unified Team for Ministry

Teamwork is needed in the congregation anytime two or more people must work together and depend on one another. (Review the section of chapter 2 on team building.) Think of managing the team-building process as a four-step sequence of (1) sharing personal history in group settings as an icebreaker and fellowship builder, (2) affirming group members' gifts for and contributions to ministry, (3) goal setting for ministry projects and programs, and (4) celebrating the developing sense of unity (figure 4.1). It's important to treat team building as a continuing practice and to use the model as a design factor in every meeting in order to develop and maintain unity.

Figure 4.1

TEAM-BUILDING MODEL

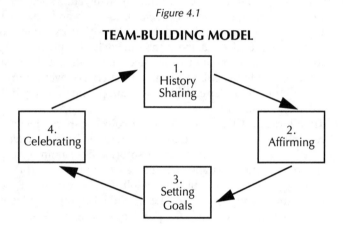

One key attitude in team building is making ministry results "the captain of the team." That is, group or congregational goals become the focus of team building with individual goals and other concerns becoming secondary. Several ingredients are basic to developing an effective ministry team: (1) a clearly defined congregational dream; (2) settings where people feel free to risk their ideas and opinions; (3) cooperating rather than competing; (4) a commitment to congregational goals.

The team-building model helps workers get acquainted, divide responsibilities, build group cohesion, heighten morale, increase creativity, and deepen loyalty. Independence then becomes interdependence. That's team building!

Solving Problems

Every organization faces problems. Volunteer organizations grapple with tough issues gingerly because these groups are glued together by a fragile bond called trust. Problem solving, then, involves the entire congregation and demands skilled management.

Problem solving can become a creative instead of a frustrating experience if a good method is used.

- Begin with a concise and precise statement of the problem under consideration. Include a broad description of an ideal solution as well. Both need and hope are identified by this step.
- Brainstorm possible solutions by "goal wishing." Completing the sentence "I wish that . . ." generates many options and lessens our tendency to defend our ideas. After all, anything can be wished for.
- Take an excursion in your mind. Great inventors and creative thinkers throughout history have used ideas and images from unrelated sources to solve their problems. For example, Edwin Land's daughter fretted about the time delay for processing photographs. This complaint stimulated him to invent the Polaroid camera. Thinking deliberately about material or events unrelated to the problem under consideration can provide the key link for solving a problem.
- Try a force fit. Choose an idea from your excursion, focus on it, return to your problem, and see if something from the excursion idea helps break through to a new solution by examining its positive possibilities first and then its negative potential. If the possibilities outweigh the pitfalls, a solution is available. Personal commitment, group endorsement, and planning the details of implementation complete the problem-solving process.[3]

Managing Ministry Meetings

Business managers complain that they spend as many as one thousand hours yearly in meetings. While ministers may not spend that much time in meetings, we work with volunteers in our meetings and must guide our meetings well or lose our volunteers.

Extra meetings must be avoided. Meetings are necessary when (1) congregation-wide concerns need to be discussed, (2) consensus building is demanded, (3) verbal reports must be shared, (4) esprit de corps needs to be cultivated, and (5) members need to be trained en masse. Don't call meetings when (1) the same information can be shared as well in writing, over the phone, or by electronic means; (2) essential participants will be absent; (3) leaders can't get prepared; and (4) the results will not justify participants' time and energy.

Not all meetings are the same. Basically, the structure of a meeting should match its purpose.

- *Information meetings* convey basic facts and require good communication skills and a variety of methods for sharing data.
- *Problem-solving meetings* focus on difficult questions and demand participative and consensus-building skills.
- *Procedural meetings* announce policies and call for abilities to enhance psychological ownership.[4] Agenda and handouts should be prepared beforehand and, in some cases, circulated in advance.

Most effective meeting managers have a plan or model they use in guiding the progress of the meeting itself. One helpful meeting management model moves from (1) *evaluating* the group's progress toward its mission, (2) *creating* a range of options and resources for dealing with challenges, (3) *deciding* which alternative to recommend for the congregation's consideration, and (4) *implementing* the congregation's ministry decisions and programs (figure 4.2). This approach provides a "picture in the mind" for leaders of conferences and meetings to use during work sessions.

Figure 4.2

MEETING-MANAGEMENT MODEL

Chairing Decision-Making Meetings

Formal decision-making meetings can be intimidating for the inexperienced or uncertain chairperson. Some straightforward principles can be helpful.

- Limit discussion to one subject at a time.
- Provide every member equal right to speak, offer motions, hold office, and vote.
- Allow for full and free debate.
- Protect the rights of both the majority and the minority.
- Set a climate of teamwork, cooperation, and consideration.

The duties of the chairperson usually include (1) keeping the meetings moving according to agenda; (2) knowing your congregation's formal documents, such as its constitution and bylaws and its adopted parliamentary law, such as *Robert's Rules of Order*, well enough to maintain orderliness; and (3) acting fairly and, if possible, preserving harmony.[5]

Relating to Church Staffers

Every church has a staff. Ninety-nine percent of church staffers nationwide are volunteers. How church leaders treat one another and work together is an important climate setter for congregations. Several principles contribute to good staff relationships.

- Church staffers are people, not roles. Respect the God-created uniqueness of fellow church leaders. Help them grow, meet their needs, and reach personal and congregational goals.
- Recognize that there are different kinds of relationships on church staffs. Some staffers' relationships revolve around what sociologists describe as "identity bonds." That is, my personality and gifts for ministry complement your gifts for ministry so that together we form a well-balanced team. Other staffers relate around "task bonds" and, therefore, focus on goals and work to be done.
- Effective staffs blend specialist and generalist roles. The crucial issue here is that someone—usually the pastor—must maintain a corporate perspective and view the congregation's ministry in its broadest scope. Some church administrators must fill a generalist role for the congregation while others may specialize in particular ministries.
- The larger the staff, the higher likelihood there is of relational tension. That's not to say that large staffs will inevitably disagree. But relational bonds, or primary interpersonal ties, multiply geometrically and become increasingly complicated as additional staffers are added.[6] Most of us have been led to believe "the more, the merrier" in staff resources. The fact is that where more staffers are involved, there's more potential for relational complications in staff relationships.
- Job descriptions provide a formal statement of congregational expectations for employed and volunteer staffers.
- Adopt a healthy management style with staffers. Provide both freedom and security for workers. A dictatorial management style majors on structure and security while stifling freedom. Managers who use a "path of least resistance" approach supply freedom but no security. Balanced styles are more apt to undergird both freedom and security.

- Take a developmental stance. Every staffer has some limitations, but most of us can grow with assistance and encouragement.
- Provide forums for communication and mutual nurture. Structured meetings with friendly atmospheres allow for information sharing, joint learning, teamwork, and supervision.

Delegating Ministry Opportunities

Delegation offers two positive opportunities to church managers. First, delegation allows ministers to multiply their ministries by involving others. Second, delegation lets others learn by doing. When is delegation called for?

- When someone else does the job better than you.
- When it saves the church time and/or money.
- When someone can be trained by means of the experience.

Good delegation demands a clear description of the opportunity and its limits, a large enough and complete enough task to challenge the person, a realistic time span for finishing the task, and agreed-upon checkpoints for reporting on progress. When delegating, let the task go; don't breathe down someone's neck while he is trying to share your work burden.

Supervising Fellow Church Members

Directly observing good supervision isn't a common experience. But several years ago I saw a first-rate example of supervision, and I was the guinea pig for the entire process. I had gone to the teaching hospital at Nashville's Vanderbilt Hospital for an eye examination. There I was treated by an ophthalmologist and a young intern on the first day of rotation in the eye clinic. The doctor would carefully explain what he was going to do and what he'd be looking for. After checking me himself, he would turn me over to the trainee and ask, "What do you see?" Sometimes the doctor would say, "See that? If his eyes were abnormal, they would . . .," and he'd proceed to describe what a diseased eye would look like. The step-by-step process and the careful instructions kept my usual "doctor's office anxieties" at a minimum. Suddenly, I became very worried. The doctor announced that he was ready to dilate my eyes and asked the intern, "Will his pupils get larger or smaller?" I was horrified when the intern answered incorrectly. I knew more about this process than the young doctor-to-be! Then my lesson in good supervision emerged. The ophthalmologist patiently and gently explained the physiological reaction that would take place. His attitude calmed me and taught the intern without embarrassing him. Good supervision combines gentleness with firmness.

81

This experience demonstrated supervision for me. Supervision, especially in a volunteer organization, is a supportive relationship. In other words, supervision calls for a comfortable but structured relationship. Typically, we have thought of supervision as a boss-employee tie with authority as the lever for change. Supervision is actually more of a mentor-novice relationship. The mentor serves as sponsor, guide, guru, model, and cheerleader. The novice, on the other hand, receives encouragement, nourishment, guidance, and proven ways of working. Supervision is a reciprocal relationship—like a two-person rail cart that requires both persons' efforts to move it down the track. The result of supervision is growth for both the novice and the mentor.

Supervision blends learning by example, practice, and feedback. (1) Pastors and other church staff ministers who supervise volunteer leaders and workers must be willing to put their ministry on display and allow others to look over their shoulders. The opportunity for novices to observe and question is an invaluable learning experience. (2) The practice of ministry is learning by doing. Much of it is on-the-job training. What's second nature to the veteran in ministry can be broken down into bite-size hunks for the less experienced. (3) Feedback extends self-evaluation into objective, behavior-based change. Feedback allows failure to become a base for learning. Effective supervisors affirm first and then confront with caring directness.

Several mistakes are common to supervision in the church:

- Trying to become supervisors without having been supervised
- Selecting workers too hastily
- Allowing jobs to expand without planning
- Failing to keep work assignments clear
- Bossing rather than coaching
- Avoiding necessary discipline
- Neglecting to train workers

These mistakes can be deadly for congregational health whether the supervisees are church staff ministers or volunteer teachers, officers, and committee workers.

Dealing with Difficult People

Every church has members who are abrasive to the larger congregation. They aren't emotionally unbalanced; they're just relationally out of step with the mainstream of the church. *These folks may become a threat to congregational health if they try to take control of the congregation's atmosphere and mission. In fact, controlling behavior is, perhaps, the distinguishing mark of the difficult person.*[7]

Difficult people fall into two broad categories: *aggressives* and *passives*. Aggressive controllers include *hostile persons, cliques,* and noncommunicating "*crazy makers.*" Passive controllers count in their numbers *apathetic persons*, *lonely people*, and *traditionalists*. Aggressives try to dominate the agenda of their congregations; passives place a drag on the mission and momentum of their congregations.

Which of these six difficult types is hardest to work with in ministry? All are tough to deal with, but the most difficult depends on you. Generally, the most offensive persons to us reflect the darker, more shadowy sides of our own personalities. We often have difficulty with the same aspect of the behavior of others that we fear in ourselves.

A general strategy for coping effectively with difficult persons must be broad based and constructive. Consider these actions.

- Pinpoint the problem. What exactly is the issue that's calling out the controller(s) and creating the tension in the congregation?
- Rate the relationship. How strong are the ties between the controller(s) and the leaders of the congregation?
- Count the costs of negative behavior within the congregation. Can the controlling actions be ignored, or must they be confronted?
- Search for a solution. What options are available for dealing with controlling behaviors?
- Covenant for continuity. Can an agreement be reached that will allow the congregation to advance toward its ultimate mission?

Each of the difficult persons mentioned above displays controlling actions differently. *Hostiles*, for example, control their groups by daring to "be bad" in an institution that has a "nice" self-image. Their belligerence and demanding confrontiveness set the emotional tone for relating. If we avoid conflict or naively assume the hostiles will ease the tension, we give the hostiles an important measure of control.

Cliques control a congregation's atmosphere for good or ill. Negatively, cliques gather for protection, revenge, or warfare. Positively, cliques lend status or share information with their members.

Crazy makers control communication processes by changing the subject, overloading the conversation with multiple issues, and contradicting. When we try to communicate with crazy makers, we are thrown off balance and feel "crazy." Crazy makers cause us to feel uncertain; therefore, they maintain leverage over us.

Apathetics exercise control in two passive modes. They withhold energy from the congregation's goals. They divide a congregation's focus between internal ministry to the apathetics themselves and outreach to others.

Lonelies control the attempts of others to build relationships by seeming to invite friendship and then holding others at arm's length. Additionally, they control many well-meaning helpers who develop a guilty conscience when their relationship-building efforts don't work.

Traditionalists worship the past so much they try to control a congregation's future. They seek to preserve by resisting all but emergency changes.

Several attitudes and actions provide a repertoire for reinvolving difficult persons in the congregation.

- Accept difficult persons as worthy of attention without approving their attempts to control.
- Build and maintain an open and up-to-date relationship with difficult persons.
- Try to look at the church through difficult persons' eyes. Anticipate their behavior patterns.
- Spare the entire congregation unnecessary strife by working behind the scenes with difficult persons.
- Use Christian love as an antidote for controlling behavior. Remember that love also includes firmness.

Shaping the Organizational Climate

Every congregation or institution takes on its own personality, aura, or atmosphere. This climate is apparent to the discerning eye. Some church climates are sunny, others stormy. Some are pleasant, others ominous and threatening. Climate, variously referred to as the informal organization, norms, the organizational unconscious, and the intangible congregation, sets the tone of congregational life and ministry.[8] Climate is the organization's internal religion, its beliefs binding it together, and the molding force of its unique character.[9]

Leaders develop the congregation's climate by articulating its dream, building trust and teamwork, keeping lines of communication open, developing positive ceremonies of recognition and rites of passage, and valuing the membership. The larger and more diverse the congregation becomes, the more challenging—and more important, shaping—the organizational climate becomes.

◾ SECTION TWO ◾

HOW A MINISTER PERFORMS ADMINISTRATIVE RESPONSIBILITIES

Chapter 5

PERSONNEL ADMINISTRATION

William G. Caldwell

C hurches should employ personnel only after careful study of how to choose them and following adoption of appropriate policies and administrative guidelines. Proper treatment of personnel has become increasingly important as legal and ethical issues have developed. Churches can no longer ignore concerns that are being faced in other places of employment.[1]

Most congregations spend at least half of their income for paid staff. These costs are found in several places in the budget rather than in one general account. The total amount of staff compensation generally includes items like salaries, hourly wages, total benefits, worker's compensation, Christmas bonuses, and Social Security. When calculating staff costs, the ministers, support personnel, secretaries, custodians, food service workers, musicians, child-care staff, and employees of any subsidiary programs directly managed by the church, such as a kindergarten, should be included.

It is not possible, however, to say 50 percent is the minimum or maximum amount that should be budgeted for personnel. Each congregation must determine its staff needs (paid or volunteer) and balance the costs among other financial priorities, like missions, facilities, and church programs.

Since such a sizable percentage of expenditures relates to the church staff, it becomes imperative that the church understand the dynamics of personnel management. It is a spiritual responsibility not only to use God's money wisely but to be a partner in the life and work of each staff member regardless of the tasks assigned.

Establishing a Personnel Committee

A personnel committee or another similar group studies the staff needs of the church, develops personnel policies, and administers the policies on behalf of the church. This group should be made up of six to nine church members with the pastor serving ex officio. These members should be spiritually mature, sensitive to the needs of persons, and willing to become knowledgeable in human resources development.

The personnel committee (or team) is responsible to the church for developing and recommending policies relating to the paid staff members and their work. Their duties include the following:

1. Study the needs for future personnel.
2. Develop and keep current all position descriptions.
3. Develop and maintain an organization chart and personnel policies.
4. Develop a process for personnel employment.
5. Recommend to the church a salary and benefit plan, consulting with the finance committee.

Developing Personnel Policies

Every church, regardless of size, should have personnel policies. In the small church with a bivocational pastor, policies will be very simple, but larger churches will want to develop a personnel policy manual. However, both need policies that assure productivity and avoid organizational and legal problems.

Policies should cover as many aspects of personnel administration as possible. Differences in policies for ministerial and support staff should be clearly identified. Any unwritten policies, which have become tradition, must be dealt with. Consider this list of areas to be included:

- Insurance provisions—health, life, worker's compensation, and disability
- Retirement provisions
- Social Security provisions
- Vacations
- Holidays
- Leave provisions—sickness, death, study time, military, jury duty, etc.
- Time away for professional development and leadership for other groups
- Salary and benefits plan
- Performance analysis procedures

A church may need to consider additional areas. See the sample personnel policy handbook at the end of this chapter. After the policy manual has been developed, it is wise to present it to the church and implement it at a specific date. This should allow time for staff members to be informed concerning the document and to understand its use. New staff members should be instructed concerning its contents and asked to sign a form indicating that they have read it. The personnel committee should conduct an annual review to keep the policies up-to-date and applicable when circumstances warrant changes.

Designing a Staffing Plan

Every church needs a written process for developing a staff based on its vision and approach to ministry. There is no magic formula for doing this. No predetermined membership size or budget amount can be used to add a staff member. The changing nature of a church or the community must be taken into account along with the financial and human resources available.

The personnel committee should consider questions like these:

1. What task is to be accomplished with this new staff member? Does the task match our objective? Do we have adequate resources?
2. Why is it important to the church? Is this position really needed? Would a part-time position work?
3. Where will the new staff member work? Is office space currently available?
4. When will the staff member begin work?
5. What skills will this person need?
6. What will happen if we don't get this person?

Writing Job Descriptions

An important part of any personnel process is the writing of job or ministry descriptions. Equally as important is using these descriptions regularly and keeping them updated and accurate. Good job descriptions assure that persons know what is involved in a job, clarify expectations of the job, provide lines of authority for supervision, and improve morale as persons feel good about what they are expected to do.

The supervisor should be involved in writing job descriptions. In some cases this would be in conjunction with a committee assignment. A job description should include four pieces of information: the job title, a principal function statement, identification of the person's supervisor, and a listing of the responsibilities and duties in a summary fashion.

Although the job description is written before the search process begins, it is often helpful to allow the new employee to have input into the document when beginning work. The basic assignment would not change, but some of the new person's abilities might be better used. When a vacancy occurs, the job description should always be evaluated and revised. Samples of job descriptions are included at the end of this chapter.

Developing a Salary Plan

Establishing a salary plan is often overlooked in dealing with staff personnel. Many churches pay "whatever it takes" when dealing with a new staff member. In larger churches with several staff members, this can be a serious problem because there is no attempt to base salary provisions on the responsibilities of the job. Any church can benefit from a formal, well-thought-out process for determining salary amounts.

Here are seven things to consider in developing a salary plan.

1. Use current, accurate job descriptions for each position. Knowing the responsibilities and duties of each person is the only way to begin to know a salary amount.
2. Rank each full-time position according to the level of responsibility. For example, supervision of others, independent decision making, and highly technical skills indicate high levels of responsibility. Positions with similar responsibilities should have a similar rank.
3. Survey comparable community and church positions to discover salary amounts. In conducting the survey, it is important to ask about positions according to the work being done, not the title being used. The base or beginning salary for each position is what is needed.
4. Decide on a beginning salary amount for each position starting at the bottom of the ranking. Make certain that the position identified as having the least responsibility is still provided a living wage in your community. Part-time positions will have to be adjusted accordingly. The beginning salary will take into account any minimum requirements for experience and training.
5. Consider a maximum salary for each position. Some plans use a 25–35 percent range between the minimum and maximum amounts. This would allow for a dollar-amount step increase for each year a person is employed. A percentage-based amount can also be used for salary adjustment. The increase should be determined based on continued service, additional training received, performance goals achieved, or a combination of these.
6. Adjust the salary amounts annually to reflect the community cost-of-living changes. If it is determined that a 3-percent increase is necessary to keep up with inflation, then all beginning salaries in the plan would be increased by that amount, and present salaries would be adjusted accordingly.
7. Merit raises or additional salary increases should be addressed according to church policy. Employees should fully understand how these increases are determined.

Filling Staff Vacancies

Staff vacancies are filled primarily in two ways: through an application-and-hiring process and through a search-and-call process. The former is used to fill nonministerial positions while the latter is used to fill vacancies for pastors, associate pastors, ministers of education, ministers of music, and other ministerial positions. Usually the supervisor is responsible for securing support staff members and reporting their employment to the proper committee or to the church.

These two processes require different procedures. First, the steps for application and hiring:

1. Prepare/update job description, qualifications, and salary plan.
2. State requirements for religious faith, moral conduct, or church affiliation as applicable.
3. Prepare an application form and solicit applicants (see figure 5.1).
4. Conduct interviews with applicants meeting qualifications.
5. Test for job skills if appropriate.
6. Prepare a reference follow-up form and secure references on selected applicants (see figure 5.2).
7. Choose the best person for the job and conduct an in-depth interview. Follow up on references, discuss details of the job, review salary and benefits, and determine whether to offer the job. Other tests may be appropriate after the job is offered, such as drug testing or physical examinations. In small to medium-size churches, the person to whom the worker will report usually conducts the interviews and approves hiring. In larger situations the screening process to this point may be done by someone else. Either way, the supervisor of the new worker must be involved in the final screening, interview(s), and choice of the worker.
8. Review all information and make a choice. (See the information in figure 5.3, "Evaluating Potential Employees.")

The search and call of staff ministers is a more complicated process. Procedures vary from denomination to denomination and even from church to church. Some churches don't conduct a search because a new minister is assigned to them. The following information describes typical procedures.[2]

The personnel committee or administrative team responsible for recommending personnel will begin the search to fill the approved position. There also is the possibility that the committee or congregation will ask that a special ad hoc search committee be appointed/elected to assist in seeking the new staff member.[3]

Where are prospective staff ministers found? Many religious organizations and denominational offices have minister relations departments that assist churches with prospective workers. Seminaries and divinity schools always provide this service. Résumés are kept current and on file to provide personnel committees with helpful information.

Calls can be made to friends and denominational workers in other areas to secure names of prospects. Encourage church members to share names of people who have impressed them.

Churches often employ staff members who are already employed by other churches. They should not, however, overlook faculty and staff members from seminaries and colleges and employees of denominational agencies. Sometimes these well-qualified people will feel God's call to return to the local church.

Churches should not hesitate to interview and call recent graduates who have prepared for ministry. Many of these well-trained and highly motivated people are ready to make a lasting contribution to God's work in the local church. If the prospect has had church staff responsibilities before or during school days, the possibility for significant contribution is greatly enhanced in the first full-time church.

Once recommendations have been obtained and evaluated, full information must be secured for the most promising prospect(s). Some feel that the prospective staff member should be thoroughly investigated before any formal contact. Others prefer a conference call or an informal, get-acquainted visit in the home or office of the prospect. It seems best to have consent from the person before beginning any formal investigation.

In the contacts/conferences that follow, great care should be given in describing the church, the position, other staff members, the people, prospects for growth, and how the prospective staff member can aid the church. Discuss negative as well as positive factors related to the position and the church. If God leads the church and the prospect to each other, this honesty and openness will have long-term dividends.

Above all, do not make unrealistic promises or develop unrealistic expectations. Good decisions are based on accurate information and clear understandings of the ministry potential for the person and the church.

A poor decision can be detrimental to the fellowship, future growth, ministry, and financial program of the church. Churches need God-called men and women to provide leadership. Consequently, the search committee and the congregation will be called to prayer in seeking the leadership of the Holy Spirit in this strategic matter. Don't rush the process until there is a strong consensus that God is leading.

Here are specific questions that the prospective minister and the search committee should ask themselves in the evaluation process:

1. Does the prospect display leadership skills? Today's churches demand people who can lead. Is the prospect too slow to keep up with the people or so visionary as to be too far in front? Does the staff member have basic traits of leadership such as truthfulness, honesty, willingness to work, interest in people?

2. Is there an overwhelming sense of God's call evident in the prospect? The dynamic church in today's society demands a high calling from God.

3. Is there a strong commitment to teaching and preaching God's Word? This is absolutely imperative in the life of a prospective leader.
4. Is the person flexible while remaining true to the Bible? "Rolling with the punches" seems to be a necessary trait of church leaders. Changing programs to meet needs is most helpful in today's churches.
5. Is the prospective staff member a generalist? This trait is helpful in local churches. A staff member who is interested in and helpful toward all church programs is important.
6. Are there indicators of continued growth in the individual? Staff members need an ongoing program of education and updating of knowledge. This is a key point of leadership in progressive churches.
7. Is there an evident love for people and their needs? The staff member who stays secluded day after day will have a difficult time in relating to the real-life needs of people.
8. Is the person capable of being an example of morality to the congregation? Issues of personal morality must be addressed.

After committee members conclude that the prospect may be the person God would have in their church, they are ready to take the final step in the search process. This step is twofold.

First, the prospect must come to the same conclusion. There must be enough interest to make a visit, meet the people, and—along with the church—consider the possibility of an invitation to join the staff. After this has been done, the prospective staff member will need to seek God's will in the matter.

Second, church members should have an opportunity to meet the prospective staff member. Leaders with whom the staff member would have the most exposure should assuredly dialogue with the prospect. The future effectiveness of the staff person can be harmed or enhanced by the way this get-acquainted visit is conducted.

At the conclusion of the visit, the church also will need to seek God's will and decide whether to invite the prospective minister to join the staff. If an invitation is extended, compensation according to the salary plan should be stated clearly to both church and future employee. There should be a general agreement as to the position expectations and performance standards. If the church approves and the staff member accepts, both parties then begin to establish the new partnership.

Orienting a New Employee

The new staff member needs a knowledgeable person to assist in getting acquainted. The logical person to do this is the immediate supervisor. Some explanation of what has happened since the last person in the job left may be helpful. In the case of a new pastor, the search committee chair or other assigned person(s) should assist with the orientation.

Here are the things you should include when orienting a new staff member. Make adjustments depending on the level of experience and background of the individual, and spread activities over several days.

1. Introduce staff members and tour the church facilities.
2. Tell how the staff is organized to carry out the church's programs and ministries.
3. Describe the church's programs, ministries, calendar of events, and schedule of services; interpret the personality of the congregation; review the church's history.
4. Review how the church operates through its various organizations, councils, or committees.
5. Explain specific policies on drug use, sexual harassment, and ethical conduct.
6. Explain employee benefits, personnel policies, salary plan, pay dates, work hours, holidays, and other pertinent items. Special tax considerations for ministers should be discussed.
7. Review and explain job duties.
8. Tour the community; introduce the new person to important business contacts relating to the job, such as the postmaster, printer, bank officials, and social service representatives.

The Staff as a Team

One distinguishing feature of an outstanding church staff is unity of purpose. This unity should include all members of the staff, support staff members as well as ministerial staff members.

If a church staff is to be effective, it should have the characteristics of a competitive sports team.[4] Members will form a cohesive whole that is greater than the sum of its parts. Staff members will be interdependent with each person supporting others on the staff. This interaction is stimulating and enjoyable to all involved.

In most team sports each member relates to every other team member. Instead of hierarchy, as in a military structure, there should be broad-based equality. One member may be more important than others for victory, but all recognize one another as equals. Good relationships, then, will be foundational to effective ministry. (See chapter 17 for additional information on staff relations.)

Today's most productive church staff teams have four key characteristics that mark their effectiveness:

1. *Appreciation*. Churchwide love and appreciation for the individual staff member lead to staff security in work and in relationships; these lead to an enhanced team effort.

2. *Responsible Freedom.* This is freedom to be creative, freedom to innovate, freedom to pioneer, and freedom to fail. A loving congregation will understand that the staff leader may sometimes miss projections, fail in developing an organization, or misread the needs of the people.
3. *Understanding.* Staff members grow through an understanding of themselves, others on the staff, and the people they lead. They grow as they understand the objective of the church and its goals. They grow by playing on the team to achieve those goals.
4. *Cooperation.* All staff members pull together to support one another's work as well as of the total church life. This cooperative spirit nurtures staff members in their own sense of purpose and fulfillment as servant leaders.

INDEX TO RESOURCES

Personnel Forms

Job Descriptions

Personnel Policies

William G. Caldwell

Figure 5.1

APPLICATION FORM

_____Church

Date	Position you are applying for:

Are you available for:
   full-time _____
   part-time _____
   temporary work _____
Were you referred by a current or former employee? yes ___no___
If so, who? _____

I. PERSONAL DATA

Name (last)_____(first)_____(middle)_____
Address (street) _____
(city) _____
(state) _____
(zip) _____
How long at this address? _____
Phone Number _____ Social Security Number _____
Prior Address _____ How long? _____

II. EDUCATION

(Complete only if job has educational qualifications.)
High School Diploma: yes_____ no_____ ; if yes, when?_____
Business College: yes_____ no_____ ; where located? _____
University or College: yes_____ no_____ ; if yes, did you graduate? yes_____ no_____
What was your major? Minor? _____
Name and location of college _____
School or college activities in which you engaged? _____

III. EMPLOYMENT HISTORY

(Start with present or most recent job.)
Are you presently employed?   yes _____ no _____
May we contact your present employer? ____ now ____ later ____ no
   1. Name of Employer _____Address _____ Worked from ____ to ____
      Supervisor _____ Monthly salary or hourly rate: start _____ end _____
      Type of work performed _____ Reason for leaving_____
   2. Name of Employer _____Address _____ Worked from ____ to ____
      Supervisor _____ Monthly salary or hourly rate: start _____ end _____
      Type of work performed _____ Reason for leaving_____
   3. Name of Employer _____Address _____ Worked from ____ to ____
      Supervisor _____ Monthly salary or hourly rate: start _____ end _____
      Type of work performed _____ Reason for leaving_____

IV. JOB DATA

Name of Employer _____ Address _____
(Check areas in which you have had experience or training.)

_____ Typing (Speed _____WPM)   _____ Receptionist
_____ Word Processor   _____ Writing and Editing
_____ Transcribing Machine   _____ Supervisor
_____ Bookkeeping   _____ Custodian
_____ Duplicating Machine   _____ Other: _____

96

Figure 5.1

APPLICATION FORM (continued)

V. CHURCH LIFE

Denomination_____

Name of Church (where you hold membership) _____

Location _____

What church activities did (do) you participate in? _____

What positions in a church have you volunteered for or been employed for: _____

VI. WORK HISTORY

Have you ever had a license suspended or revoked by a professional body or state agency?
_____yes _____ no.   If so, explain circumstances _____
_____

How many days were you late to work last year? _____

How many days were you absent from work last year? _____

VII. CRIMINAL RECORD

Other than a minor traffic offense, have you ever been convicted of a crime? yes ___ no ___
If so, please explain: _____

Are you currently involved in any legal proceedings? yes ___ no ___
If so, please explain: _____

VIII. REFERENCES

(Do not list relatives or former employers.)

1. Name _____ Address_____
   Occupation _____ Years Known _____
2. Name _____ Address_____
   Occupation _____ Years Known _____
3. Name _____ Address_____
   Occupation _____ Years Known _____

IX. ADDITIONAL INFORMATION

Please give us any additional information you desire about your education and experience (include any special talents). Please list any personal characteristics that you feel would prepare you for this position.

Employment terms: I understand that this church is an "at-will" employer and that employment may be terminated at any time with or without cause. This status is not to be altered unless we enter a contract that specifically addresses and replaces the "at-will" employment status.

Applicant's Signature _____Date_____

REFERENCE RELEASE

The information I have provided is accurate and true, and I understand that any false information is grounds for termination. I authorize the verification of this information with all former employers, references, and other appropriate persons. I will not take action against anyone releasing the requested information.

Applicant's Signature_____Date_____

Figure 5.2

EMPLOYMENT REFERENCE CHECK

Name of Applicant _____

Position under consideration_____

Person contacted for reference _____

Firm/Church_____ Phone _____

Employment period covered: From_____ to _____

The above person has given your name as a reference and signed a release giving us permission to contact you. Please complete the confidential questions below and return in the enclosed, postage-paid envelope. Thank you!

Person conducting reference check _____ Church_____

1. In what capacity did you know the applicant and for how long? ____

    _____

    Were you the immediate supervisor? _____yes _____no

2. What was the job title? _____

    What specifically was done as a part of the job? _____

    _____

3. How would you rate

    (a) performance? _____

    (b) supervisory abilities? _____

    (c) independent work? _____

    (d) creativity? _____

4. How did this person get along with others? _____

    _____

5. Any unusual work habits?_____

    _____

6. What were the circumstances under which the person left? _____

    _____

    _____Is this person eligible for rehire? yes_____Any

    qualifications? No _____Why _____?

    _____

7. Describe the strong points? General _____

    Technical _____

8. Are there any negative aspects or weaknesses? _____

9. Did this person have the skills required for the job? _____yes _____no

    If not, explain. _____

10. Please list any other names we might contact for a reference.

    Name _____ Address _____ Phone _____

    Name _____ Address _____ Phone _____

    Name _____ Address _____ Phone _____

11. Any additional comments:

    Signed _____Title _____Date _____

Figure 5.3

EVALUATING POTENTIAL EMPLOYEES

1. Is the applicant a Christian? Participating in a local church? Living and acting responsibly? Does applicant have a good character and reputation?
2. Is the applicant neat? Alert? Have good posture? Good facial expression?
3. Is the applicant tactful? Courteous? Confident? Warm? Enthusiastic? Cheerful? Optimistic? Animated? Humorous?
4. Does the applicant have good pronunciation? Enunciation? Vocabulary? Grammar? Have good expression? With clarity? Act in an organized manner?
5. Does the applicant have good educational and professional backgrounds? Can do the job at an acceptable level now or with training?
6. Has the applicant exhibited mental effectiveness? Good personality? Skill in getting along with people? Good insight?
7. In short, beginning with your initial contact, did you immediately sense that this person would fit in well and is qualified for the job?

Figure 5.4

PASTOR

Principal Function: The pastor is responsible to the church to proclaim the gospel of Jesus Christ, to preach the biblical revelation, to engage in pastoral care ministries, to provide administrative leadership in all areas of church life, and to act as the chief administrator of the paid staff.

Responsibilities

1. Plan and conduct the worship services; prepare and deliver sermons; lead in observance of ordinances.
2. Lead the church in an effective program of witnessing and in a caring ministry for persons in the church and community.
3. Visit members and prospects.
4. Conduct counseling sessions; perform wedding ceremonies; conduct funerals.
5. Lead the church in planning, organizing, directing, coordinating, and evaluating the total program of the church.
6. Work with deacons, church officers, and committees as they perform their assigned responsibilities.
7. Act as moderator of church business meetings (unless a layperson is elected as moderator).
8. Cooperate with denominational leaders in matters of mutual interest and concern; keep the church informed of denominational development; represent the church in civic matters.

9. Serve as chief administrator of the paid church staff; supervise the work of assigned paid staff workers.

Figure 5.5

EXECUTIVE PASTOR

Principal Function: The executive pastor is responsible to the church to assist the pastor with the day-by-day management and oversee spiritual, emotional, and relational health of the pastoral ministers and other staff as needed. This position will work with the senior pastor to focus attention on the vision and direction of the church.

Responsibilities
1. Work with the senior pastor and other leadership to carry out vision and direction for the church. Provide supervision for assigned staff.
2. Assist in hiring and dismissing staff as needed.
3. Provide leadership to ministry teams as assigned.
4. Approve and submit budget requests from ministries that report to the executive pastor.
5. Perform weddings, funerals, baptisms, and Communion when called upon by the pastor.
6. Preach and provide pastoral ministry as requested by the pastor.
7. Perform duties and other assignments as requested by the pastor.

Figure 5.6

MINISTER OF EDUCATION

Principal Function: The minister of education is responsible to the church, supervised by the pastor, for providing staff leadership to the entire church educational program. This involves assisting church program leaders in planning, conducting, and evaluating a comprehensive ministry of Christian education in support of the mission and objectives of the church.

Responsibilities
1. Lead the church in planning, conducting, and evaluating a comprehensive program of Christian education.
2. Serve as educational resource person and advisor to the leaders of church program and service organizations.
3. Serve as educational resource person and advisor to the committees of the church as requested.
4. Work within the church process to select, enlist, and train qualified leaders.

5. Coordinate the production of informational and public relations materials, such as church publications and news releases.
6. Develop special educational and training projects such as camps, retreats, and study seminars for various age groups within the congregation.
7. Lead the church to be aware of the educational and curriculum materials available and lead the church to choose the most suitable.
8. Prepare an estimated annual education budget and administer the approved budget.
9. Assist the pastor in planning, conducting, and evaluating congregational services as requested.
10. Serve on the church council or coordinating group.
11. Supervise appropriate church staff members as assigned, such as age-group directors, recreation leaders, educational secretary, and custodian.
12. Cooperate with denominational leaders in promoting activities of mutual interest.
13. Keep informed on methods, materials, principles, procedures, promotion, and administration as related to the education program.
14. Perform other duties as assigned by the pastor.

Figure 5.7

MINISTER OF MUSIC

Principal Function: The minister of music is responsible to the church, supervised by the pastor, for the development and promotion of the music program of the church.

Responsibilities

1. Direct the planning, organizing, conducting, and evaluating of a comprehensive music program including choirs, vocal and/or instrumental ensembles.
2. Supervise the work of assigned paid staff workers.
3. Cooperate with the church process to enlist and train leaders for the church music ministry, including graded choir workers, song leaders, and accompanists for the church education organizations.
4. Lead in planning and promoting a graded choir program; direct and coordinate the work of lay choir directors; direct adult, youth, and other choirs as needed.
5. Serve as a member of the church council or coordinating group; coordinate the music program with the organizational calendar and emphases of the church.
6. Assist the pastor in planning all services of worship.
7. Arrange and provide music for weddings, funerals, special projects, ministries, and other church-related activities upon request.
8. Plan, organize, and promote choir tours, mission trips, camps, festivals, workshops, clinics, and programs for the various choirs.

101

9. Supervise the maintenance of the music library, materials, supplies, musical instruments, and other equipment.
10. Keep informed on music methods, materials, promotion, and administration.
11. Prepare an estimated annual music budget and administer the approved budget.
12. Cooperate with denominational leaders in promoting activities of mutual interest.
13. Perform other duties as assigned by the pastor.

Figure 5.8

BUSINESS ADMINISTRATOR

Principal Function: The business administrator is responsible to the church, supervised by the pastor, for administering the business affairs of the church.

Responsibilities

1. Establish and operate an efficient plan of financial record keeping and reporting; develop bookkeeping procedures.
2. Prepare financial information for the finance and budget committees and treasurer of the church.
3. Serve as resource person regarding legal and business matters of the church; study annually the insurance program and make recommendations, if any.
4. Serve as church purchasing agent, approving and processing requisitions and purchase orders.
5. Maintain records on church staff personnel; establish and maintain records of equipment and facilities.
6. Administer church-adopted policies and procedures concerning the use of all church properties and facilities.
7. Assist building committee in its relationships with architect, contractors, and others in building, remodeling, and equipping church buildings.
8. Work with the property and space committee in preparing an annual budget of maintenance and equipment needs.
9. Supervise workers in the maintenance and repair of all physical properties; establish and implement cleaning, painting, renovating schedules; operate within approved budget.
10. Supervise the operation of food services.
11. Supervise assigned office personnel.
12. Perform other duties as assigned by the pastor. Several of the duties are usually included in the minister of education's position description when the church does not have a business administrator. Many of the jobs indicate supervision by the business administrator. This would change to office manager, minister of education, building superintendent, or other staff person if there is no business administrator.

Figure 5.9

MINISTER OF YOUTH

Principal Function: The minister of youth is responsible to the church, supervised by the minister of education, for assisting church program organizations to develop a comprehensive program of youth education.

Responsibilities

1. Counsel with church program organization leaders in planning, conducting, and evaluating a youth education ministry and in enlisting appropriate youth workers.
2. Conduct special training projects for youth workers in proper relationship to discipleship programs.
3. Advise in the use of program materials, equipment, supplies, and space by youth groups in all church program organizations.
4. Work with the director of the recreation service to provide needed services.
5. Plan and conduct special projects (such as camps and retreats) for youth program organization groups.
6. Work with organization leaders to coordinate visitation for the youth division and lead workers to visit prospects and absentees.
7. Develop a proposed budget for youth ministry and administer it when approved.
8. Work with program leaders and teachers and appropriate staff members to resolve philosophical, procedural, and scheduling problems in the youth division.
9. Perform other duties as assigned by the minister of education.

    Note: This description could be used for any age-group specialist; simply substitute the appropriate age group for "youth."

Figure 5.10

SECRETARY/ADMINISTRATIVE ASSISTANT

Principal Function: Perform general office work, under the supervision of the business administrator, in relieving supervisor of minor executive and clerical duties.

Responsibilities

1. Prepare documents; type sermons; use word-processing equipment as required.
2. Perform general office work; maintain supplies and various files; keep records and compile these into periodic or occasional reports.
3. Review, open, and distribute mail; prepare routine answers without direction for approval and signature; answer routine letters in absence of the supervisor.
4. Act as required during supervisor's absence in making decisions or taking any necessary action not requiring supervisory approval.
5. Exercise tact, courtesy, and diplomacy in receiving callers, in person or on the telephone; keep calendar of appointments.

6. Notify committee members of meeting dates.
7. Edit and prepare bulletin copy.
8. Order literature and office supplies.
9. Assist in training new office workers.
10. Perform other duties as assigned by the business administrator.

Figure 5.11

ORGANIST AND MUSIC ASSISTANT

Principal Function: The organist and music assistant, supervised by the minister of music, serves as organist of the church and assists in the music ministry.

Responsibilities
1. Play for all services of the church, both regular and special.
2. Serve as accompanist for choirs, ensembles, and soloists in regular and special rehearsals and performances, as assigned.
3. Play for weddings and funerals, as requested, and with the approval of the minister of music.
4. Assist in planning worship services, choir rehearsals, and special music events.
4. Plan and give direction to a training program designed for developing organists and pianists in the church.
5. Maintain a regular schedule of organ practice and study.
6. Prepare workbooks and study materials for the graded choirs as assigned.
7. Perform other duties as assigned by the minister of music.

Figure 5.12

MINISTER OF EDUCATION AND MUSIC

Principal Function: The minister of education and music is responsible to the church, supervised by the pastor, for the development and promotion of the educational and music programs of the church.

Responsibilities
1. Direct the planning, coordinating, conducting, and evaluating of comprehensive educational and music programs based on program tasks.
2. Supervise the work of assigned paid staff members.
3. Lead in enlisting and training volunteer workers.
4. Organize and direct a churchwide visitation program.
5. Assist the pastor in planning all services of worship; arrange and provide music for weddings, funerals, special projects, ministries, and other church-related activities upon request.
5. Maintain personnel records of all paid staff workers; maintain music library, materials, supplies, musical instruments, and other equipment.
6. Serve as the purchasing agent for the church as assigned.
7. Develop projects such as mission trips, festivals, youth camps, retreats; plan activities for senior adults.

8. Edit church publications as assigned.
9. Assist the chairpersons of the various church committees; serve as ex officio member of church committees as assigned.
19. Prepare an annual program ministry budget for approval; administer the approved budget.
11. Keep informed on educational and music methods, materials, promotions, and administration.
12. Cooperate with denominational leaders in promoting activities of mutual interest.
13. Perform other duties as assigned by the pastor.

Figure 5.13

MINISTER OF ACTIVITIES/DIRECTOR OF RECREATION

Principal Function: The minister of activities/director of recreation is responsible to the church, supervised by the minister of education, for leading the church in planning, conducting, and evaluating a program of recreation for church members and other persons in the community.

Responsibilities

1. Direct the planning, coordination, conducting, and evaluation of recreation activities in the church.
2. Coordinate and administer activities in the church's recreation center, as assigned by the church.
3. Work with the church process to recruit and enlist workers for the church's recreation program.
4. Plan and coordinate training for all volunteer recreation workers.
5. Coordinate the recreation activities with the calendar and emphases of the church.
6. Serve as recreation resource person and advisor to organizations of the church as requested.
7. Lead the church to provide equipment and supplies needed in the recreation activities.
8. Supervise the inventory, care, repair, and storage of recreation equipment and supplies.
9. Provide representation for the church in planning, conducting, and evaluating recreation activities that involve other churches and groups.
10. Prepare a proposed recreation budget and administer it after approval.
11. Perform other duties as assigned by the minister of education.

Figure 5.14

FINANCIAL RECORDS ASSISTANT/FINANCIAL SECRETARY

Principal Function: Maintain the church financial records and prepare financial reports, under the supervision of the business administrator.

Responsibilities

1. Receive, count, and deposit all church offerings, with appropriate committee help.

2. Post receipts and disbursements of all accounts according to financial system.
3. Post offerings weekly to individual accounts; file envelopes.
4. Prepare bank reconciliation statements monthly.
5. Prepare monthly and annual financial reports for finance committee and church business meetings.
6. Prepare quarterly and annual tax reports.
7. Check and total all invoices when approved; inform responsible persons of their budget expenditures.
8. Receive and answer queries concerning financial matters; maintain files of invoices, correspondence, and reports.
9. Prepare and issue checks to staff members, designations, and organizations in accordance with church policy.
10. Mail pledge cards, stewardship letters, and envelopes to new members.
11. Requisition and prepare all forms and records for the annual stewardship emphasis.
12. Perform other duties as assigned by the business administrator.

Figure 5.15

RECEPTIONIST/OFFICE ASSISTANT

Principal Function: Prepare documentation, use computer, and perform general office work under the supervision of the business administrator.

Responsibilities
1. Prepare documentation; use word-processing software.
2. Perform general office work; maintain files and supplies; keep records and compile these into periodic reports.
3. Keyboard copy for reproduction.
4. Receive visitors; arrange appointments and keep calendar of appointments.
5. Receive and distribute incoming mail.
6. Answer the telephone.
7. Assist in mailing out the bulletin.
8. Perform other duties as assigned by the business administrator.

Figure 5.16

CLERK-TYPIST

Principal Function: Maintain office files, records, and schedules; make requisitions, prepare reports, and type copy, under the supervision of the business administrator.

Responsibilities
1. Maintain office files, program records, and schedules.
2. Fill out requisition forms.
3. Prepare reports periodically or as directed.
4. Do routine typing and compose routine letters.

5. Correct mailing lists; prepare mailing labels as needed.
6. Operate photocopy machine.
7. Prepare documentation, as assigned.
8. Answer telephone and serve as receptionist, as assigned.
9. Perform other duties as assigned by the business administrator.

Figure 5.17

FOOD SERVICE DIRECTOR

Principal Function: Oversee the operation of the kitchen and dining areas for all food services, under the supervision of the business administrator.

Responsibilities

1. Plan meals; purchase, prepare, and serve food for all scheduled meals and snacks and for social functions as requested.
2. Supervise assigned personnel; enlist and direct volunteer workers; train workers in proper food preparation and service.
3. Maintain high standards of sanitation in cleanliness of cooking utensils, dishes, glasses, silverware, and in food handling, preparation, service, storage, and so forth, to assure compliance with local health and sanitation laws; maintain clean work areas, storage bins, and so forth.
4. Prepare proposed food service budget; administer it when approved, maintaining accurate records in costs and operation.
5. Maintain up-to-date inventory of food supplies.
6. Arrange for the servicing, repairing, and replacing of equipment in the kitchen as needed.
7. Work with the building superintendent on table and room arrangements for all meals and social functions.
8. Perform other duties as assigned by the business administrator.

Figure 5.18

CUSTODIAN

Principal Function: Maintain clean buildings and grounds; make minor repairs, under the supervision of the business administrator.

Responsibilities

1. Sweep, mop, buff, clean, and wax floors according to schedule; dust furniture and equipment; wash walls and windows and vacuum carpets as scheduled.
2. Maintain clean restrooms; replenish tissue and towels; empty waste cans.
3. Request cleaning and maintenance supplies and equipment as needed.
4. Operate heating and cooling equipment according to schedule and instruction.
5. Open and close building daily as scheduled.
6. Mow grass; trim shrubbery; maintain clean church entrance, sidewalk, and parking areas.
7. Check with church office or supervisor daily for special assignments.

8. Move furniture; set up tables and chairs for suppers, banquets, and other similar occasions; set up meeting areas for regular and special activities.
9. Make minor electrical, plumbing, and equipment repairs as requested.
10. Paint walls, furniture, and equipment.
11. Perform messenger service.
12. Perform other duties as assigned by the business administrator.

Figure 5.19

SAMPLE PERSONNEL POLICY HANDBOOK

PERSONNEL POLICY HANDBOOK
_____ Church

CONTENTS

CHURCH EMPLOYEE CATEGORIES

Employee categories are defined below. These terms will be used throughout this handbook in relation to certain practices and benefits.

1. Called Staff

Full-time: Positions relating to the primary ministries of the church that include but are not limited to:

- Pastor
- Minister of Education and Administration
- Minister of Music and Outreach

Part-time: Persons employed to direct a ministry of the church for a specified number of hours each week that include but are not limited to:

- Organist
- Pianist
- Children's Minister
- Youth Minister

2. Support Staff

This category includes office personnel, custodians, kitchen employees, etc.

Probationary: A period of 60 days will apply to all categories of support staff.

Regular: Employees who have been with the church more than 60 days and who work at least 37 hours a week.

Part-time: Employees who have been with the church more than 60 days and who regularly work at least 20 hours per week but less than the normal full-time schedule.

Temporary part-time: Employees who do not normally work on a regular schedule or who may be employed for a relatively short period.

EMPLOYMENT PROCEDURES

1. Called Staff

a. Personnel committee selects a subcommittee to help recruit for each vacant position with the exception of the pastor.

b. Review and/or possibly amend the position description. Recommend any change in the position to the church.

c. Develop selection criteria based upon the perceived job, experience, and educational requirements of the position. A pay-benefit study may be conducted.

d. Dissemination of pertinent position information to possible resources (e.g., seminaries, denominational offices, past staff members).

e. Review all applicants against the selection criteria. Additional information may be requested as the review process proceeds.

f. Recommend to the full personnel committee a priority listing of applicants based on qualifications. The full committee may amend the listing.

g. Interview and/or review "in view of a call" the applicants in priority order.

h. Recommend the most qualified applicant to the church.

2. Support Staff

a. When a vacancy occurs, the supervisor will review and/or possibly amend the position description.

b. The supervisor will review all applicants in view of the qualifications needed for the position and select the one who will best suit the job.

TERMINATION PROCEDURES

1. Voluntary Termination

a. Two (2) weeks written notification must be given prior to the effective date of resignation. Failure to make proper notification could result in the loss of any accumulated benefits.

b. In the case of called staff, the resignation must be announced at a church meeting.

2. Involuntary Termination

a. Any church employee may be terminated involuntarily for unsatisfactory performance, failure to support church programs, failure to adhere to established personnel procedures, or behavior unbecoming a Christian (as determined by vote of the church).

b. Support staff may be terminated by his/her supervisor with the approval of the personnel committee.

c. Called staff members may be terminated by the church. Such action may be initiated by the pastor and the personnel committee.

d. Called staff terminated involuntarily may be given up to three (3) months severance pay and benefits as determined by the personnel committee.

OTHER EMPLOYMENT AND INTERIM POSITIONS

1. A called or full-time employee may not be employed in another job (inside or outside the church) without the written consent of the pastor and personnel committee.

2. The personnel committee and the pastor may employ an "interim" or "supply" staff worker in the event that a staff position is vacated.

WORKING RELATIONSHIPS

1. The pastor will supervise all called staff members.

2. The minister of education and administration will supervise all support staff members and the day care director.

3. The minister of music and outreach will supervise the organist and pianist.

LEAVE OF ABSENCE

1. *Support staff.* A leave of absence must be approved by the supervisor and the personnel committee.

2. *Called staff.* A leave of absence must be approved by the pastor, the personnel committee, and the church.

SCHOOL ATTENDANCE

School attendance during normal working hours must be approved by the pastor and personnel committee.

WORKING CONDITIONS

1. Normal office hours are 8:00 a.m.–5:00 p.m. All full-time employees are expected to work a minimum of 37 hours per week. Part-time employees will post a schedule of working hours not adhering to the normal working hours.
2. Breaks:
   a. A lunch break will normally be one (1) hour. Longer periods of time must be approved by the supervisor and normal hours adjusted.
   b. A fifteen (15) minute break may be taken in the morning and one in the afternoon. Working hours may not be adjusted for shorter breaks.
   c. Overtime is considered an exceptional working condition and must be approved by the supervisor and/or the personnel committee if compensatory time or pay is to be granted.
   d. All work will normally be performed in the location appropriate for the activity (e.g., all office work is to be done in the office). Any deviation from this pattern must be approved by the supervisor and/or personnel committee.
   e. Full-time called staff members will be allowed two (2) days off per week (not to include Sunday). Only one day will be taken between Monday and Friday and must be scheduled on a permanent basis with exceptions being scheduled at least one week in advance. Days off not taken may not be accumulated.

PAY POLICIES

1. Called staff and support staff will be paid biweekly. Pay periods will end on Saturday for support staff and on Sunday for called staff.
2. Checks will be issued on Wednesday following each ending pay period.
3. Initial employment pay benefits will be recommended by the personnel committee to the finance and stewardship committee. The finance and stewardship committee will approve and/or amend the pay benefits, based on the financial resources of the church, and include these with the position description for final approval by the church.
4. Raises/benefits will be recommended to the finance and stewardship committee by the pastor and personnel committee.
5. Raises/benefits for the pastor will be recommended to the finance and stewardship committee by the deacons.
6. Raises/benefits for all staff will be reviewed annually in time to be included in the January 1 budget.
7. The church participates in the Social Security program for all employees. Qualified ministers relate to Social Security on an individual basis as self-employed persons.
8. Worker's compensation insurance coverage shall be provided for all employees and ministers.

BENEFITS FOR FULL-TIME CALLED STAFF

The church will need to decide if accumulated time served at other churches will be a factor related to the benefits listed. For instance, if a person has served 20 years in a full-time position, many churches will recognize the entire amount while others will recognize one year for every three years served. This is unique to the church but should be considered because ministers are penalized when they move to a new location if they are treated as if they had no prior service.

1. Vacations

After six (6) months of service—five (5) working days and one (1) Sunday.

One (1) to four (4) years of service—ten (10) working days and two (2) Sundays.

Five (5) to ten (10) years of service—fifteen (15) working days and three (3) Sundays.

Ten (10) years plus of service—twenty (20) working days and four (4) Sundays.

Vacations may not be declined during successive years.

Vacations not taken within the year of eligibility will be lost except as approved by the personnel committee in writing.

2. Sick Days

Provisions for sick days are determined by the personnel committee.

3. Revivals and Speaking Engagements

Four (4) weeks including Sundays (not consecutive) may be taken to serve as guest minister or a leader or participant in training conferences, classes, conventions, etc. Consecutive Sundays must be approved by the personnel committee.

4. Holidays

Nine (9) holidays* per year as follows:
New Year's Day
Memorial Day
Good Friday
Independence Day
Labor Day
Thanksgiving Day and the following Friday
Christmas Eve and Christmas Day
*When the holiday falls on Saturday and/or Sunday, adjustments will be made.

5. Leave of Absence

A leave of absence without pay may be granted upon the approval of the personnel committee and the church. A leave of absence may not be granted for more than 45 days.

6. Military Leave

Military leave, not to exceed two (2) weeks, will be granted to any person who is active in the National Guard or Reserves.

7. Bereavement Leave

Three (3) days bereavement leave may be granted in the death of an immediate family member: spouse, children, and parents. Additional time may be granted by the personnel committee.

8. Maternity Leave

A leave of absence not to exceed twelve (12) weeks may be taken. The church shall continue only insurance benefits during such leave. No salary will be paid during the leave of absence except for remaining sick leave and vacation time. Additional time with or without pay may be granted by the personnel committee.

9. Study Leave

Upon completion of each ten (10) years of service, the pastor and other full-time called staff become eligible for a study leave.

The pastor may be granted up to twelve (12) weeks leave in addition to other time off with full pay to engage in study. Other full-time called staff members may be granted up to nine (9) weeks in addition to other time off.

The personnel committee may secure an interim supply for the staff member on leave.

A study leave agenda must be approved by the personnel committee.

10. Jury Duty

Employees are encouraged to cooperate in civic responsibilities. The worker on jury duty will receive full pay in addition to jury fees.

11. Anniversary Recognition

Anniversary recognition shall be observed on the first, fifth, tenth, fifteenth, etc., anniversaries. A churchwide reception will be held to recognize each minister on these occasions.

12. Family Leave

Family leave provides job security as long as the leave does not exceed 12 weeks in a 12-month period. The personnel committee or team will be responsible for administering this leave according to the legal guidelines.

BENEFITS FOR FULL-TIME AND PART-TIME SUPPORT STAFF

1. Vacations

Five (5) working days may be taken after six (6) months of service.
Ten (10) working days may be taken after one (1) year of service.
Fifteen (15) working days may be taken after ten (10) years of service.

Organist and Pianist Vacations

One (1) week may be taken after six (6) months of service.
Two (2) weeks may be taken after one (1) year of service.
Three (3) weeks may be taken after ten (10) years of service.
Vacations may not be declined during successive years.
Vacations not taken within the year of eligibility will be lost except as approved by the supervisor and personnel committee.

2. Sick Leave

Five (5) working days per year are allowed for the illness of the employee or immediate family. Upon completion of three (3) years service, two (2) weeks are allowed. Additional time off may be granted by the personnel committee.

Organist and pianist sick leave. One (1) week per year is allowed for the illness of the employee or immediate family. Upon completion of three (3) years service, two (2) weeks are allowed. Additional time off may be granted by the personnel committee.

3. Holidays

Nine (9) holidays* per year as follows:
> New Year's Day
> Memorial Day
> Good Friday
> Independence Day
> Labor Day
> Thanksgiving Day and the following Friday
> Christmas Eve and Christmas Day

*When the holiday falls on Saturday and/or Sunday, adjustments will be made.

4. Bereavement

Three (3) days bereavement leave may be granted to an employee in the case of a death in the immediate family: spouse, children, and parents. Additional time may be granted by the personnel committee.

5. Absences

The supervisor must be informed prior to the employee's absence. Absences for personal reasons are discouraged but in emergencies must be approved by the supervisor.

6. Maternity Leave

A leave of absence not to exceed twelve (12) weeks may be taken. The church shall continue only insurance benefits during such leave. No salary will be paid during the leave of absence except for remaining sick leave and vacation time. Additional time with or without pay may be granted by the personnel committee.

7. Jury Duty

Employees are encouraged to cooperate in civic responsibilities. The worker on jury duty will receive full pay in addition to the jury fees.

8. Family Leave

Family leave provides job security as long as the leave does not exceed 12 weeks in a 12-month period. The personnel committee or team will be responsible for administering this leave according to the legal guidelines

Chapter 6

OFFICE ADMINISTRATION

Bruce P. Powers

The church office is the nerve center of a congregation's life. It is a support system for church staff members and volunteer leaders, a communication center for church life, and a business location for transacting church affairs. It is at the center of support services for church administration and congregational leadership.

Purpose of the Church Office

The purpose of the church office is to provide support services that assist the congregation in achieving church-approved goals. Under the guidance of designated leaders, tasks will be organized and performed in such a manner as to enable a church and its leadership to function effectively and efficiently. The church office is the administrative center for the congregation as well as the major contact point for members throughout the week.

Checkpoints for Office Administration

There are five major areas to consider: location, environment, facilities, equipment, and work systems. General guidelines for each of these will be given. Keep in mind, however, that you will have to determine specific ways to apply these in your situation. The number of church staff members, the availability of facilities, and financial considerations influence the extent to which a church can provide centralized support services.

Location

Where is your church office? It should easily be accessible by church members *and* by persons not familiar with your facilities. Parking should be nearby; access by young and elderly should be easy; directional signs should point the way; and the area should be convenient to other offices and workrooms.

Pretend you are a newcomer to town and that you are going to the church office to get information about worship services. Drive up to your church and approach it as a newcomer would. What would you see? Where would you park? What entrance would you use? What signs tell you where to go? What would you think of the church before even reaching the office?

Environment

As you walk in your church office, what impresses you? Does it appear orderly? Would you know where to stand or sit or where to get information if you were a stranger? How would you be greeted and by whom?

The personality of an office is just as important in relating to people as your personality is to you. The environment of your church office elicits a positive or negative feeling that can give confidence or create doubt. The impressions one receives can inspire trust or encourage suspicion about the quality of the church's programs, ministries, and leadership.

Most often mentioned in office manuals are the needs for:

- Clean and uncluttered work areas
- Clean and attractive reception/waiting area
- Clean and well-maintained furnishings
- Clean and well-maintained floors, walls, and ceilings
- Adherence to published office hours
- Warm, personal greeting when a guest enters

Office consultants would tell many of us to clean up, throw away, paint, and spend some money on attractive furnishings.

Office Facilities

A church office can be a corner of a room; or it can be a suite of offices, workrooms, and storage areas. No matter the size, everything must be inviting and functional, and it must help you do your job! The church office must not be a catchall location for old literature, athletic supplies, out-of-date equipment, and a place to retire used furniture that someone donated.

A basic administrative guideline says, *a place for everything, and everything in its place.* This is pretty good advice. You need a reception area, work stations (desks or tables), walkways, work areas, and storage facilities. Each of these requires decisions about what is needed, where it should be located, and how best to manage the work flow.

Reception Area

This area should be immediately inside the entrance to the office and should be separated from the work area by a reception desk, counter, planter, or some other device. Items needed: at least two comfortable chairs, a table, lamp (or good overhead lighting), a place to hang coats, and a trash can. Keep some current church literature and brochures about your church on the table.

The secretary or receptionist should have line-of-sight vision of the entrance in order to greet any visitor immediately. Seats in the reception area should be arranged so that persons who are waiting are not looking directly at the work areas; in this way jobs can continue without office workers appearing rude. Guidelines for the reception area are in figure 6.1.

Figure 6.1

GUIDELINES FOR THE RECEPTION AREA

1. Greet each visitor and determine what he or she needs.
2. If the visitor has an appointment, ask the guest to be seated while you notify the appropriate person.
3. If the person has an information or work request, determine immediately whether you can handle the request or need to refer it. Most requests will be routine, and you can handle according to established procedures. If you are not sure how to handle a request, write down the information and inform the person when and to whom you will channel the request.
4. When a visitor is kept waiting, tell the person you are sorry and give a reason if appropriate. Don't let a person sit and wonder why the delay.
5. Keep a record of visitors, requests, and work you perform on a drop-in basis. Use a daily calendar or appointment sheet. This is invaluable if you are asked to tell about something that was said or done, if you need to assess the work flow in the church office, or if you need to recall the details later when you report on work that someone had requested.
6. Keep the area fresh and clean. Live plants, up-to-date reading materials, a box of tissues, and attractive furnishings will make a good impression for your church.

Work Stations

Desks, tables, and chairs should be at a comfortable height: desks, 29–30 inches; typing or keyboard tables, about 26½ inches; and chairs, adjustable from 17 to 21 inches. Chairs must be comfortable in size and in design. It is unwise to use cheap chairs to save a little bit of money and lose efficiency due to poor back support.

The size and design of furniture should be appropriate for the work to be performed. Consider the size and number of machines and other devices that must regularly be within reach of the person working at a particular place. If you are outfitting a new office, consult with an office supplier to determine what might be appropriate in your situation. If you are evaluating a current arrangement, discuss needs with those who use the equipment. Be sensitive to expressions of back and shoulder discomfort, eye fatigue, and inability to concentrate for extended periods—symptoms often related to the design of work areas. Guidelines for work areas are in figure 6.2.

Figure 6.2

GUIDELINES FOR WORK AREAS

1. Determine what needs to be done at each work station, the appropriate furniture, the necessary equipment, and the resources that need to be nearby.
2. Design each work area so that all major items such as phone, computer screen, and primary reference materials are within a radius of about three feet from the worker. A swivel chair with rollers is preferable for many situations; this allows quick, easy access to secondary resources (file cabinet, supply shelf, etc.) within about six feet.
3. Locate large and/or noisy operations away from the central office. In a small church this may be in the next room. In a big church locations most appropriate for the operations should be selected. Be sure to check the lighting, power, heating/cooling, and communication needs for remote office functions such as printing, addressing and mailing, literature processing, and such before making any final decisions.
4. Storage areas of often-used supplies should be in the immediate area where they are used. For example, printing supplies should be in the printing/duplicating area and financial materials in the area or office where such matters are handled. In a small church you need a main storage cabinet; this would be located so that a secretary could secure paper or printer supplies without leaving the phone or reception area unattended. For all storage areas, label the location on each shelf or in each drawer for all items kept on hand. When the supply of a certain item is low, it will be easy to determine what is needed and reorder. A storage area for coats, umbrellas, lunches, and other items belonging to workers should be provided in a convenient but out-of-sight location.
5. Arrange work stations so that there is a minimum of distraction to a worker when someone walks by. In general, arrange a walkway on one side of a work area rather than through it. Whenever possible, arrange a divider at least 54 inches high between work stations to provide privacy, to control the noise level, and to avoid distractions. Make sure that all areas have good overhead lighting (preferably natural light fluorescent) and adequate ventilation.
6. Evaluate your office arrangement whenever new workers come or there is a change in work assignments, equipment, or quality/quantity of work. Experiment with various arrangements by using a computer design program or graph paper to sketch out the possibilities.

Office Equipment

The administrator's concern with equipment primarily is at the point of how best to speed up the work. An office could function without any electronic or technological assistance, but how nice it is to have labor-saving devices that improve efficiency and provide better quality. Each church has to determine what it is willing to invest in order to make its work easier, get it done faster, or do more of it.

One caution: the quest for improved efficiency through the use of electronic and technological devices must not result in a loss of the *personal touch of ministry* extended to people through the church office.

Church office equipment generally helps us to do one of the following:

- Word processing
- Financial reporting
- Data filing and sorting
- Duplicating and printing
- Communicating

In each of these areas, there is a great variety of equipment ranging from simple, cheap, and slow to complex, expensive, and fast.

Work can be done well at a number of levels. Consider word processing: it can be done by hand, word-processing program on a computer, or by using oral/character recognition processors. Prices range from less than a dollar to thousands of dollars. Personnel time may range from ten minutes for a letter to about three minutes; a second or revised copy takes from ten minutes to about 30 seconds. Consider the following options when making decisions about equipment.

Word Processing

While some offices still use word-processing equipment other than computers, most have upgraded to desktop units and/or servers with stations. The real value of the computer is that corrections and changes can be made on a screen and fresh, original copies produced quickly. Visit a computer dealer or office store to compare work speed, print quality, and price ranges for various options.

Another consideration is the storage that is available with many electronic devices. After items are prepared the first time, they can be stored on a disk or hard drive until you need them again, desire to revise them, or choose to delete them—all with very little time and trouble. In addition, you can easily copy files and send them to someone via e-mail or take them with you on portable drives for use elsewhere.

For example, consider the worship service bulletin. Prepare it one time and store it; the next week, push a button, and it will appear on a screen. Type over the parts with the new date, hymns, sermon title, and announcements; press a button and a perfect master is printed. You just saved more than three-fourths of the time it would have taken to prepare one without the saved version.

Financial Reporting

The same examples given for word processing could be given for financial reporting. The only difference is that much more time can be saved. Rather than using an accounting journal, entering figures by hand, and performing calculations on a desktop calculator, a computer works this way:

1. A spreadsheet or budget form is displayed on the screen.
2. Figures are entered using the calculating keys on the computer keyboard.
3. All entries are automatically calculated or readjusted in a matter of seconds at the push of a key.
4. An accurate report is printed at the push of a key.

Data Filing and Sorting

Two types of filing cabinets are in general use in church offices. One is the traditional stacked-drawers model that files materials front to back. Another style—called a lateral file—opens on the side, and file folders are placed side by side as if on a shelf. This design makes it easy to get to a large number of files without pulling and pushing drawers. If you wish, you can pull down a sliding cover over the materials.

Sorting devices for information are rather rare. Usually, materials will be sorted before filing, as in the case of a prospect list sorted by age groups and then left in that form in a notebook, card file, or folder. To help with this task, most administrators have used codes like colors or symbols to facilitate what basically has been a manual operation.

Many well-designed computer programs have revolutionized filing and sorting. With any information that must continually be updated, combined, sorted into parts, or in any way rearranged, a filing program on your computer will prove invaluable. Computer programs can also be used for membership rolls, financial records, sermons, prospects, visitation records, sick lists, and appointment schedules—in fact, for anything you might normally write on paper and stick in a file folder. All of this is encoded by typing the information on a screen, then recording it in an electronic file system. The most useful systems save the information internally and also allow you to transfer the data from machine to machine through a network or on a disk.

A membership record can be programmed to print out names sorted by ZIP code, age, vocation, and so forth. A talent file within seconds can provide prospects for a vacant position. A sermon file can display a message preached in the past; it can be updated, added to, parts deleted, and a fresh, *new* sermon produced in a short period of time. Do you need to list new members in an alphabetical file? Simple. Type the information and tell the computer to insert it in the correct places. The insertions are made, and all material is automatically sorted to produce an accurate, up-to-date list. Want a fresh copy? Press a button.

Duplicating and Printing

A great variety of equipment is available to make multiple copies. For the usual items such as bulletins and newsletters, an office printer/copier is suitable. If you want color printing, paper of different sizes and textures, or if collation is needed, more sophisticated equipment is required. Commercial printers often are used when thousands of copies are needed or if sophisticated materials such as brochures or newsmagazines are produced. Consequently, you must determine the types of materials that need to be duplicated in your office and those that might be taken to a printing specialist.

In order to make decisions about duplicating and printing in your office, list the items and the number of copies that need to be made during a typical month. Then discuss your needs with an office supply specialist.

Communicating

The basic equipment for communication is the telephone. However, the traditional use of one line with several extensions has been replaced by several options that are more efficient and very cost-effective.

Of course, there is still the need for basic local and long distance phone services; in addition, however, churches are increasingly installing a high-speed Internet connection and a communications network connecting workstations and various buildings and offices. When planning for renovation of offices or building a new facility, consult with a communication specialist to assure that future as well as present needs will be met. Guidelines for communication equipment and services are in figure 6.3.

Figure 6.3

GUIDELINES FOR COMMUNICATION EQUIPMENT AND SERVICES

1. Invest in quality equipment supported by good service. Inquire about the reputation of dealers in your area before making *any* decisions. Visit or call several churches similar to yours and discuss the good and bad features of their systems. Inquire about costs, reliability, and suggestions based on their experiences.
2. In a small office, consider one desk phone and extensions as needed, either wired or wireless.

3. In larger offices that have several rooms and/or private working areas, you must have a primary phone to receive and direct calls or an automated system that provides instructions and offers choices for callers. Switchboards no longer are large and unsightly; they may take little more space than the phone and a large box of tissues. Discuss options for this with several vendors and secure proposals with specific bids. Consider leasing *and* purchasing before you make a final decision.

4. Buy or lease at least one long-range cordless phone with an intercom feature. This can be used as an extension phone. Whenever someone has to work away from his or her desk, the portable handset can be carried. The church phone can be answered from this handset, or the person with the phone can be paged from the location of the phone's base. If several people regularly work in the office, consider a system with multiple handsets that can operate from the same base. Many churches also have cellular phone service for maintaining contact with the office when staff members are making visits or attending to a crisis.

5. Purchase a system or subscribe to a service that will answer calls and take messages. This device can be used very effectively to "tend the office" and to provide information about the church and scheduled activities when the office is closed. Callers can be greeted by a recorded message, then asked if they would like to leave a message for someone. *Note*: Make your recorded messages short and personable, then tell callers how to leave a message. Frequently check the messages and always respond promptly.

6. Consider placing answer-only phones and/or pay phones in locations where a phone is needed but use cannot be monitored, such as in a fellowship hall or in a gym.

7. A facsimile (FAX) machine is useful to send or receive copies needed quickly. This feature can be purchased as part of a multiple-use office machine or can be attached to an office computer. Discuss options and look at equipment at an office supply store.

8. Scanning devices connected to computers can be used to transmit printed materials into electronic files for storage, editing, printing, or transmitting to other locations via the Internet or FAX.

9. Consider a multiple-use device that combines several functions such as phone, FAX, message center, and printer. Office supply stores can provide information as well as describe how properly equipped computers can perform these same functions.

Audit of Equipment Needs

Whenever there are questions about the efficiency and effectiveness of office functions, an audit can help to determine what equipment is appropriate for the job. The forms in figures 6.4 and 6.5 can be used to evaluate either proposed or existing equipment needs.

Figure 6.4

GUIDELINES FOR AN EQUIPMENT AUDIT

1. Determine:

   - What needs to be done?
   - Who will do it?
   - How fast does it need to be done?
   - What level of quality is necessary?

2. According to the availability of resources, choose the most efficient equipment for the work that needs to be done. Consult with several vendors (such as office equipment, computer supply, and communication companies) to get acquainted with equipment options and to secure recommendations. Meanwhile, discuss needs with knowledgeable business persons in your church.

3. Evaluate possibilities with workers who would be affected.

4. Work through the normal decision-making channels in your church to secure and/or replace equipment.

5. Use only reputable dealers that have a reputation for service and attention after a sale. Avoid trading after-the-sale assistance to save a few dollars; the best price must be determined over the life of the equipment.

6. A fireproof safe or filing cabinet is absolutely necessary for keeping valuable records.

7. As you add or change equipment, consider keeping at least one back-up computer. Volunteers helping out in the office can use it, and you will have a back-up machine when the other equipment doesn't work or is being serviced.

8. When considering computer applications, keep in mind:

   - Even with a good computer, you still need good manual skills and procedures. Computers operate best when office information systems are well designed and understood.
   - A new computer or program will not be a perfect match for your present methods; adjustments in work flow and duties will likely be necessary.
   - Computers help *good* workers. They can only extend and enhance the skills of those using them. Don't count on a computer to make up for poor performance of a worker.
   - While adjusting to new computers or programs, demands will be greater for those learning how to operate the equipment and use the system. Be patient.
   - You must evaluate the specific needs of your office. Then, if you desire to move toward new computer applications, evaluate the programs (software) that are available. Find those that best meet your needs, *then* consider the equipment (hardware) that will operate the programs.

Figure 6.5

EVALUATION OF EQUIPMENT OR SOFTWARE

EVALUATION OF EQUIPMENT OR SOFTWARE FOR:_____(job)
NAME OF EQUIPMENT OR SOFTWARE:_____
VENDOR OR SUPPLIER:_____

EVALUATION (USE A SCALE FROM 1 to 10)

Requirements for This Item	References from Users	Vendor Literature	Demonstrations You Have Seen	Comments for or Against
SPEED				
QUALITY				
EASE OF USE				
EASE OF LEARNING				
EASE OF MAINTENANCE				
POINT AVERAGE	ESTIMATE THE VALUE OF THIS ITEM BASED ON THE COST:		__SUPERIOR __GOOD __FAIR __POOR	
SIGNED	POSITION			

Work Systems

On the following pages you will see a variety of work systems that could be used in your office. Each of them obviously must be part of a larger operation; everyone and everything in an office must work together for the benefit of the church.

Review these ideas, consider your existing systems, then determine what you might want to revise. In some cases you can take the suggestions and use them with very little adaptation. In others, you will want to consult the suggested resources and then work out your own version. Either way, good administrative practice requires that those who are involved in doing the work be involved in making decisions about how to improve.

Office Protocol

Review and determine the guidelines in your office for the items listed in figure 6.6. Write in the general expectations. Discuss them with those involved; then prepare a final copy that can be distributed and used as a set of guidelines for office protocol.

Figure 6.6

GUIDELINES FOR OFFICE PROTOCOL

Office hours
Dress code
Reception duties
   How to greet callers:
   On the phone
   In person
Titles: when and what titles to use (Mr., Mrs., Dr., Rev., etc.):
   In reference to ministerial staff
   Church members
   Outsiders
How to handle requests
Message-taking procedure
How to handle emergencies
What to do when someone is angry or demanding:
   Member
   Visitor
   Business or civic representative
   Vagrant
What to do when you:
   Are sick
   Are angry
   Have a conflict with a co-worker
Expectations about supervision
Expectations about confidentiality

Telephone/Communications

1. If possible, the same person should do all the answering, forwarding of calls, and message-taking. In case this person is unable to answer, agree that anyone in the office will answer after three rings. Be sure all personnel are trained in how to answer the phone and what to say. Few things are worse for your church's image than for a caller to hear a gruff, "Hello!" followed in a few seconds by, "I don't know."

2. Identify the church, then yourself, and ask, "May I help you?"

3. Do not keep a person waiting. If a caller cannot be helped or connected right away, arrange to take a message or to call the person back. Avoid placing a person on "hold."

4. If there are many people who work in your office, use a sign-in and sign-out sheet so that the receptionist/phone attendant will know who is available. Also, persons in conference must notify the attendant when they desire not to be disturbed.

5. Maintain a log for all outgoing long-distance calls. This will serve as a checklist when the bill comes and assist with determining the budget allocation for phone services.

6. Develop a policy regarding the use of church phones for private purposes by workers or by members. What local and what long distance calls are appropriate to receive? To make?

7. If your church has a cordless or cellular phone, it can be taken when someone is on an errand in the building. If there is only one worker, the phone can be answered in the normal way without anyone being aware where the person is. If there are several workers, the person with the cordless phone can be paged if necessary.

8. Prepaid calling cards are useful when ministers and other church personnel are on church-related business away from their local calling zone.

9. Limit personal calls, both incoming and outgoing, to necessary messages. Also, be careful about letting business calls turn into pleasure calls.

10. Use an answering and message telephone or service when there is no one in the office. Listen and respond to messages first thing upon returning.

11. Publish your office telephone number along with the church's name and other contact information in all church-related publications. In a large church you may wish to provide and publish separate numbers for some of the offices or ministers. If you have a Web site or participate in one, be sure that current information is posted.

12. Many of the principles listed above also apply to communication via e-mail and cellular phones. Review all forms of communication used in your office and determine those that apply.

Filing and Storing Records

1. Keep ready-reference materials—those items that need to be stored and used in the church office—in sturdy folders or file cabinets/containers within easy reach of workers. In some cases, such as the membership roll and a dictionary, reference materials can also be maintained on a computer. Categories of ready reference materials and possible filing options are given in figure 6.7.

2. Records that must be retained either for the benefit of the church or to fulfill legal obligations usually are not in the ready-reference category. They must be filed and stored but may be placed in a secure location adjacent to or near the work areas. These are materials such as bank records, historical documents, deeds, and business contracts. The usual rule is this: keep all valuable and/or historical materials in a fireproof vault or safe box and all other records either in or near the church office. A record retention schedule in figure 6.8 gives an approximate time to keep different types of materials.

3. Separate mail into categories: personal, church, and "to whom it may concern" items, such as catalogs and sales brochures. Handle the personal, send the church items to the appropriate person for action, and make an *immediate* decision whether to save or discard the junk mail. Items that

Figure 6.7

READY REFERENCE MATERIALS

ITEM	FILING OPTIONS		
	Journal or Notebook	**File Drawer or Similar Device**	**Computer* File**
To-do list	X		
Correspondence		X	
Purchasing records		X	
Leadership list	X		X
Organizational records		X	X
Membership records	X	X	X
Record of contributions	X		X
Financial reports	X	X	X
Prospect list		X	X
Sick list		X	X
Visitation list		X	X
Business meeting minutes	X	X	X
Inventory of equipment	X	X	
Personnel records—individuals		X	
Employment/personnel data		X	
Business contracts		X	
Legal data		X	

*The use of a computer compresses significantly the amount of space required as well as making the information easy to recall, tabulate, and revise. Items saved on a disk, however, should always be backed up with a spare copy. You can, of course, print copies of the information whenever desired.

come in bulk, such as supplies and literature, should be labeled with the person's name and location to which the items are to go.

4. If items will not be saved, use or circulate them as appropriate and then discard.

5. Keep records of key decisions made, instructions received, actions taken, and *any* significant or unusual activities in which you are involved. *This is absolutely necessary for effective administration.* Do not count on remembering the facts when something goes wrong, when someone wants to know exactly what is happening and why, or when a business sends an order and no one knows exactly what leader requested the items. For general records, record notes in your datebook, on a desk calendar, or in a computer file. For major actions, prepare records and file as appropriate.

6. For expenditure of church funds, always follow a church-approved financial plan. Maintain either a purchase order system or a journal in which all transactions are recorded, along with the person approving. For petty cash disbursements, require a receipt for the item, signed by the person being reimbursed. For additional guidelines related to financial matters, see chapter 7.

7. Maintain regular backups of all important documents stored on office computers. Again, back up on a regular basis, and keep one set of back-up files in a vault or other waterproof and fireproof location.

Figure 6.8

RECORD RETENTION SCHEDULE

Keep at Least Three Years

Deposit Records, Bank Statements, and Processed Checks
General Correspondence
Inventory of Equipment (after new one is prepared)
Purchasing Records
Financial Statements/Reports to the Congregation
Organizational Records (A summary should be included in the church
    minutes at least once a year and in an annual denominational report.)

Keep at Least Five Years

Insurance Policies (after expiration date)
Record of Individual Contributions
Individual Personnel Records (after person has left employment)
Tax Records—Employees
Business Contracts (maintenance and supply items/services)

Keep Permanently

Historical Items (charter, constitution and bylaws, pictures, etc.)
Legal Items (deeds, contracts, bonds, incorporation documents, tax re-
    cords, and other related items)
Church Business Meeting Minutes
Audit and Financial Reports

Master Membership Record
Employment/Personnel Records
Annual Report of Church Activities
Some denominations provide a microfilm service to preserve church
   records. Contact your denominational office to inquire.

Mailing and Shipping Services

1. Establish a routine for receiving and processing incoming mail.
Determine whether all mail except that marked personal will be
opened and sorted by the assigned person. All mail addressed to a
specific person should be placed in an agreed-upon spot. Financial
items such as bills and statements should be placed together for the
treasurer. Nonspecific mail should be processed according to established procedures.

2. If incoming mail is centrally processed, open all mail first, attach
any enclosures to the enclosed letter, check to see that the letterhead
has the return address information that is on the envelope (if not,
staple it to the letter), stamp the first-class mail with date received,
sort it, and then handle as agreed upon.

3. When there are several workers in an office, consider having a
mail and message pickup point. Normally, this location would be near
the phone attendant so that messages could easily be put in the appropriate place. Additional boxes and/or locations could be arranged
for key church leaders and for employees who may work in other
locations.

4. A pickup point also is a good location for a collection box for all
outgoing items. Determine the mail pickup time(s) in your area and
post the time(s) by which mail must be in the box to be picked up
and/or delivered to the post office or other service facility.

5. Consult with your local post office as well as with other delivery services. Secure information about rates and specifications for the
various classes of mail. Discuss the types and frequency of mailings
from your church, and get recommendations for how best to secure
good service at the least cost. Make notes and place in a file for quick
reference.

6. Arrange the writing, editing, printing, and addressing activities
for each major item mailed on a regular basis. Set the schedule so that
everyone knows exactly what must be done, when, and by whom in
order to get items to the post office at the appointed time. A sample
preparation schedule is included in chapter 11.

7. A postal scale will be of great assistance in determining the amount of postage to affix to letters and packages. This often saves a trip to the post office.

8. In most churches it is a simple matter to keep first-class and a variety of other stamps in a box, replenishing when necessary. However, when many letters and packages are mailed, a postage meter is preferable. The actual cost can be determined and the postage printed on a label, just like at the post office. The amount for postage is subtracted automatically from the amount of credit in your account. You can even include your church's imprint on the label, if you wish. This service is available also on the Internet, through the United States Postal Service Web site (*www.usps. com*). Consult your postmaster for more information.

9. Make a file for Mail and Delivery Services—Special. Secure information about special handling and next-day delivery from the post office. Get a small supply of certified and registered mail materials so that they can be prepared at your office. Find out if next-day delivery is available to and from your post office. Also contact parcel delivery services such as FedEx and United Parcel Service (UPS) to determine if they pick up and deliver in your area. Request information about rates, pickup and delivery points, and schedules. Make sure the person who handles the church's mail is thoroughly familiar with all options.

Communications within the Office

Effective interoffice communications make work easier. When personal contact is important, call or talk with persons directly. When this is impossible or unnecessary, choose one of the following methods:

1. Use voice mail, instant messaging, or an interoffice message form.

2. Arrange for a central mail and/or message pickup point, as described in the section on mailing and shipping services.

3. Consider connecting your office computers in a network. Then all interoffice communication can be sent, reviewed, and filed electronically. Consult with a computer or office supply specialist for information and costs.

4. Whenever you send an outside letter or message that includes information needed elsewhere in the office, send a copy to the appropriate person. This can be done easily by sending a photocopy. If messages are sent via e-mail, send a copy to appropriate persons.

5. For internal communications, e-mail is the easiest and quickest way to send multiple copies. For written messages, standard memo forms are available at office stores or forms can be designed and printed for your church.

6. Dictation is easier and more efficient if a recording device is used. Rarely is dictation given personally anymore. New devices make it easier and more convenient for the person who sends information and for the person who transcribes. Devices are available that can be carried easily

from office to car to home, offering a time-saving option for busy church workers. The recorded information can then be left for dictation, with the typist being able to start and stop the message as necessary in order to prepare the desired material. Increasingly, however, ministers use personal computers to prepare documents. When the material is ready, you can print out the finished copy or send the file to an office worker for processing.

7. When you are asked to give a word-of-mouth message to someone in your office, especially from a member of the congregation, write it down. Next time you are in the office, place it on the message board or in the recipient's in-box. Alternatively, jot the message into an e-mail and send it. If the message relates to an emergency, contact the recipient in the quickest manner.

8. When distributing committee meeting minutes and other such reports, make enough extra copies to send to key staff persons. Increasingly, churches are sending minutes and related information via e-mail, using a distribution list for each group. It is a simple matter to add key staff members to this list; this will keep them informed with little extra effort.

9. Purchase standard office forms or develop your own for all regular information recorded and/or distributed in your office. If a suitable form is not available from an office supply store, prepare the form as you want it to look; leave lines and spaces where the desired information can be inserted. This form can be duplicated in your office, or it can be sent to a commercial printer. It can also be set up on a computer, which will allow for easy data entry and distribution. If desired, pads of your custom-designed form can be made either by the printer or in your office. Inquire at your office supply store about the way to bind forms in a tear-off pad.

10. Memos and forms that will be filed in a notebook should be duplicated on punched paper. Paper can be bought by the ream with holes already punched for very little extra cost. In addition, keep a heavy-duty paper punch in the church office.

11. All church staff members should tell the receptionist/phone attendant when they will be out or unavailable during office hours. Additionally, emergency contact information for key personnel and emergency services should be readily available.

Minutes of Business Meetings

The following procedures are helpful in maintaining an accurate accounting of important information in the life of the church. While these steps are specifically for business meeting minutes, the same process could be used for processing any records for which the church office is responsible.

1. The clerk or other authorized person should take the minutes.

2. The minutes should be prepared, typed, and reviewed for accuracy.

3. Send a copy to the presiding officer/pastor for review.

4. Minutes of the previous meeting should be read, corrected as necessary, and approved at the next regular business meeting.

5. An official copy and two photocopies should then be distributed as follows: the original to a chronological file of church business meeting records; a copy for the clerk's file; and a copy retained for ready-reference in the church office. If files are prepared and stored electronically, back up the files each time new records are added.

6. Store *official* minutes in a secure, fireproof location, under the care of an appointed staff member or church officer. Minutes may be recorded electronically or may be stored in bound volumes, notebooks, or in file folders by the year or by several years, depending on the number of pages. If the service is available in your denomination, consider having copies made and stored in a permanent historical collection.

7. Keep the office copy of minutes in a notebook or computer file for easy use. Retain these copies on a reference shelf in the office for three years or longer if there appears to be a need.

Membership and Organizational Records

1. Determine a scheduled time each week when all regular files are updated. Here is a sample plan:

Monday	Compilation of Sunday visitors
	Sick list
	Church membership requests (sent and received)
Tuesday	Organizational files (attendance records,
	visitors, new members, drops, etc.)
Wednesday	Prospect file and visitation list
Thursday	Master membership file
	Specialized files (newcomers to community, newsletter
	mailing list, college students away, etc.)

2. Whenever possible, combine other tasks with the above activities. For example, when processing requests for church membership, also fill out a form that will add the person to the church mailing list, place the person's name on the prospect list for church organizations, give the minister(s) pertinent information, and notify the new member committee.

3. Evaluate the present system for handling these routine tasks. If there are no established procedures, write the exact steps that are to be completed and review them with those who are involved. Look for ways to cut and combine steps. Finally, adopt the procedures that will best serve your office. Once this has been done, work can be delegated or shared with other workers or with volunteers. The procedures become the basis for training and for determining the exact duties to be done.

4. Maintenance of membership and organizational records requires the use of standard forms and other supplies. One person should be respon-

sible for determining the materials used regularly and maintaining an adequate supply.

5. Consult with your denominational bookstore or an office supply store to determine the best binders, holders, files, and other supplies to manage these materials. Often there are specialized devices that save time and effort.

6. Computers provide an effective and speedy way to manage records and produce reports. Your denominational office or a theological school should be able to provide information about record management programs and suppliers.

Chapter 7

FINANCIAL POLICIES AND PROCEDURES[1]

William G. Caldwell

C hurches have two limited resources: money and people. Using these resources wisely requires each church to budget wisely, to subscribe the budget, and to use the funds from these limited resources in keeping with the wishes of the congregation.

Research in the giving patterns of church members indicates that a minimal percentage of the membership gives most of the budget money and that perhaps as many as half of church members give nothing during a twelve-month period. The church, through its leadership, has a keen responsibility in planning effective ministry budgets and spending the tithes and offerings of the people. The highest level of integrity is called for when caring for God's money that is given through a local church.

Mission efforts and worthy programs often suffer from inadequate funding. Without financial planning, churches can be strapped with unrealistic debt, ballooning personnel costs, and rising maintenance and utility charges.

Training a Committee

A stewardship or finance committee, or some similar group, should be selected and trained to give vital leadership in financial matters. The committee will seek to develop distinctive Christian stewards through all areas of the church's life and work. It will endeavor to permeate all teaching, preaching, training, and mission work with biblical concepts of stewardship. This process must be developed and implemented on a year-round basis. It is obvious that church members do not automatically become distinctive Christian stewards when they come to know Christ, but they do become learners and disciples. This committee can help a church give attention to this aspect of discipleship.

Members of this committee should give evidence of being dedicated Christian stewards. They should also reflect a growing commitment to Christ. The characteristics of a distinctive steward have been described as one who makes Christ Lord, acknowledges God as owner of everything, and accepts responsibility as trustee of God's bountiful blessings. A member of the stewardship committee will demonstrate a redeemed life in giving, reflecting the teachings of the church in tithing or systematic giving as well as being one who manages personal money well.

Committee members should also be concerned with the growth of the church, particularly its needs and opportunities. They should be adept at informing others of these facts. Committee members should be spiritually mature persons who have the confidence of other church members. They should participate fully in the activities of the committee as well as in all stewardship functions of the church. Members of this committee should be carefully selected and elected according to the procedures of the church.

Developing a Budget

The best approach to budgeting is to start over each year and develop a budget based on fixed costs with variables being assigned funds in order of their priority. In a local church this plan of assessing needs and resources is called ministry budgeting. This is a process by which a church plans its spending around the ministries it conceives as God's will for its life. This involves the vision and mission understanding of the church. Since budgeting is an evidence of our interpretation of that will, we carefully study its processes.

Ministry budgeting is based on people. The size of a church has little to do with the ministries it performs; however, planning does. This process may be used by a church of a hundred members just as easily as it can be used by a church of a thousand members or more. It is important to identify what people value before determining an appropriate budget and challenging members to a higher level of giving. The committee asks important questions:

1. What are the ministries our church will be engaged in next year to accomplish the mission God has given us?
2. How much will these ministries cost?
3. Is there a better way to get the job done?

In essence, each church needs to rediscover what it is to do and find ways of getting that job done. Ministry budgeting is an effective way of doing the job. Guidelines for developing a budget are given in chapter 8.

Presenting the Budget for Church Approval

Methods of presenting the budget can be changed from year to year. Using audiovisuals, panel discussion, and congregational discussion can heighten interest in the budget. Major changes in budget format, additional staff, or new buildings should be thoroughly explained and discussed until all questions have been answered. Save enough time for a discussion period.

Some churches adopt the report of the budget committee and the new church budget at the end of the discussion period while it is fresh on people's minds. Other churches wait several days before the vote is taken in a worship service to allow for more thought and prayer about the decision.

Underwriting the Budget

From the time a budget is adopted and underwritten, there is a time of prayer, education, and promotion. Many varied and productive plans are available to assist in this significant task—stewardship lessons in Sunday school and tithing testimonies and stewardship sermons in the worship services.[2] An individual commitment will be sought from each church and Sunday school member. Whether this is done through the mail or by a personal visit, it is important that everyone be given the opportunity to indicate financial support for the ministries of the church.

Accounting for the Budget

A procedure for receiving and expending funds is critical to the integrity of the church's financial plan. Anytime money is received, at least two church members should be present to assume responsibility for those monies! Money should be counted in a place where reasonable security can be maintained. Again, at least two members should be present during the counting of the money. As soon as possible it should be deposited in the church's bank account. Under no circumstances should money remain in the church or in a home overnight.

A procedure for the accounting of church funds should follow this schedule:

- Receive monies from all sources within the church.
- Count the money and fill out appropriate records (see figure 7.1).
- Deposit all money.
- Post member contributions and provide each member an annual record of his or her giving.
- Record all financial transactions.
- Make a monthly report to the church.

Figure 7.1

COUNTING COMMITTEE REPORT

Date: _____

BUDGET OFFERINGS	Sunday School	Worship Service
Money in Envelopes		
Not in Envelopes		
Other		
Total		

DESIGNATED OFFERINGS		Amount
	Total	

Total Cash	Total checks	
Grand Total		

CASH COUNT		Sunday School	Worship Service
Currency:	$50.00		
	20.00		
	10.00		
	5.00		
	1.00		
Change:	.50		
	.25		
	.10		
	.05		
	.01		
Total		$	$

Approved by	Date

A current practice among some churches is to secure a bond from a bonding company for each person who has fiduciary responsibility. This is a prudent business decision that all churches should follow. In no way does bonding question the honesty of the person who handles church funds. It is simply good business practice.

Using Purchase Orders

Some churches control spending by using a purchase order system. When instituting such a system, it is essential that all persons in the church who might purchase for the church are made aware of the need to secure approval in advance. Vendors from whom the church might purchase items should be notified of the requirement that a purchase order must accompany all orders. The notification should include the information that after a specified date, the church will not be responsible for payment unless a purchase order has been received. The church will decide which budget accounts do not require a purchase order—such as salaries, missions, and building payment.

For purchases less than a specified amount, authorized persons can buy needed items and receive reimbursement from a petty cash fund (figure 7.2). For more costly items and those that must be ordered, a request is given to the financial secretary or the fiscal representative of the stewardship committee. This request may be oral or written according to church

Figure 7.2

PETTY CASH SLIP

No. _____

Received of Petty Cash $_____

For_____

_____

Charge to budget acct. # _____

Signed_____ Date _____

Approved _____ Date _____

Figure 7.3

PURCHASE REQUISITION

Please purchase for _____

Name _____

Committee or program to be charged _____

Purpose or use _____

Deliver to _____

Notify _____

Date needed _____

Preferred vendor _____

Remarks _____

Quantity	Description	Unit	Total
		Total	

Signed _____

Approved by _____

Received by _____

---

policy. (For a purchase requisition form, see figure 7.3.) After a request is received and approved by the designated church purchasing agent, a purchase order form (figure 7.4) is prepared and delivered. The number on the purchase order must then appear on the invoice before payment is made.

Checks will be drawn against the general bank account of the church when a check requisition like the sample in figure 7.5 has been completed and authorized. Normally, payroll checks are not drawn with a check requisition. All other checks, however, should have this approval safeguard before being issued.

Many churches require two signatures on each church check. Usually the treasurer and one other member of the stewardship or finance committee are authorized to sign checks.

Figure 7.4

PURCHASE ORDER

No._____

TO [   ] SHIP TO

This number must appear on all correspondence, invoices, shipping papers, and packages.

DELIVERY

Date	Req. No.	Terms	Ship via	F.O.B. Point
Quantity	Please enter our order in accordance with prices, delivery, and specifications given			Price

Signed _____

Approved _____

Received by _____

Figure 7.5

CHECK REQUISITION

(Name of Church)

Address _____ Phone_____

Make Check to _____

Address _____ City_____State_____Zip_____

Amount of Check $ _____

Purpose of Check _____

Budget Account Number_____

Approved by _____

Preprinted forms similar to those illustrated in this chapter are available from office supply stores. They can also be ordered with the name of your church or organization imprinted.

The Annual Audit

There is a growing trend toward securing an annual audit conducted by an independent firm of public accountants. There are several benefits:

- Credibility of the financial statement
- Assistance in developing good and meaningful financial statements and reports
- Professional advice on controls and other administrative matters
- Compliance with legal requirements

In addition, an experienced accountant can provide the technical assistance for establishing suitable record systems that reflect the needs of specialized church activities and simplify treasury functions. The audit establishes in-depth information provided in the financial statement.

If the church has never had an audit, the initial cost will be greater than subsequent audit costs. A base for assets and liabilities will be established and future audits will be constructed from that base. Some churches use an audit committee that reviews procedures during the time between professional audits.

Designated Accounts

Many churches have no fiscal problem with designated accounts. Churches usually seek to include all regular activities in the budget. For special purposes, however, members sometimes give funds designated for a particular cause. These funds are placed in a restricted account and used only for the specified purpose. Major difficulties and misunderstandings can be avoided by having a policy drawn by the stewardship or finance committee and adopted by the church. One problem often faced in the absence of a policy is the giving of a gift for a specified purpose that does not fit into the church's priorities. Then the church risks losing the gift or changing its priorities. See the sample designated accounts policy in figure 7.6.

Figure 7.6

DESIGNATED ACCOUNTS POLICY

Purpose: To provide procedures for the establishment, activity, and closure of a designated account.

Establishment

1. A designated account will be established upon a written request to the church administrator, the approval of the finance committee, and, if appropriate, the approval of the church.

2. The purpose of the account must be specific and consistent with the church's tax exempt purpose. It must comply with all IRS rules and regulations.

3. A minimum opening deposit of $100 is required.

Activity

1. The finance committee will be responsible for reviewing distributions to ensure compliance with the account's purpose.

2. Upon fulfillment of the purpose of the account, the account will be closed, and any unused funds will be transferred to the general budget account or another account specified at the designated account's establishment.

3. When the account balance is less than $100, it will be closed unless it has a periodically recurring purpose.

4. If the account is inactive for six months and with no immediate plans for its use, it may be closed and funds transferred to the specific account. Prior to closure, the establishing party will be notified, and finance committee approval will be required.

Chart of Accounts

A simple but extremely helpful device for proper budget coding is called a "chart of accounts." Each line item in the budget should have a corresponding descriptive paragraph telling what items are to be charged to that particular budget number. The stewardship or finance committee prepares, evaluates, and updates the chart of accounts (figure 7.7).

Special Gifts

The stewardship or finance committee will possibly have a subcommittee to seek and encourage special gifts. However, it is important to understand that designated gifts received by the church must be used for the purpose of designation or refunded to the donor in case the purchase or use is changed. Another important factor is that because of changing tax laws and different state requirements, many church members may be unaware of tax advantages that are available to the giver. The committee should plan to inform church members of these advantages toward the end of each year. The church may also want to consult with a person who specializes in helping nonprofit organizations determine the best use of noncash items that are given to the church. Gifts that are to be sought are:

Real Estate. Giving a home, farm, or other property will allow a federal income tax deduction for its full value and avoid capital gains tax if the property's value has increased. Property can also be used to fund a trust that returns regular income for the life of the donor.

Figure 7.7

CHART OF ACCOUNTS

Assets and Fund Balance 100
101 Cash in Bank A
102 Cash in Bank B
110 Petty Cash
120 Transfers to (from) Other Funds
190 Fund Balance
Designated Receipts 200
210 Missions
215 Organ Gifts
225 Debt Retirement
230 Other
Designated Disbursements 300
310 Missions
315 Organ Gifts
325 Debt Retirement
330 Other
Undesignated Receipts 400
410 Budget Receipts
412 Loose Offerings
Undesignated Disbursements Missions 500
510 World Missions
520 Local Missions
530 Other Missions
Educational Ministry 600
610 Sunday School
613 Discipleship
615 Music
619 Denominational Literature
621 Vacation Bible School
625 Mission Organizations
      (Including Related Youth Groups)
630 Youth
644 Honoraria

648 Conventions and Conferences
651 Library
655 Scouts
660 Kindergarten
General Operations 700
706 Public Relations
712 Denominational Retirement
718 Insurance—Property
721 Kitchen
728 Office Supplies
735 Postage
738 Hospitality
745 Payroll Taxes
750 Utilities
756 Laundry
759 Ordinances
764 Altar Flowers
769 Employee Hospital Insurance
772 Miscellaneous
Property and Debt Retirement 800
810 Building Equipment
820 Building Maintenance
825 Office Equipment and Maint.
830 Grounds
840 Debt Retirement
Personnel Salaries; Allowances 900
910 Pastor
915 Minister of Education
920 Minister of Music
925 Church Secretary
930 Education Secretary
935 Organist
940 Nursery Coordinator
945 Nursery Assistants

Memorial Gifts. Often families, respecting the wishes of deceased loved ones, request that memorials be established. Sometimes these are in the form of an endowment, where the amount given remains intact and is invested. The proceeds can then be designated for specific ministries of the church.

Gifts in Kind. Gifts in kind, such as jewelry, crops, livestock, works of art, coin collections, antiques, and royalties, can be the perfect answer to giving interests. Mortgages, leases, and notes can also be donated.

Cash. If deductions are itemized on a federal income tax return, gifts of cash up to 50 percent of adjusted gross income can generally be deducted.

If more than 50 percent of adjusted gross income is donated one year, the excess amount may be carried over.

Securities (stocks, bonds, mutual funds). There are three ways generally recommended for giving securities so that the gift benefits the charitable organization as well as the giver. The church should develop a policy on how these items are to be liquidated so that the proceeds can be used.

1. Give a security that has appreciated and qualifies for long-term capital gains status.
2. Give the capital gains portion of an appreciated security and retain the amount of original cost.
3. Sell a depreciated security, deduct the loss, and donate the proceeds from the sale.

Life Insurance. Many people do not realize that life insurance policies or dividends paid on the policies make practical gifts. There are several ways to donate life insurance:

- Give policies no longer needed for their original purposes.
- Give a fully paid-up policy, and deduct its replacement cost.
- Give a policy on which premiums are being paid and deduct the approximate cash value, plus all future premiums paid.

A Systems Approach to Financial Record Keeping

Churches of all sizes are moving rapidly toward a systems approach to all record keeping, especially financial records. Personal computers are being used in smaller churches while large churches are going to more sophisticated hardware and programs. Installing a computer, however, will not solve all of the financial problems of a church. If good records are not in place already, adding a computer will likely compound the problem.

If a church decides to purchase a computer or upgrade present equipment, it is necessary to consider all of the needs of the church that might be impacted by such equipment. A committee composed of representatives of all areas of church life should be used to identify all possible uses. A search for software to accommodate the needs should be done prior to purchasing any equipment.

Several companies are producing software to meet the financial recordkeeping needs of a church. Included in the program should be the capability to do all bookkeeping functions, individual member contributions, payroll, and monthly statements. In addition to financial records, the computer should have the capacity to accommodate all educational organization records, membership rolls, master prospect file, and other needs identified.

Above all, we must remember that the purpose of giving must be more than paying bills or funding an institution. We must be doing the work of Christ through the mission and purpose of the church.

Chapter 8

PLANNING AND BUDGETING

Bob I. Johnson

I nsanity has been described as doing the same thing in the same way
and expecting different results. Does that thought have anything to
say to the church when it comes to planning and budgeting? Consider
your own experience to find an answer. If a church comes to either planning or budgeting and does it in the same way as in the past, it should
expect similar results. But times have changed. Planning no longer relies
on thick notebooks with finely tuned plans and a call for extensive detail.
Both planning and budgeting have to be projected with more fluidity than
in the past. Decisions must be made not so much about specific and detailed plans but with putting the church in a position to react positively to
ministry opportunities that may not have been thought of when the planning took place.

John, a usually quiet church member, made an appointment to speak
with his pastor about an idea for ministry that had captured his thinking.
He worked for a sheriff's department where he related closely to the pris-
oners, often transporting them to long-term facilities. John would engage
these persons in conversation and learn about their lives. From this he
felt compelled to see if there were something he could do to help children and youth avoid the pits into which others had stumbled. So he went
to the pastor with an idea for an exercise and sports program during the
summer.

His church just happened to have worked its way through a self-study
that produced a new focus for the coming years. The church also had put
in place a new structure that called for a coordinator of ministries to deal
with just such possibilities. The focus that would drive the church for the
foreseeable future was on young families. John's idea fit into this focus.
The coordinator of ministries worked with John and helped others become
involved in the ministry. The church already owned a building for such
uses as well as vans for transporting the children. When this ministry was

planted in the heart of one caring church member, everything was in place to implement it.

Hear the words of Jesus: "On this rock I will build my church, and the powers of death shall not prevail against it" (Matt 16:18 RSV). In moving a church toward knowing and claiming this mind-boggling promise, planning and budgeting play strategic roles. All business and service organizations engage in these two functions. The church, however, is unique in the entire world and thus needs a specific word about how it addresses its future and uses its financial resources.

In planning and budgeting, the church will be saying something significant to itself, its community, its larger world, and ultimately to God, who birthed and sustains the church. This chapter is designed to offer practical help to do this. It will also seek to emphasize the impact these functions can have on the church's witness and story it seeks to tell.

Planning

Nothing takes the place of a good beginning in any effort, large or small. The approach you take to planning is most important in determining the outcome of such an effort. For example, if you rely solely on the planning model that studies the congregation, the geographical communities surrounding the meeting place, and the resources available to that congregation for ministry, then the results will probably highlight the weaknesses, liabilities, and shortcomings of the congregation. If this is the sole approach, then the effect may be rather negative. Planning ought to help the church enhance its statement about what it wants to be and do under God.

Earlier you read about ways to help a church clarify its vision and enhance its ministries. This chapter builds on that concept, showing how to provide leadership for decision making and, then, for implementing plans. It would be helpful to consult resources on change along with the material in this chapter. See the bibliography for suggestions.

Principles for Leaders of Planning

Some basic principles should undergird any planning in the context of the church or related entity.

1. *Maintain the biblical meaning of church.* The purpose of a church is to be the people of God, a communion of saints, a called-out people in the community. The number one requirement for an administrator is to keep clear focus on the biblical meaning of church.

Unlike other organizations the church has the undeniable promise of God that through the Holy Spirit the church will be directed and empowered for its mission. The Spirit gives power to overcome opposition forces and provides a spirit of love and self-control.

2. *Emphasize being, then focus on doing.* Danger lies in a planning process consisting primarily of setting goals and objectives, listing and choosing from alternative strategies for reaching the goals, performing the tasks, and evaluating the results. The primary danger lies in assuming there is an ideal to be reached and that it can be accomplished by marshaling the forces to do something. Foundational to doing is being; therefore, emphasis should be given to being God's people.

3. *Keep data in its perspective.* Data is important, but to base your planning solely on data that has been collected may send you off in the wrong direction. The danger is that the more data a congregation collects, the greater the potential for confusion. This approach can also enslave congregations to the supposed inevitability of demographic trends of population growth or decline. For example, a local church may select a particular demographic trend and on that basis justify withdrawing from active ministry efforts in certain areas.

Certainly correlation between demographic trends and church growth exists. Some churches, however, grow in the midst of a declining population. Some churches decline in the midst of a swelling, unchurched population.

4. *Focus planning on the relational nature of the church.* In relation to the community, the church's task is to provide an arena where people can understand the forces affecting their lives, be confronted by the living God, and get a correct perspective on time and eternity. In short, the church must focus on its relationship to God and to people.

5. *Keep planning as a means to an end, not an end in itself.* It is fairly simple for a church to focus on lesser things and to miss the main thing(s). A church may fall prey to an overreliance on administrative structure, financial planning, and the desire to eliminate risks. Planning can become an end in itself because it may be more interesting and safer than getting on with *being* the church. Planning should be seen as risk-taking decision making.

6. *Major on the strengths of the church.* Strengths are present in every church and precisely so because God has empowered believers to develop them. For a church to deny its strengths for all practical purposes means that it denies God. This is not to be an ego trip because the strengths are gifts from God and as such belong to the entire congregation.

Good planning begins with helping a church proclaim its strengths because good planning begins with God. To ask, "What are our needs? What are our problems?" is to ask the wrong questions first.

7. *Base your planning on a set of stated values.* The congregation should affirm those things that are dear to it—values, in other words—and focus on these for the thrust of planning. Like no other time, the church is exposed to a public evaluation of its values. Planning provides an opportunity for the church to demonstrate a moral and value-based reason for existence.

Guidelines for Planning

The principles of planning listed previously should permeate the church's attitude and total process. The following guidelines are a sequential, step-by-step process that may be expanded or rearranged to suit your situation.

1. *Prepare for planning.* A key person in planning is the pastor. The pastor, in working with key leaders and the congregation as a whole, should be aware of the need and the timing for planning. The pastor is the person who knows the values of the church and expresses those values in a variety of ways. The basic philosophy and values of a church have far more to do with its achievements than do its economic resources, organizational structure, or various other aspects.

In the business world the effective companies seem to have developed cultures that have incorporated the values and practices of their great leaders with those shared values surviving for decades after the passing of those leaders. The enduring contribution of a chief executive comes through the formation of values that guide the organization.

In preparing for planning, emphasize the church's story. Every congregation has one; it permeates the group life of the church and is the interpreter of past, present, and future. Story is the primary medium by which the identity, goals, perceptions, and strategies are communicated. Try asking, "How come?" and you will probably get a story from the church's past. The story can enhance an appreciation of the rich background of the average congregation.

The local church that recounts its story gains many benefits. By focusing on strengths, achievements, and vision, members are able to identify and reinforce who and what the church is today. Story reveals what is important and facilitates group discussion of church life. It will also reveal something of the pain and needs in the life of the church. But most importantly, story can help the church identify its mission and place in the world.

In preparing for planning, perhaps one way the church can be made aware of its story is to set up group meetings in which people are allowed to share the parts of the church's story that have most influenced their lives. In a church with significant numbers of new people as well as many who have been members for many years, a time when both groups can share dreams and aspirations would be helpful. This helps people get to know one another better and understand how the church is perceived and how they might fulfill the mission of the church.

2. *Establish purpose in planning.* Establishing purpose means to develop a clear statement of a church's purpose or focal mission. This statement serves as an umbrella under which the church functions in day-to-day and year-to-year ministry. Consider this example: "The mission of our church is to be a worshipping, redemptive body in Christ, whose field is the world and whose ministry includes the whole person." Most every church with a Web site will include a purpose statement in the information it provides.

A check of several such Web sites will provide examples from which you may learn.

A church may look at what others have adopted, but each church should formulate its own unique statement. Try stating it as briefly as possible, but remember that this is a statement of purpose, not a slogan, such as "Family of Love." Consider displaying the statement in an appropriate place in the church building.

Such a statement should enable the church to move forward in planning its response to the future to which God is leading. If a church has no such statement at present, involve as many people as possible in the study of Scripture, history, and other church documents in writing such a statement. The pastor may find it appropriate to preach sermons on the subject. When it comes to the actual writing of a statement, a smaller group works better.

Another step in establishing purpose and direction in planning is to develop objectives. Two approaches are currently being used in relation to church objectives. In one view, objectives state the church's timeless intention to act. They are statements of ultimate ends toward which a church aims its energies. They express the congregation's understanding of the kind of church God wants it to be. Here is how one congregation wrote its mission statement:

Our objectives are to be:

1. A covenant fellowship of Christians filled with the Holy Spirit.
2. A worshipping fellowship in which God encounters people.
3. A congregation of witnesses for Christ both in this community and throughout the world.
4. A fellowship of maturing Christians whose learning results in responsible living.
5. A church that unselfishly ministers to persons in the community in Jesus' name.

Another approach makes objectives more specific. Here objectives are stated in a sufficiently clear fashion that it is possible to know when they have been achieved. Thus, a local congregation that is effective in mission is seen as having a compelling passion for the achievement of very clear, intentional goals. In this approach, objectives should focus on specific groups with which the church wants to be on mission, like young adults or homebound elderly.

Whatever approach you take in the use of terms, lifting the church's collective vision above the mundane through the eyes of mission objectives leads us beyond ourselves. When a church is effectively on mission, that congregation is a group of persons living beyond selfish preoccupation. This develops corporate strengths, lifts vision, and makes new levels of living possible as new surges of energy animate congregational life.

As a part of establishing purpose in planning, keep in mind the individuals involved. Encourage members to remember that people are important. Hold up the truth that while a plan for the church is being developed, people can also grow and develop individually as Christian persons. Be aware of ministry opportunities that encourage individual growth.

Additionally, establishing purpose in planning involves a simple but fundamental matter. The purpose is not to set the future in concrete, restricting freedom and flexibility. Rather, it is to develop an informed plan that, in the congregation's best judgment, will enable the church to live out its story responsibly and courageously. *Long-range, or strategic, planning* usually begins about halfway through the current plan so that a new plan is in place before the current one expires.

Short-range, or annual, planning usually deals with working out details for up to a year. This process begins several months prior to a new church year and transposes long-range plans into specific, action-oriented plans related to ongoing church programs. Short-range goals, a coordinated calendar, and budget allocations should result from this type of planning.

Operational planning is regular planning done quarterly, monthly, and weekly to implement plans. This is the type of planning regularly done in meetings of the church leadership team or cabinet, coordinators and/or ministry team leaders, and the church staff.

3. *Involve people in long-range planning.* In most churches the church council (or cabinet/leadership team) will be a work group already in place that can lead the planning process. The church council is normally charged with duties such as helping the church understand its mission and define its priorities, coordinating studies of church and community needs, recommending to the church coordinated plans for ministry, and evaluating progress in the priority use of church resources.

Whether you use an existing committee or form a new one, whatever group you choose to use should represent the best available human resources. These people should possess various strengths. They should be encouraged to think of the potential possessed by the church and the central fact that planning begins with God and depends on God for its completion.

Planning should be more than collecting data and/or allocating resources. It should bring out the best in everyone for the sake of the church. Planning should be forward-looking and innovative. It should encourage the emergence of new ideas, creativity, and new solutions to problems.

Use as many people as possible in the planning process. For example, Telling the Church's Story (figure 8.1) provides a work sheet that can be used for group discussion and/or a survey for members of the congregation to express themselves in positive ways about the church's future.

Although warning has been given about basing one's long-range planning solely on the data collected in the community, knowing the community is important. By all means, bring into the planning process those

Figure 8.1

TELLING THE CHURCH'S STORY

List the *best* things you know that have happened in the life of our church to make its story exciting.

1. _____ 4. _____
   _____   _____
2. _____ 5. _____
   _____   _____
3. _____ 6. _____
   _____   _____

Suggest one or more possibilities for ministry the church has which can help make its future story exciting.

1. _____ 4. _____
   _____   _____
2. _____ 5. _____
   _____   _____
3. _____ 6. _____
   _____   _____

I am interested in being a part of the church's exciting story by participation in:

1. _____
2. _____
3. _____

(Optional)
Name: _____ Phone no. _____
Address: _____

church members who have special relationships with local government, community agencies, and businesses. Use these sources, but avoid dumping too much information on the committee at the outset. Formulate a limited number of realistic questions to collect information you believe pertinent to your church's forward look. Ask the people to collect only the information they feel is relevant to the church.

Participation in the planning process includes the church gathered to consider the finalized plans. After all the study, discussion, praying, and formalizing of plans, another important step follows: bringing the congregation together to hear the results. The way the planning team presents its report is important. Advanced information should be given. Copies of the plans should be available to any who wish to see them. Clarity of presentation and information should receive high priority. Questions should be anticipated and answered during the presentation.

It should be made clear that, once adopted, long-range plans become the direction-setters for the church. People, in effect, are committing themselves to participate in fulfilling the approved plans. If the plans are well done, they should provide a motivational atmosphere for people to join in living out the story of the church on mission.

4. *Simplify the process.* Use four simple steps for long-range planning:

1. Assess the church's current situation.
2. Determine primary direction for the future.
3. Study strengths related to the biblical concept of church.
4. Determine major objectives/goals that will assist the church in achieving its mission.

In the *first* step the planning team looks at certain statistics realistically. Church consultants usually say that the average attendance at the Sunday morning worship service is an indication of the strength of the church, not Sunday school enrollment or church membership. Look realistically at participation in organizations, commitment to stewardship of time and money, attitudes about needs and opportunities for ministry, and progress during the past year.

The *second* step has been discussed previously in this chapter; however, an additional comment should be added. In determining primary direction, the church needs to decide such things as the maximum mission potential available in the community, the total number of people to be served in the coming five to seven years, and the fundamental type of church the members want to become.

The *third* step has to do with a study of key strengths of the local church. This may be done by comparing the church with a predetermined list or by comparison to standards derived from biblical principles and current church-life factors.

The *fourth* part of the process, before taking the plan to the church for adoption, is to develop strategies to help the church reach its stated goals effectively.

The planning process will identify many specific needs and hopes toward which the church can direct its ministry. It is important to be selective, however, so that human and material resources are challenged but not stretched beyond capacity. To overload a church with objectives and goals could overwhelm people and diffuse the strength of the congregation so that the church ends up helping no one with anything.

5. *Maximize the results.* One temptation following the planning process is to put the plan on the shelf or in the desk drawer while those who have worked hard on it take a rest. Make sure proper assignments are made and leaders of programs, councils, and teams are clear on their duties. Have regular times to evaluate progress and check up on procedures for achieving the specified goals.

Look to see if the expected results are being achieved. Are improvements being made? Are new people being reached? Is the church making better use of its resources? If the church has said it needs to reach out to single adults, is it? Is the congregation building on the strengths it already has?

A final word: Be thorough in planning the strategies of the plan. Strategies are the specific actions designed to accomplish the goals or objectives the church has chosen. You not only want to know what can go right with them but also what can go wrong with them. This way you can work to keep the possible wrong things from ever happening.

Budgeting

Budgeting is the process of allocating resources toward goals by expressing the church's focal dream in dollars. Budgeting is one very notable way of expressing the church's story, past, present, and most of all, what it wants to be in the future.

Set the Tone for Good Budgeting

Solid financial resources are required for today's effective churches. A biblical approach to stewardship undergirds the development of solid financial resources and helps persons grow in their own understanding of stewardship. Saving money and the efficient use of money do not constitute an adequate stewardship theology.

A responsible biblical approach to stewardship encourages local congregations to view stewardship as an *investment of financial resources*. It is an investment of money to (1) enlarge mission outreach in the community, (2) maximize the effectiveness of the local church, and (3) increase the number of households that contribute financially to the life and purpose of the church. It is important that the church understand that its task is not to save money or simply to spend money. The congregation must view itself as investing its funds so that the church may truly be on mission.

At this point it must also be said that each new generation expresses its stewardship of money uniquely. For example, the oldest generation generally shows a loyalty to the institution. They give just because it is the institution of the church to which they are giving. Younger generations typically give to causes and to ministries that involve their friends. In budgeting and in promoting the budget, attention should be given to communicating in generation-acceptable terms.

Setting the tone for budgeting includes worship services built around the theme of Christian stewardship. Sermon possibilities include:

- Christian Stewardship as a Lifestyle (Luke 12:13–21)
- Acknowledging Our Source of Being (Prov 3:5–6)
- Being Found Faithful (Luke 22:7–23)
- Growing Commitment to Cooperative Giving (2 Cor 8:1–14)
- Trustworthy Stewards (1 Cor 4:2)

Setting the tone also includes developing positive attitudes for the missionary purpose of the church. Although it is not easy to maintain a worldwide view of the church's mission, such an intentional effort pays rich dividends. To develop such positive attitudes for mission support, leaders must possess deep convictions and genuine enthusiasm.

Mission support is directly related to one's attitude toward the people of the world. To believe that all people are created in the image of God is to believe that all people are important and worthy of the church's mission focus. Because it is easy for a congregation to lapse into self-centeredness, leaders must consistently encourage and proclaim a worldview of mission responsibility.

Cooperation and trust lie at the heart of mission education and financial support. Such attitudes grow out of fellowship, common convictions, and mutuality that involve Christians in a relationship with God and with other people. A cooperative attitude is endowed with a sense of belonging—being involved in something bigger than and beyond ourselves. It validates commitment to Christ and to the concept of the priesthood of all believers.

Examine the Mission of the Church

This issue has been discussed earlier in this chapter. It is mentioned here because of its importance to the church's stewardship of resources. If the church doesn't understand its purpose, then budgeting will become somewhat ambiguous at best.

Usually money follows mission. Occasionally the church may be the recipient of a large amount of money for which it has to determine purpose; however, the truth is usually the opposite. In many cases the reason the congregation does not have enough money is that it has not effectively defined and put into practice a mission purpose. It may have become preoccupied with maintenance and forgotten about mission. People want to give to *mission* more than they want to give to *maintenance*.

Many times it is rather easy to get people to give money to build buildings. The reason for this may be that the buildings are specific and concrete ways for people to see how their giving is being used. This may lead to the judgment that it's easier to build buildings than to support mission causes.

Congregations that have been specific in stating and practicing their mission objectives tend to have much less difficulty in financing those objectives and goals. Instead of asking, "Our budget is behind; we are cutting every cost possible. Would you please help us catch up?" try saying: "Our church is seeking to reach and help many people. The money you are giving is being invested wisely in people ministries. Thanks for your giving." In summary, the church whose story includes a small mission focus tends to raise a small amount of money. The church whose story includes substantial mission purpose tends to raise substantially more money.

Assess Potential Financial Resources

One of the major leadership responsibilities in church finance is to anticipate the sources of income for the church. It is important to know how much money the church might reasonably expect to receive during the period covered by a new budget.

Usually most of a church's income will come from the undesignated gifts of members. Such gifts are given through church offering envelopes in the Sunday school and/or the worship services. A smaller proportion of total income is received as designated gifts for special causes. Each church, however, should study its giving pattern, as designated gifts may be more prominent in one church than another. Other sources of income for some churches include rental fees from facilities or parking lots, memorial gifts, interest income on money invested, trusts, wills, and capital gifts.

A church can do an analysis of the occupational and generational groups that are present in its life and ministry. Research can then be done with the local census bureau or county planning agency concerning the average income in your region for the occupational categories that are present in the congregation. With this data the church can reasonably assess the potential financial resources available to it—usually 10 percent of the total estimated income of the congregation.

The church should be aware that, with effective financial management, any money now used for indebtedness will be available for other purposes within a few years when debt obligations are met. One such church carefully planned well in advance how it would divide its money after a loan had been paid off. Part of it went for mission purposes, and another part went for needed repairs and air-conditioning of its educational building.

Develop the Ministry Budget

Two primary ways to develop a budget are described on the following pages. First is a line-item approach and second, a ministry-based approach. Read the details and consider the potential for your situation; then choose the better approach for your church.

Line-Item Budgeting

Line-item budgeting is the most common type of budget used by a church. In this kind of budget, allocation is made for each type of item where there is anticipated expenditure without regard for the particular ministry the item supports. Line-item budgeting may be done by a committee working through three important studies.

1. *What is the present situation?* This is an analysis of the church's past and present giving patterns. Look at the total undesignated gifts for each of the last five years. Determine the percentage of increase or decrease that might be expected if nothing changes.

2. *What is the potential?* Study the church's giving potential. If the potential is significantly greater than the present giving level, determine what steps would be necessary to improve financial support.

3. *Develop a proposal that will challenge the congregation.* Study the programs and budgetary needs of the church. Are there any items/areas to add or delete? What were the expenses last year? Determine the approximate amount that will provide for anticipated expenses plus some growth; compare this total with the anticipated level of support. Adjust figures for the various line items up or down to arrive at a reasonable projection of what the church will be able to do for the anticipated income.

A schedule for developing the budget is in figure 8.2. You will need to determine any additional items that need to be scheduled and assign specific dates for the actions. See figure 8.3 for an example of a line-item budget worksheet used by a small church.

Ministry-Based Budgeting

In this approach emphasis is placed on the fullest participation of people possible. This process involves more people than traditional budgeting by requiring a larger budget development team and extensive use of church leaders and organizations. Emphasis is also given to priorities in planning. Church entities must discover needs for ministries and project solutions. In all stages, priorities are to be determined.

Ministry-based budgeting emphasizes understanding and purposeful giving. It involves more people and communicates more clearly the ministries to be supported. Written explanations are included with each ministry area.

Eight steps are called for in the ministry-based process. The pastor, staff, and others charged with the spending of funds are responsible for the first two steps. The budget or finance committee will have primary responsibility for steps 3, 4, and 5. Then, as appropriate for your situation, all leaders related to the budgetary process will be involved in the final steps.

1. *Analyze ministries.* This is an appraisal of how well the church is performing its work and will be valuable to the budget committee.

2. *Propose ministry actions.* This is to include written proposals of ministries from staff members, church committees, and organizations. See figure 8.4 for a sample proposal form. It calls for a description of the ministry, why it is needed, the cause, any implications for future ministry, and an alternative approach that could be used, as well as when the money would be spent during the year.

3. *Evaluate ministry actions.* After all ministry-based proposals are presented in written form, the budget development team carefully and prayerfully evaluates them in light of the church's missional purpose. Now is a good time for this group to ask how these proposed ministries will help the church live out the story it wishes to tell. Priority rating must be given to each proposal. In many instances this can be done by asking questions

such as, "To what degree does this program make a contribution to the purpose of the church?"

4. *Prepare the budget.* Now is the time to make decisions. List proposals in broad categories and begin determining the overall requirements for supporting the proposed ministries. Make adjustments among items and within categories according to the priorities determined in step 3.

A budget usually is organized into categories that represent the major areas of a church's ministry, such as:

- World Missions Ministries
- Pastoral Ministries
- Educational Ministries
- Music Ministries
- Support Ministries
- Buildings and Grounds Ministries

In the simplest budget an amount would be specified for each of the major categories. For most churches, however, each category is divided into specific programs, projects, or areas of work, as illustrated in figure 8.5.

While not ignoring past giving, a total amount budgeted should usually include a challenge for growth in giving. If stewardship education is practiced and the budget clearly expresses the mission of the church in an exciting and understandable way, then members will rise to the challenge. (It should be noted that the quality of the relationship between the pastoral staff and the congregation affects people's response also.)

5. *Present the budget to the congregation.* Interpreting the proposed ministries to the church is a highly important step. This is where the church members see what their giving will help the church accomplish. Visual presentations through PowerPoint, posters, videos, and drama can be effective. Such presentations help broaden the members' view of what the church is doing and plans to do. The budget can also be interpreted effectively through a budget fair or ministry expo—a festive, informal event for the entire church family. Personal demonstrations and attractive displays depict the various programs and ministries of the church.

In most churches every member needs an opportunity to review the proposed budget prior to any discussion. One method of communication is by direct mail. The mailing should be accompanied by a letter of explanation and any other relevant information. A far better way to reach each home is through visitation. Visitors can deliver commitment cards, encourage members, listen to concerns, and improve understanding. In some cases ministry needs will be discovered that were not previously known or met.

6. *Promote the budget.* Adoption of the budget will not ensure that giving will always follow. Members must be taught, encouraged, and led to make giving commitments.

7. *Report on ministry progress.* Regular budget reports should include all important financial data, but they should also become ministry progress

reports. Events such as interviews, prayer periods, testimonies, visual aids, a review of plans, and reports on the number of people involved in specific ministry can be helpful.

8. *Review and evaluate.* More than just beginning again, the entire budgeting process should be analyzed and needed changes and improvements made.

The flowchart in figure 8.6 shows the process of ministry-action budgeting described above. This process requires a minimum of ten weeks and should be completed in the sequence described.

Additional figures are included for reference. See figure 8.7 for a way of interpreting the World Missions section of the budget. A similar paragraph would be written to interpret each major category. Figures 8.8 and 8.9 are other forms that may be used in this budget development process.

Figure 8.2

BUDGET PLANNING SCHEDULE

Week 1 Finance team distributes lists of (1) amounts spent during the last twelve months, and (2) the previous year's budget, asking committees and organizations to submit budget requests by priority and by monthly estimates.

Week 3 Ministry teams and organizations send budget requests to the finance team.

Week 4 Finance team meets to discuss requests and to propose a budget.

Week 6 Finance team and a leadership council meet to discuss requests and to recommend a budget to the church membership.

Week 7 Finance team mails proposed budget and a letter of explanation to church members.

Week 8 Church members discuss the proposed budget at a church business meeting.

Week 10 Finance team mails amended budget and letter of explanation to church members.

Week 11 Church members decide on the budget at a called church business meeting.

Week 12 Bible school teachers present a lesson on stewardship.

Week 12 Finance Team mails pledge cards and a letter of explanation to church members.

Week 13 Finance team sponsors Pledge Day and a commitment luncheon at the church. All choirs sing at the morning worship service.

Week 13 Finance team mails follow-up letters to members who did not turn in pledge cards.

Figure 8.3

BUDGET WORK SHEET

	Current Budget 20XX	Actual/ Anticipated Totals This Year	Committee Requests	Proposed Budget 20XX
UNDESIGNATED RECEIPTS	$ _____	$ _____	$ _____	$ _____
PROPOSED DISBURSEMENTS				
Missions				
World Missions	$ _____	$ _____	$ _____	$ _____
Associational Missions	$ _____	$ _____	$ _____	$ _____
Local Missions	$ _____	$ _____	$ _____	$ _____
Total Missions	$ _____	$ _____	$ _____	$ _____
Educational Ministry				
Sunday school & Discipleship	$ _____	$ _____	$ _____	$ _____
Vacation Bible School	$ _____	$ _____	$ _____	$ _____
Women's ministries	$ _____	$ _____	$ _____	$ _____
Men's ministries	$ _____	$ _____	$ _____	$ _____
Students	$ _____	$ _____	$ _____	$ _____
Total Education	$ _____	$ _____	$ _____	$ _____
Property	$ _____	$ _____	$ _____	$ _____
Debt Retirement	$ _____	$ _____	$ _____	$ _____

General Operations

Travel Allow-ances	$ _____	$ _____	$ _____	$ _____
Seminars/Convocations	$ _____	$ _____	$ _____	$ _____
Retirement Plans	$ _____	$ _____	$ _____	$ _____
Insurance	$ _____	$ _____	$ _____	$ _____
Kitchen	$ _____	$ _____	$ _____	$ _____
Music & Equipment	$ _____	$ _____	$ _____	$ _____
Office Equipment	$ _____	$ _____	$ _____	$ _____
Postage	$ _____	$ _____	$ _____	$ _____
Church Supplies	$ _____	$ _____	$ _____	$ _____
Payroll Taxes	$ _____	$ _____	$ _____	$ _____
Utilities	$ _____	$ _____	$ _____	$ _____
Contingencies	$ _____	$ _____	$ _____	$ _____
Total General	$ _____	$ _____	$ _____	$ _____

Personnel

Pastor	$ _____	$ _____	$ _____	$ _____
Church Secretary	$ _____	$ _____	$ _____	$ _____
Janitor/Custodian	$ _____	$ _____	$ _____	$ _____
Total Personnel	$ _____	$ _____	$ _____	$ _____
TOTAL PROPOSED BUDGET	$ _____	$ _____	$ _____	$ _____

Figure 8.4

A MINISTRY ACTION PROPOSAL

For_____ Subject _____

1. A description of proposed plan and how it relates to the church's basic purpose:

_____

_____

_____

2. Why this ministry is needed:

_____

_____

_____

3. The costs to the church (in detail):

_____

_____

_____

_____

4. What this will mean to the church in opportunities and cost in two to seven years:

_____

_____

_____

5. An alternative plan/other options:

_____

_____

_____

Figure 8.5

BUDGET WORK SHEET

	Current	Proposed
1. World Missions Ministries		
Cooperative Missions	$ _____	$ _____
Associational Missions	$ _____	$ _____
Direct Missions	$ _____	$ _____
Children's Home	$ _____	$ _____
Local Missions	$ _____	$ _____
Total	$ _____	$ _____
2. Pastoral Ministries		
Pastor's Salary	$ _____	$ _____
Housing & Utilities	$ _____	$ _____
Associate Pastor's Salary	$ _____	$ _____
Housing & Utilities	$ _____	$ _____
Administrative Assistant	$ _____	$ _____
Radio & Television	$ _____	$ _____
Deacon Care Program	$ _____	$ _____
Revival	$ _____	$ _____
Total	$ _____	$ _____
3. Education Ministries		
Minister of Education's Salary	$ _____	$ _____
Housing & Utilities	$ _____	$ _____
Administrative Assistant	$ _____	$ _____
Sunday School	$ _____	$ _____
Discipleship Training	$ _____	$ _____
Men's Organizations	$ _____	$ _____
Women's Organizations	$ _____	$ _____
Leadership Training	$ _____	$ _____
Total	$ _____	$ _____

4. Music and Worship Ministries

Minister of Music's Salary	$ _____	$ _____
Housing & Utilities	$ _____	$ _____
Organist's Salary	$ _____	$ _____
Music & Supplies	$ _____	$ _____
Special Programs	$ _____	$ _____
Worship Supplies	$ _____	$ _____
Total	$ _____	$ _____
Grand Total	$ _____	$ _____

Figure 8.6

FLOWCHART

Steps That Make Ministry-Action Budgeting
a Simple Committee Procedure

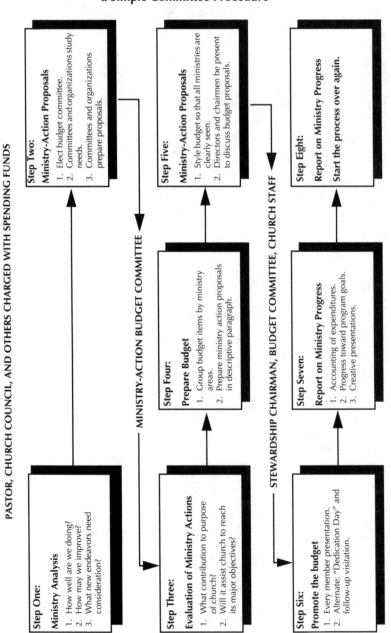

PASTOR, CHURCH COUNCIL, AND OTHERS CHARGED WITH SPENDING FUNDS

Step One:

Ministry Analysis

1. How well are we doing?
2. How may we improve?
3. What new endeavors need consideration?

Step Two:

Ministry-Action Proposals

1. Elect budget committee.
2. Committees and organizations study needs.
3. Committees and organizations prepare proposals.

MINISTRY-ACTION BUDGET COMMITTEE

Step Three:

Evaluation of Ministry Actions

1. What contribution to purpose of church?
2. Will it assist church to reach its major objectives?

Step Four:

Prepare Budget

1. Group budget items by ministry areas.
2. Prepare ministry action proposals in descriptive paragraph.

Step Five:

Ministry-Action Proposals

1. Style budget so that all ministries are clearly seen.
2. Directors and chairmen be present to discuss budget proposals.

STEWARDSHIP CHAIRMAN, BUDGET COMMITTEE, CHURCH STAFF

Step Six:

Promote the budget

1. Every member presentation.
2. Alternate: "Dedication Day" and follow-up visitation.

Step Seven:

Report on Ministry Progress

1. Accounting of expenditures.
2. Progress toward program goals.
3. Creative presentations.

Step Eight:

Report on Ministry Progress

Start the process over again.

Figure 8.7

SAMPLE BUDGET INTERPRETATION

WORLD MISSIONS MINISTRIES
FIRST CHURCH

As we interpret our part of the Great Commission, mission ministries fall into five areas:

1. Cooperative missions give us a real part in a worldwide ministry in co-operation with others. Through cooperative missions, we support thousands of missionaries, hospitals, schools, and homes for children and older persons in our region and around the world.

$50,500

2. Associational missions keep us aware of the desperate needs that are closer to home and give us a real sense of participation in ministry as these needs are met.

$7,500

3. We have direct relationship with a chaplain who ministers at the jails and institutions in our area.

$3,600

4. We have a special part in the ministry of three children's homes where over two hundred children are ministered to annually.

$2,000

5. Local benevolences are increasing due to the discovery of growing needs in our community and due to a greater need for our church to become involved.

$3,600

Our World Mission Ministry Total—$67,200

Figure 8.8

BUDGET REQUEST FORM

Ministry Plan and Request for Allocation of Resources

1. Name of Ministry:_____
2. Ministry Objectives: _____
   _____
3. General Plan of Action (activity, date, responsible person, etc.):
   _____
   _____
4. Necessary Program Costs (the funds you have to have):
   Description and Amount Needed

   _____ $_____   _____ $_____
   _____ $_____   _____ $_____
   _____ $_____   _____ $_____
   _____ $_____   _____ $_____
                                    Total $_____

5. Discretionary Program Costs (what you would like to do if you had the money):

   Description   Amount   Rank
   _____ $_____   _____
   _____ $_____   _____
   _____ $_____   _____
   Total $_____

TOTAL BUDGET REQUESTS $_____   Date_____
Requested by: _____   Position _____

Figure 8.9

WORKSHEET FOR FINANCIAL SUPPORT OF THE MINISTER
(Duplicate and Use a Separate Sheet for Each Staff Member.)

	This Year	Proposed for Next Yr.
I. Ministry-Related Expenses		
1. Automobile Allowance	_____	_____
2. Convention Allowance	_____	_____
3. Book Allowance	_____	_____
4. Continuing Education Allowance	_____	_____
5. Hospitality Allowance	_____	_____
TOTAL EXPENSES	_____	_____
II. Protection Benefits		
1. Insurance		
a. Life	_____	_____
b. Long-Term Disability	_____	_____
c. Medical	_____	_____
2. Retirement	_____	_____
TOTAL BENEFITS	_____	_____
III. Basic Compensation Personal Support		
1. Cash Salary	_____	_____
2. Housing Allowance	_____	_____
TOTAL COMPENSATION	_____	_____

Chapter 9

DESIGNING AND MANAGING FACILITIES

William G. Caldwell

One of the most significant and far-reaching decisions churches ever make is the location and design of facilities in which the congregation will meet. A location with poor visibility or accessibility will create problems for the church as it attempts to reach people. The same problems will exist if the design of the facility does not relate to the community where it is located. For these reasons it is essential that a church give careful consideration to its facilities.

Many of these considerations will relate to the need to buy, build, rent, borrow, or add space as a part of the ministry to the community. The church must be involved in feasibility studies, growth trends and patterns in the community, and demographic studies in order to determine what to do about facilities.

Determining Purposes of Facilities

The church must make some decisions about the basic use of church property before it can adequately determine its building and equipment needs. Most churches would feel that property and facilities should be used for worship, education, and fellowship. But each congregation needs to determine its own goals and then relate the use and maintenance of property and facilities to best meet those goals. The best decision relates to balance among all three areas.

Some churches would emphasize worship space needs over education space needs or vice versa, while others would give priority to fellowship. Many churches with limited resources will decide to build multipurpose space that could be used for all three purposes. The flexibility of space should be a key factor in determining priorities in this day of high building and financing costs.

Another consideration related to the purpose of facilities would be weekday use and the extent to which outside community groups should be allowed to use the facilities. A church that uses its facilities six or seven days a week will be faced with significant decisions about materials to use in construction as well as maintenance considerations. A church that is involved in sharing the use of its facilities regularly with community groups such as scouts, senior citizen groups, community interest groups, and others will need to face additional considerations concerning the scheduling and maintenance requirements.

Construction of large buildings for recreational purposes has caused churches to evaluate further their purposes and objectives for ministry. Providing such facilities calls for additional property (including outdoor recreation provisions), large financial commitments (including building and equipment, plus personnel for programming and maintenance), and proper policies for their use. Even the remodeling of existing space for recreational purposes requires the same considerations.

Whatever the decision about the basic use of property and facilities, the church must develop some system of priority use for what it owns. Failure to do so may completely defeat the basic purpose of what the church is about. Jesus' instructions about planning before building illustrate what happens to those who do not calculate all that is involved before beginning a project (Luke 14:28–30).

Designing Facilities

The design of a church facility is determined by the purposes for which it is to be used. A careful study of several factors will enable those who oversee the project to develop an appropriate facility.

Secure Sufficient Land

The first decision a new or an existing church will make about facilities relates to the land needed for its purposes. Various committees or task forces will assist in this process to help people relate to a vision for the church facility. A new church will be deciding where it will locate facilities from which to conduct its ministry. An existing church will be deciding if its present location is sufficient for its ministry or if it will need to move to another location because of inadequate land availability at the present site. Buying too much or too little may be poor stewardship.

A number of factors will be involved in decisions concerning site selection, zoning restrictions, and the amount of land needed. These factors will vary from place to place. For example, a church in Manhattan would almost ignore parking requirements because of mass transit, but zoning requirements would be very significant.

1. *Size and shape.* Because of the varied activities in which churches engage and requirements for parking, the suggestion of a minimum size of five acres is frequently given. Another suggestion is to allow two acres for every 300 people in attendance. (This involves projecting the future growth of the church.) The best shape is a rectangle or a square.

2. *Topography and drainage.* The land should be fairly level with a slight slope for drainage. Sites with problems in this area would require more space so that drainage could be designed properly. The cost of preparing a site for building and other uses must be considered.

3. *Easements and utilities.* An investigation must be made of the kinds of easements or other access to the property that exist. Setback requirements for buildings must also be determined. If utilities are not presently available at the site, an estimate of the cost of bringing them in must be made.

4. *Zoning requirements.* An important consideration for any site would be the zoning classification. Restrictions concerning parking, building height, types of structures, and uses of buildings must be investigated. An attempt to change the zoning classification after land is purchased may not be successful.

5. *Accessibility.* The location must be readily accessible to the persons the church intends to serve. It should be at the intersection of major travel arteries within a reasonable driving time of those persons. Traffic patterns during the week should be analyzed. Several entrance/exit points must be obvious. The location of buildings on the property should provide a feeling of openness, and the places to enter the buildings must be prominent. Provisions for persons with disabilities are essential.

6. *Visibility.* Closely related to accessibility is the need for the location to be seen easily by the people who pass by. The often-repeated statement remains true: "If you need a sign to point people to your location, your church should be where the sign is." Signs that can convey a changing message will add to the visibility of the church.

7. *Parking.* Adequate parking is a must for most churches. Too many churches rely on street parking when provisions should be made on the property for people to park. Many cities have ordinances that require a minimum number of off-street parking spaces, and the church might consider exceeding the minimum if it expects people to drive to the facility. The parking should be within reasonable walking distance of the building, and it should be integrated with the landscaping to provide an attractive appearance.

Multiple services require provisions for traffic control as people are coming and going at the same time. Provisions for guest parking and parking for the disabled must be made. Churches with limited space may justify the expense of parking structures to provide sufficient parking. A good site selection would be adjacent to a good-neighbor business or office space with parking facilities not used on Sundays.

8. *Previous land use.* Environmental laws and contaminated land make this essential. The cost of cleanup can be significant.

9. *Security.* Is the land in a fairly safe area and what are the businesses or buildings nearby? Would people feel comfortable traveling to and meeting at the proposed location?

Survey Program Needs

The church's program needs should be the starting point of facilities design. What needs to be done to accomplish the purpose of the church? This presupposes some basic understanding of what the work of the church is. When this is determined, then the question of programs and activities can be dealt with. All churches do not have to have every program that has ever been designed. Each church should prioritize what it will be able to do to accomplish its purposes.

The process of surveying what the church has done in the past and what it is doing currently is necessary if the church is to plan adequately. The only way to know how to build a building is to determine what you intend to do in it.

The careful analysis of present and projected program space requirements is essential. Educational guidelines for space for learning are important here. Denominational resources should be consulted. The church will likely appoint a survey committee of competent individuals, representing various aspects of church life, to conduct this analysis. The committee should be organized so that it will be able to study all aspects of the church life. Subcommittees should be assigned to the basic areas—education, recreation, worship, and so forth—so that they can focus on specific needs. Use questionnaires to secure information from church members concerning their ideas about church programs. Remember that adequate storage and work areas will be needed for all programs.

The entire committee should be involved in analyzing and evaluating the material developed by the subcommittees. The assimilation of the survey information should be provided in a condensed form for the church membership, along with recommendations for congregational action.

A broad range of church members should be involved in the survey process. Since the study looks at present activities as well as future possibilities, it is necessary to include as many people and ideas as possible. The decisions made concerning program needs should be based on accurate information and assessment of the work of the church. This will provide a proper basis for developing facility needs according to a priority arrangement.

Determine Community Needs

A part of the ministry of any church grows out of those things it intends to do to meet specific needs in the community. This may include provisions for day care for working parents, after-school care for older children, a school program, senior citizens programs, recreation programs for the community, and other types of activities that would affect the design. Public relations problems may have to be dealt with if the church is viewed as a threat to the community rather than an asset.

Many denominational offices offer a community survey instrument for churches to use in determining needs. Again, the approach to this kind of survey must be based on the understanding the church has concerning its purpose in ministry. Decisions concerning programs to meet community needs are just as vital as those concerning church needs. Sometimes they are even more crucial because of the additional funds, facilities, and personnel involved.

No church can do everything or provide every service that a particular community may need. The committee's thorough survey will provide the kind of information necessary for the congregation to decide what they can do and what must be left to others. Many programs will not require additional facilities; decisions about them can be made apart from facility considerations.

Any community ministry decision must be made deliberately after carefully considering all available information. Many churches have entered specific ministries without all the facts and have been unable to sustain the work. Such activities have caused churches to lose credibility in the community. Where facility additions are required, it is even more imperative that a church gather all the needed information and weigh it carefully before deciding to start a community ministry.

Prioritize Facility Needs

Decisions concerning what facilities are needed must be followed by decisions concerning what should be done first. The long-range projections for community development as well as the population of the ministry area of the church must be taken into consideration. The ministry area will be determined by the church's reach into the community and its programs of ministry. What the church does first will have a definite effect on what it does later.

Whether to build worship, educational, or recreational space first must be carefully analyzed by the committee and the congregation. The church that builds a large, permanent worship center first may never fill it up. A growing church may go through two, three, or more temporary worship centers before it decides about the permanent structure. In the meantime, facilities must be available to conduct the various ministries of the church.

Unless the church decides to relocate and build everything new, present structures must be looked at from the viewpoint of the feasibility of their continued use. Sometimes the decision will be to tear down and build anew in the same place. The soundness of existing buildings must be evaluated by structural engineers. Local building codes must be studied to determine the extent to which existing buildings must be brought into line with current codes if extensive remodeling is undertaken. In some cases the needs can be met by simply rearranging a few walls for more functional use of a building. In other cases the inside of the entire building will need to be torn out and new walls put in.

A *long-range master plan*, designed with the help of an architect and based on the priorities that the church assigns to facility needs, becomes a goal or a vision toward which the members work. Even those who may not be in complete harmony with the first stages will work at accomplishing them so that the future developments can be worked on sooner. The plan should remain flexible enough to permit adjustments if community or ministry needs change.

The basic purpose and objectives of the church must be evident in the way facility priorities are set. The special significance of church buildings makes them different from commercial buildings. Because church buildings are dedicated to God's work, the church's priorities must reflect its spiritual ministries and the service it provides to the community. These priority decisions will be reflected in the policies regulating the use of buildings that will be considered later.

Prepare Financial Costs

The construction costs and interest rates have created significant problems for churches that need to build facilities. Through the years many different kinds of financial programs for building have been used. The results have not always been good for the church. Interest payments have risen higher than missions giving. These problems point out the need for churches to plan carefully for the financing of any facility improvement.

There are tax considerations a church must include when purchasing land and improving facilities. Although churches are basically tax exempt, local taxing authorities may have regulations about land that is not yet used for church work and about certain improvements that may require tax payments. A church must investigate these possibilities early in the process of providing facilities.

Accumulating as much cash as possible before building is a must. The establishment of a building fund in an interest-bearing account is the first step to take. Encouraging people to give to the fund over and above their regular budget giving will help in increasing the giving. The use of promotion ideas such as "Double Tithing" and "Fifth-Sunday Building Fund Offering" will help. A major fund-raising activity for many churches has been the three-year pledging campaign in which people are asked to pledge and then give weekly to the building fund. Many firms as well as denominational groups have specialized in this area of fund-raising for churches. Information from these groups should be sought before beginning a campaign.

How much cash should be raised before beginning construction? Some recommend that all of the funds should be in hand first. Other advisers recommend a pay-as-you-go operation, while still others suggest from one-half to two-thirds of the total amount needed should be in cash. Each church will be different in terms of its needs and ability to pay for buildings. A high interest rate, especially if the repayment is to be done over several years, could cause the total amount to be two or three times the original construction cost. A church must face the stewardship considerations of this kind of expense. There will be times when the immediacy of the building need will offset the additional cost. Waiting may mean lost opportunities.

A significant fact for the church to remember is that it is easier to raise funds for building the facility than to raise funds for debt retirement after it is completed. The continual emphasis of the effort should not be on the building itself but on the people who will be involved and who can be reached by this effort.

The best approach is to develop a sound financial program that can be explained to the church. It will likely incorporate a cash fund-raising approach along with a feasible, limited-payment plan for financing the remainder of the costs. Such a plan should include all of the anticipated costs related to the building project: land costs and site preparation; architectural and engineering fees; construction costs; furnishing costs; and anticipated maintenance, program, and personnel costs for the use of the facility.

Develop Design Drawings

The selection of an architect is a crucial decision for the church. Visits should be made to buildings designed by architects being considered. The one selected should be familiar with church buildings, have experience in designing church facilities, and be willing to listen to what the church has established as the needs to be met and the priorities to be followed. Some denominations can provide a list of qualified architects. The wrong decision here will further complicate an already difficult process.

The committee will need to spend time with the architect to make certain that the approach the church is taking is fully understood and that it can be implemented. Any problems should be worked out before proceeding with the project. Agreement should also be reached concerning the architect's involvement in the construction process, such as the extent of supervision to be provided.

Step One: Develop Property Utilization Plans. The best arrangement of the proposed facility along with any future buildings should be identified on the available property. It should be evident that there is enough space to provide for all that is planned on the property and that the proposal will fit the topography of the land.

Step Two: Develop Program Graphic Plans. These plans will show the allocation of the square footage of the floor space to the various age groups and programs that have been determined by the survey. The evaluation of these plans will determine if the needs that should be met are being provided for in the proposed facility. Other facilities should be visited to benefit from the development of their floor plans.

Step Three: Develop Detailed Drawings. The drawings will provide the schematic design for all the areas included in the construction: foundation, plumbing, electrical, heating and cooling, roofing, ceiling, wall and floor treatment, and so forth. This would include decisions concerning types and colors of walls and floor coverings to assure a proper "look" for the facility and good maintenance capabilities. The specifications relating to all of these components must be stated in the way the church wants the facility finished. These become the criteria on which the bids for construction are developed. Careful evaluation of these drawings and descriptions must be made.

With all of these things accomplished, along with the appropriate review and approval, the church will be able to construct a facility that will meet the ministry needs it has envisioned.

Managing Facilities

It is not enough for a church to design and construct good facilities. The church must also be in the business of managing those facilities in order to derive the maximum benefit from their use. It is poor stewardship indeed if the facilities are not cared for and used in the intended way. Many factors are related to effectively managing facilities.

Develop Facility and Equipment Use Policies

Who should determine policies for the use of church facilities and equipment? Since a policy is a stated course of action that will be consistently followed, a responsible group should be involved in determining what each policy should be. Since procedures vary from church to church, the group to accomplish this will also vary. However, regardless of the group—the congregation, a church committee, an official board, or church officials—policies should be written and readily available when needed. This would include the identification of the person or persons responsible for their application. In small churches the pastor may have this authority; in larger churches some other staff member may be identified. In some churches some other official, committee, or team may be responsible.

Since policies assist in the delegation of authority, help in reaching the goals of the church, and lead to the uniform handling of all requests, the group developing these policies should consider the following ideas:

- Policies should be positive in nature.
- They should be simple and easily understood.
- They should be broad, allowing flexibility.

- They should be geared toward consistent application.
- They should adequately reflect potential conflicts.
- They should be kept up-to-date.

The group will determine what policies are already in effect and will probably look at what other churches have in the way of policies. Resources listed in the bibliography will provide additional help.

A church may follow some system of priorities when developing policies. Preference in scheduling should be given to church activities rather than outside groups. Larger group activities may have priority over smaller group activities in certain facilities. Meetings that are conducted on a regular basis should be considered ahead of one-time or occasional meetings. All areas of the church facilities and equipment should be covered by policy statements. The group should consider worship areas, fellowship areas, educational areas, recreational areas, kitchen, parking areas, office equipment, and vehicles in the development of policies. Several sample policies and request forms are included (figures 9.1 through 9.4).

In order to facilitate the scheduling and use of church facilities, all rooms should be numbered. A room assignment record can then be kept and used for scheduling as well as for janitorial assignments.

Plan Energy Management Measures

One of the most significant stewardship responsibilities a church has is related to the wise and proper use of energy. A lack of concern and involvement of people in energy management will result in wasteful and expensive energy use. All areas of church life relate to energy use: the scheduling of meetings, the selection of a temperature range, the type of lighting fixtures used, the turning off of lights, and equipment not in use.

In planning a new church facility, careful consideration should be given to energy use. The architect and the building committee should give special attention to:

1. *Location.* The way the buildings are situated on the property will affect energy use. A balance should be maintained between the aesthetic view of the structures and the energy-management view. Facing the building in such a way as to take advantage of the sun and using earth embankments for insulation is good stewardship.

2. *Landscaping.* The use of trees and shrubs can be advantageous from an energy-use standpoint. Careful landscape planning will result in lower utility bills. Screening the sun out in the summer and allowing the sun in during the winter can be accomplished with trees.

3. *Insulation.* Every possible part of the building should be properly insulated according to the recommended R-value for the climate. This would include ceilings, walls, crawl spaces, concrete slabs, electrical outlets, outside pipes, duct work, caulking around wall openings, weather-stripping doors, thermal doors and windows, and attic and roof ventilation.

4. *Building materials.* Building materials that provide higher energy conservation should be considered. Their use should not rule out such practical considerations as purchasing windows that may be opened when conditioned air is not required by outside temperature.

5. *Energy-efficient equipment.* The selection of heating and cooling equipment with the highest possible energy efficient ratio is a must. In addition, water heaters and other appliances should be selected for their energy efficiency.

Many energy-management measures can be taken in existing buildings. Some can be accomplished at virtually no cost. Some are expensive but will pay for themselves in a short time. Other measures should not be taken because of their expense and long payback period. An energy management committee can be established to develop an audit of how the church is presently using energy resources and to provide suggestions for improving in energy management.

Here are some *no-cost* possibilities for saving energy: set heating temperature lower; lower hot water temperature; set air-conditioning temperature higher; shut off mechanical equipment when not in use; turn off lights when not in use; remove a bulb from multiple light fixtures when safety is not a factor; and schedule meetings at the same time in facilities that are already cooled or heated.

Consider these *low-cost* options: caulk and weatherstrip around doors and windows; repair broken windows; install higher efficiency lighting where possible; use lighter colors when redecorating; use timers or photocells on outdoor lighting; lock thermostats; check efficiency of heating and cooling systems; keep filters clean and replace when necessary. Additional suggestions will be obvious when an audit is completed.

Energy management systems are available to assist churches in operating and controlling heating and cooling equipment. Many companies that install these computer-controlled systems will guarantee that the energy savings realized will pay for the equipment needed. Churches building new facilities should check on the feasibility of installing this equipment during construction. Churches with existing facilities should investigate the possibility of such equipment being installed to cut costs.

Provide Adequate Insurance Coverage

The need for proper insurance coverage by churches has long been demonstrated. The old idea of "charitable immunity" is no longer valid for a church. A church is subject to the same liability problems that face other businesses. A church needs insurance to meet its stewardship and moral responsibility as well as to meet practical and emotional needs. An insurance committee or other assigned group should carefully analyze the areas of need facing a church and select insurance coverage to meet those needs. The following categories should be covered:

1. *Personnel.* Insurance should be provided for all church employees, including staff members and other paid workers including part-time employees. Consideration should be given to accident and health insurance, group life insurance, disability income, worker's compensation insurance, and fidelity bonds for those who handle money. Related to these would be the provision for a retirement plan for all personnel. Leaving out any of these coverages would mean that the church might have to come up with funds to help an employee in need.

2. *Liability.* This insurance provides protection from financial loss due to suits or claims arising from accidents on the premises or away from the premises if they relate to normal church activity. This will include the operation and maintenance of church facilities, the alteration of church properties, the sale or distribution of food, church schools, and camps and other recreational activities. In addition, coverage should be provided for all vehicles owned by the church or used in the work of the church.

3. *Building and property.* This insurance should cover physical damage to any property the church owns or uses. Included in the coverage would be fire insurance for buildings and contents; extended coverage for windstorm, lightning, explosions, aircraft and motor vehicles, riots, vandalism, earthquake, flood, and special coverage for glass or other valuable property; theft and burglary; and church vehicles.

The committee should follow these guidelines for providing proper coverage:

- Cover all essential areas of risk.
- Cover the largest loss exposure first.
- Maintain sufficient coverage (keeping an inventory of property and equipment to establish replacement cost amounts on all property).
- Seek professional help (especially with appraisals).
- Select a reputable agent and company.
- Provide coverage for special events and activities that depart from regular programs.
- Use large deductibles where possible.
- Compare premium costs regularly to get reasonable rates.
- Review coverage periodically.

Effective work in this area will assure that a church is properly insured when the need arises so that property damaged or persons injured will be adequately covered.

Develop Good Housekeeping Procedures

What does good housekeeping mean for a church? It means keeping the physical facilities clean, attractive, and in good repair to provide a positive witness to the community. The appearance of the facilities will speak loudly concerning the congregation's feelings about the place that is dedicated to the worship of God, to say nothing of the need to protect the original investment. Good housekeeping is good stewardship. A properly planned and executed preventive maintenance program will provide good upkeep on facilities and assure their ongoing usefulness to the church as well as provide a safe environment in which to meet.

In order to keep buildings and equipment prepared for service, there are three types of housekeeping and maintenance programs that must be provided. The first is *operational maintenance*, in which the custodial or maintenance staff performs the routine cleaning of facilities and the standard placement of furnishings. The second is *in-service maintenance*, in which labor and materials are provided to place into service a damaged portion of the building or a broken piece of equipment. The third is *preventive maintenance*, in which a planned program of routine service and inspection of buildings and equipment is developed to maintain service and appearance. A church should be involved in all three types for proper stewardship.

Proper organization for this type of housekeeping and maintenance program will require the use of paid personnel (full-time or part-time) as well as volunteers. The supervisory responsibility for the work, whether it is done by paid persons or volunteers, should be delegated to a responsible individual to assure its accomplishment. In a smaller church that person may be the one in charge of a committee that has the assignment of facilities. In a larger church some staff member will be given the responsibility but will likely work in conjunction with a church committee or team.

The use of volunteers and the employment of personnel will vary according to the size of the facility. In some larger cities, contracting services are available for operational maintenance. Investigation of these services should include references from satisfied customers. Because of the unpredictable nature of church schedules, this outside contractor approach would have to be considered carefully. It may still be necessary to have a custodian on duty for emergencies.

The person in charge needs to work in several areas to make certain that the facilities are well maintained. The person in charge is responsible to:

- Develop inspection procedures for properties.
- Maintain an inventory of all equipment and furnishings (see last section of this chapter).
- Develop maintenance policies and procedures.
- Prepare budget recommendations for maintenance.
- Keep records for maintenance.
- Contract with outside maintenance firms as needed.
- Develop a preventive maintenance program, including forms and reports needed.
- Oversee budget expenditures and development of contingency funds for large items.

- Supervise personnel in the maintenance program.

The development of forms and records is an essential part of a good housekeeping program. The ability to keep up with what has been done and what needs to be done is necessary for good facility upkeep. The proper maintenance of equipment requires a record of its use so that it can be serviced at regular intervals. The sample custodian's checklist (figure 9.5) will serve as an example of the kinds of forms that will be helpful in maintaining facilities.

Other forms could be used for weekly, monthly, and periodic assignments. The frequency of use in a specific part of the facility will determine the housekeeping requirements. Use of the same room by different groups will also complicate the procedure and will need to be planned carefully.

Develop Adequate Lighting and Sound Systems

Adequate lighting and sound systems are essential because of the nature of activities conducted in church facilities. Improper lighting makes reading and study difficult and may even pose a safety hazard. An inadequate sound system will prevent persons from hearing and understanding much of what is being said in activities such as worship services, business meetings, and drama productions. However, providing good quality equipment without providing adequate training for those who operate the equipment is a mistake. Many times light and sound problems are operator related. One solution is to contract those who install equipment also to conduct training for those who will operate it.

Adequate lighting should be installed when the building is constructed. When this does not happen, it becomes necessary to correct the problems by adding additional lighting where needed. A study should be made of the various classrooms, office areas, hallways, entrances, and restrooms as well as the worship area to determine if the lighting is sufficient. Lighting needs will vary from area to area. A light meter can be used to determine if the required amount of foot candles of light is present in the more crucial areas. The ability to control lighting with spots and dimmers is especially helpful in worship areas. In classrooms and hallways, changing from incandescent to fluorescent fixtures will provide better lighting and save energy.

The acoustics of a building are also determined at the time of construction. The type of floor, wall, and ceiling materials used will affect the sound in a room. A noisy room can be deadened by placing carpet on the floor or acoustical treatment on the walls and ceiling. Other types of acoustical treatment can be used to make a "dead" room more alive. Sound systems can be installed to enable persons to hear what is being said. Unfortunately, sometimes after spending large sums of money, the hearing problem still exists. The advice of experts must be sought to provide answers to acoustical problems.

Perhaps the major problem with sound treatment relates to the worship area. The problem is complicated by the need to amplify music and the speaker by using the same system. Music should sound like it comes from all over the room, but the speaker's voice should sound like it comes from the person speaking. These two different approaches create problems for the sound system.

Proper installations will take into account the size and acoustical treatment of the building and its existing equipment and furnishings. A number of microphone outlets or wireless mikes will be necessary to meet a variety of amplification needs such as for multiple speakers, different types of choral music, and dramatic presentations. Good quality speakers can be focused to direct sound to all parts of the room. The amplifier, mixer, recorder, and other equipment must be of sufficient quality to provide the kind of sound reinforcement needed.

Maintain Sufficient Heating and Cooling Systems

The days of the hand fan have long since passed as an adequate means of keeping people comfortable at church. The key word is *comfort*. Whatever people have become accustomed to in their homes and in other public places regarding heating and cooling should be seen as the norm for the church facility.

The adequate heating and air-conditioning systems should be installed during the construction of the building. Proper maintenance of the equipment will provide for its long-term use. The type of system will determine the type of maintenance that must be done. Because of construction design, some systems will need to operate year-round to provide conditioned air in the facility. In buildings where windows can be opened, there likely will be several months during the year (depending on the climate) when the equipment will not need to be used.

The maintenance of heating and cooling equipment requires good record keeping to enable service to be done at the proper intervals. In some instances the church maintenance personnel will be able to provide the proper service requirements. In most situations the maintenance will need to be done by outside contractors who will provide the proper service within the appropriate time frame (see figure 9.6).

Develop Proper Security Measures

The need for security in church facilities has been highlighted in recent years by increasing reports of vandalism, burglary, attacks on persons, arson, and other unfortunate events. No one likes to think of the church as a fortress where everything is locked up, but proper steps should be taken to protect the church property and the lives of members.

Several factors should be considered in the internal security of the buildings. A key-control policy should be established to provide for the issuing of keys to proper persons and to keep a record of keys issued (see figure 9.7). Certain areas and rooms should be locked when not in use. These areas include offices, library and media rooms, equipment rooms, kitchen, supply rooms, and the like. All equipment should be identified with the church name and control number and should be put away when not in use.

Special precautions should be taken concerning security of confidential records, computer access, and money receiving and counting activities. Churches with weekday child care and school programs should provide training for workers in regard to security precautions for children. A plan for evacuating the buildings should be developed and publicized.

Additional consideration should be given to external security of the buildings and grounds. Doors and windows should be provided with adequate locking devices. Landscaping around the building should not block the view from windows and doors so as to provide cover for a burglar.

Outside areas, including parking lots, should be equipped with sufficient lighting for nighttime use in order to protect vehicles from theft. It is wise in some areas to provide parking lot patrols when people are in the building. A committee or special group in the church or a security service company could take responsibility for providing the patrol.

Many churches have felt a need to install an alarm system for better protection of the property, especially when no one is on the premises. There are several types of systems available for churches to use. Some simply make a noise while others are tied directly to an alarm service company or to the local police or fire station. A church should carefully investigate the types of systems available before selecting the one to install.

Maintain Grounds and Parking Areas

The appearance of the church grounds and parking areas should inspire others in the community to improve the appearance of their own property. These areas serve as a testimony to the attitude of the church members concerning the place where they worship. Grounds that are neglected may be communicating a lack of concern that is not characteristic of the church. One indication of concern is an attractive and clearly visible sign that identifies the church and provides information about church services.

Grassy areas can do much to enhance the appearance of the facilities. These areas must be fertilized, watered, mowed, and edged regularly if they are to remain attractive. Some churches assign this responsibility to the custodial staff. Others secure outside help for this purpose. This is an excellent place to use youth or others in the community who can provide this service. If volunteers are used, there must be a clear understanding of the responsibilities involved or the appearance will probably suffer.

Landscaping with trees and shrubs can enhance the attractiveness of the facilities. Professional help will be an advantage here in the selection and care of the proper plants. The choices should be made in the interest of energy considerations as well as appearance. The plants and trees chosen should enhance the beauty of the facilities without hiding them or blocking the view of drivers entering or leaving the parking area.

Walkways and parking areas must be designed to facilitate easy access to the buildings. Ramps and close-in parking should be provided for older persons and the disabled as well as guests. Covered loading and unloading areas should be considered for parents with small children and for use in inclement weather. In areas of extreme winter weather, surfaces should be treated to prevent falls.

The design of the parking areas should be planned to accommodate the maximum number of cars and still provide sufficient driveway areas. The parking angle used should be easily negotiated by all drivers. Entrances and exits should be provided in two or more locations far enough apart to prevent backup during busy traffic times. City zoning codes must be examined and followed in determining the amount of parking to be provided.

The parking area should be surfaced to provide all-weather use. Although concrete is more expensive to install, it will provide a longer-lasting and more easily maintained surface. The parking spaces should be clearly marked and kept painted so that drivers will know where to park. The feasibility of parking structures should be investigated when limited land is available or when the cost of ample land for surface parking is prohibited.

As discussed earlier, security and safety require that sufficient lighting should be provided for all grounds and parking areas. In addition, the lighting of the building or one special feature of the building such as the steeple will serve as an advertising focal point at night. All outside lights should be on a timer or a dusk-to-dawn automatic switch so that the areas are illuminated only when needed.

Additional lighting may be needed where outside grounds or parking areas are to be used for recreational purposes. Special lighting (as well as additional parking area) may be needed for church vehicles when stored on the parking lot.

Develop Inventory Policies and Procedures

Perhaps one of the most neglected areas in church facility management is a workable system for keeping up with property and equipment owned by the church. Both insurance requirements (in case of fire or theft) and good stewardship require churches to develop and maintain such a system.

A church that must continually replace hymnals, kitchen equipment, tables, and chairs because they "disappear" is not providing a good model for its members or acting as a good steward of its resources. Taking an inventory of present equipment as well as developing a procedure for keeping up with additional purchases is required.

The building and grounds or properties committee should initiate the inventory procedure. It may be as simple as counting and listing all tables, chairs, educational furniture, kitchen equipment, and so forth or as involved as securing tags or stickers with control numbers and affixing them to every item. Additionally, inventory records that include receipts and photos/videos of equipment and furnishings provide additional documentation when filing reports and insurance claims resulting from fire, flood, burglary or other disaster. Whatever approach is taken, it is necessary to maintain a listing of all items and the location of each.

Policies related to the borrowing of equipment would include a form to use in recording that information. All existing equipment should be identified as to approximate date of purchase, cost of the item, and the amount of time used in the case of motors or other items that require scheduled service.

An inventory record of all new items should be started at the time of purchase and maintained for the life of each item. Any warranty information or instructions for use should be filed in a related folder. The record form should include all information necessary for providing maintenance for the item (see figures 9.8 through 9.10). For safekeeping and to avoid possible fire loss, inventory records should be stored in a secure location, with a backup copy kept away from the church facility.

Facilities that are properly designed and managed will go a long way in helping the church fulfill its mission. A lack of attention to facilities will not only handicap the church in its work, but also it may provide a negative witness to the community.

Food Service Facilities

The extent to which a church is involved in food services will vary greatly from church to church. In some churches there will be little or no activity relating to food, whereas other churches will have several full-time personnel and an extensive operation in food services. Regardless of the extent of the activity, a number of considerations must be made for the food service operation to be effective in a church.

A church must decide what it hopes to accomplish with food service activities. This decision will affect the approach taken to serving and funding meals. When it is seen as a ministry of the church, it will be used to enhance what the church is trying to do. When properly planned and administered, a church's food service ministry will encourage fellowship, support programs, foster involvement, provide convenience, and provide opportunities for spiritual development.

Encourage Fellowship

Something about sitting down to a meal together encourages the fellowship and friendship of those who are involved. The informality that exists along with the amount of time it takes to eat a meal contributes to the opportunity for people to get better acquainted with one another. New members can be encouraged to participate in food service activities as a way to meet church members and to develop friendships.

Support Programs

Providing a meal is often the best way to get people to participate in some activities. A regular Wednesday evening meal will encourage members to attend the prayer service and other program activities that may be scheduled at the same time. A special missions emphasis, visitation programs, training sessions, or some other ministries of the church will more likely be better attended if a meal is included.

Foster Involvement

Many churches use volunteers in the food service operation. This provides the opportunity to involve people in the ministry of the church who might not be willing to serve in leadership roles. Adequate planning and scheduling will be necessary to make the most of volunteer involvement.

Provide Convenience

The opportunity to eat at church will offer a convenient way for many individuals and families to participate in church activities. This will be especially true on weeknights, when there would not be time for people to get home from work, prepare and eat a meal, and then get to the church for a meeting.

Provide Opportunities for Spiritual Development

The emphasis on physical food should not overshadow the need for spiritual food. Every meal service activity should be seen as a means to helping people grow spiritually. This brings all of the purposes together. Developing a plan for outreach and fellowship helps to focus the activity of providing food. When the food service operation is seen in this light, the ministry opportunities are unlimited.

Designing an Efficient Church Kitchen

The design of a kitchen will have a great deal to do with how it is used and how well it contributes to the effectiveness of the operation. Whether a church intends to serve meals from a potluck supper approach, a completely prepared and served approach, or a caterer approach, the design of the kitchen will help or hinder the process.

Location

The kitchen is best located on a ground floor with easy access to the outside for receiving deliveries, servicing equipment, and disposing of garbage. It must be accessible to water, sewer, electric, and gas connections and have an outside wall or ceiling access for exhaust fans. It should be near an interior corridor and directly adjacent to the dining area.

Space

The amount of space needed will be directly related to the type and frequency of meals served and to the number of people involved. A volunteer operation will require more kitchen space than a completely paid operation. The space should be adequate for storage and refrigeration of food, preparation and serving of meals, cooking equipment, washing and storage of dishes and utensils, and the movement of people. A room size equal to 20 to 25 percent of the dining area should be considered. It should also be large enough to allow for growth.

Arrangement

The way in which the kitchen is arranged will have a definite impact on its efficiency. If people continually get in the way of each other while trying to work, problems will exist. If the arrangement does not allow for an orderly flow of the activities relating to meal service, it will be difficult to operate effectively. The usual arrangement is to have the preparation area in the center with storage and dishwashing facilities to either side or at the back of the kitchen and the service area facing the dining room.

Ventilation

Adequate ventilation is essential for a good kitchen operation. The hot, odor-filled air should be exhausted and replaced by fresh air once every two or three minutes. The exhausted air should be moved directly outside. A separate heating and cooling system for the kitchen works best when tied into the exhaust system. Filters relating to the system should be cleaned and changed regularly.

Sanitation

A church must be extremely cautious about the sanitation and health aspects of its kitchen. Even though the local health inspectors may not visit the church, county health department standards should be met. The health of the people being served requires the church to be diligent in its own inspections and in the thorough cleaning of the facility. Those who work in the kitchen should have a health certificate or a food handler's certificate and should follow all the standard rules of hygiene around food.

The kitchen and storage areas should be treated regularly to prevent insects and rodents from thriving. Leftover food and garbage should be removed promptly. Any outside doors or windows should be provided with screens that are maintained regularly.

Equipment

A church must recognize that the church kitchen is not a home kitchen. This will have significant bearing on the selection of equipment as well as policies for its use. The amount and type of equipment needed will be determined by the frequency of use, number of people served, and type of service used.

For most churches commercial or institutional equipment should be installed. If a church never plans to cook a meal, however, it would not require extensive equipment. Used equipment can frequently be obtained from local suppliers or from restaurants going out of business.

Stainless steel equipment costs more but offers real advantages in upkeep and cleaning capabilities. The equipment should be purchased with a long-term outlook rather than the immediate cost factor. The amount of equipment secured should relate to the regular, normal activities of the kitchen.

On those once-a-year occasions when more equipment is needed because of an extremely large gathering, consideration could be given to renting equipment, moving the gathering to a larger facility, or using a caterer.

Walls and Floor Treatment

The construction of the kitchen should take into account the heat, moisture, and sound that will be generated as well as the cleaning and maintenance needs. The surfaces should be covered with material that provides for these considerations. The sanitation of the facility will relate directly to this consideration. If proper acoustical treatment is not done, the proceedings in the dining area or other areas of the church will be limited because of the kitchen noise. As with equipment, proper construction will be more expensive but much more effective in the long run.

Operating Food Services

Designing a good church kitchen is the beginning of a good food-service ministry. Using the kitchen in the best possible way requires careful thought and planning concerning its operation. Even a well-arranged and well-equipped kitchen will not operate itself. Proper selection of personnel, menus, and the process of serving will determine the effectiveness of the operation.

Develop Policies

Policies for the operation and use of the church kitchen are needed for the same reasons as any other church facility. Guidelines are needed to avoid problems and to define responsibilities. They should be protective but not restrictive and should be followed by all who use the food services. Most churches will find it helpful to have a committee to develop the policies. This may be designated as a kitchen committee or a food services committee or some other appropriate name. This group will consider carefully the needs of the church and the needs of the kitchen staff. The committee can also serve as a liaison between the church and the food service personnel in implementing policies and procedures. All aspects of the work of the kitchen and food services areas should be covered. See figures 9.11 and 9.12 for a sample policy statement and a food service request form.

The church should also make a decision about the procedure to follow in the matter of reservations or the number of people to prepare for when a meal is served. Most churches that serve a weekly meal will be able to forecast the expected attendance based on the time of year and special programs and will not use a formal reservation system. Those who use a reservation system will have to determine the procedure for making reservations, the deadline for canceling reservations, and the procedure for collecting from those who do not attend.

In the case of banquets or other special meals, tickets should be sold or a number of plates should be guaranteed by the organization responsible. The cost of all meals should be determined in advance and paid for by those who attend. When a program organization is providing a meal for a special purpose, the food to be served and the appropriate budget account to be charged must be decided in advance.

Enlist Personnel

The selection of personnel for the food service operation is critical to its success. Most churches will use a combination of paid and volunteer help. One person (whether paid or volunteer) should be selected as the food service director. The supervisor and personnel committee should be involved in this selection. Some of the characteristics needed by this person are:

- An outgoing personality
- Ability to work in harmony with others
- Emotional maturity
- Ability to communicate

- Interest and experience in kitchen management
- Understanding of food service purposes
- Energy and dependability

These same qualities should be looked for in other persons who will be enlisted to work.

How many persons are needed will depend on the type of food service activity in which the church is involved. A regular, weekly meal will likely involve some paid personnel who will work every week. The food service director will plan the meals, purchase the food and supplies, and enlist and direct the persons who will be involved in cooking and serving. Volunteers can be enlisted to assist with the serving and initial cleanup. It is usually wise to use paid personnel in the dishwashing operation because of the need to maintain proper sanitation procedures as well as to recognize the limitation of asking volunteers to work after everything is over.

Helpers will usually be available from within the church membership. Using youth and senior adults is a wise procedure. Enlisting volunteers from Sunday school classes, mission organizations, or other church organizations should be done for the weekly meals or the occasional banquets. Some of the tasks will require limited training, but most of the jobs to be done can be accomplished by any willing person.

Determine Serving Methods

The arrangement of the kitchen and dining facilities will affect how food is served. This should be considered in planning a facility, but it will have to be lived with once the facility is constructed. If there is not enough room or equipment to cook a meal, then it would be unwise for a church to plan anything more than a potluck dinner. If the facility planning has allowed for different approaches to serving, then the decision can be made based on the number of persons and the type of group to be served. The economics of the meal should not be the only consideration. The ages of the persons will be a factor as well as the type of group: families, children, senior adults, or others. The amount of space available and the amount of time allowed for the meal will also need to be considered since some serving methods require more space and take more time than others. The following methods should be considered:

1. *Family style.* The food is placed in bowls on the tables. Persons serve themselves. This requires enough servers to get the food to the tables while it is still hot. The cost factor is usually greater.

2. *Cafeteria.* This requires counter-serving space where food can be kept hot or cold. It offers selection, but it is not good for persons who have trouble making decisions. Cost is controlled since portions are determined by servers. It requires servers behind the counter.

3. *Buffet*. This requires serving space where food can be kept hot or cold. It allows persons to serve themselves the amount they want. The cost factor is usually greater.

4. *Plate service*. Plates with food are picked up at one location. This requires enough servers to put food on the plates as people come in. It offers portion and cost control. Taking plates to the table would require more servers.

5. *Caterer*. At times it may be best to use an outside caterer to provide the meal service.

Plan Menus

The food service director should be responsible for planning menus in keeping with the type of meal to be served and the type of group involved. The sponsoring organization should provide input based on the cost factor as well as the occasion. Basic suggestions relating to menu selection include the following: simplify the choices; balance the menu from a nutritional standpoint; contrast textures, flavors, and colors; consider the workload and personnel available for cooking; stay within budget limitations.

The trend toward healthy eating needs to be considered in planning meals. Using baked or broiled meats rather than fried is a good option. Dietary fat can be reduced by using skim milk instead of whole milk, using low-fat yogurt for sour cream, and using cocoa instead of chocolate. The desire for low-cholesterol, low-salt, high-fiber foods is valid and should be met in planning and cooking.

A regular midweek evening meal program must also be planned from the standpoint of variety since the same people will be eating every week. Some basic items can be selected and rotated over time. Seasonal items can be included when they are available. The attractiveness of the items as they appear on the plate will have a great deal to do with the taste of the food.

Purchase Food and Supplies

Because of the high cost of food, the food service director must shop carefully and wisely in purchasing food and supplies. If the amount purchased is large enough, institutional distributors will deliver to the church, and wholesale prices can usually be obtained. The wise food service director knows that one distributor cannot provide everything that is needed. Rather than purchase only what one distributor sells, a combination approach is better. This means buying from several distributors for a better variety of choices as well as using retail outlets for some needs that a wholesaler cannot meet as well.

It is best to plan so that major purchasing is done only once a week. This will save time and money. Quantity purchases can be made when price considerations and storage capabilities are favorable. Quality should not be sacrificed for price. Poor-quality food service will affect participation and probably cost more in the long run.

A food service director will discover over a period of time who the best distributors are and where the best deals can be made. Taking advantage of special sales is good when there will be a need for what is on sale in the immediate future. Any deliveries made to the church should be checked for quality and quantity of items ordered.

Determine Costs

All of the factors relating to the food service operation must be calculated when figuring the cost of meals and services. Many churches will provide for equipment, supplies, and labor through budget allocations and charge only for the cost of food when determining a per-plate charge.

A church must decide how it will provide the cost of the food service ministry. If different charges are to be made on the basis of the organization or activity involved, the policies should identify the differences. For instance, a church may have a maximum cost for families of five or more at a weekly dinner but offer meals free of charge for participants in certain community mission programs. When an outside organization or group requests food service, the church should plan to recover all of the direct costs incurred (labor, utilities, supplies, and such).

Prepare and Cook Foods

All of the activity relating to food services will be a waste of time if the food is not prepared and cooked so that it looks and tastes good. There should also be enough food prepared so that no one goes hungry. The menu selection must be done based on the amount of time and number of personnel available for cooking. The choice between using prepared foods or cooking from ingredients will also be based on the time and personnel considerations. The higher cost of prepared foods may be offset by the cost of personnel who cook.

When more than one meal is involved, consideration must be given to oven space, refrigerator/freezer space, and utensils available for multiple use. Planning ahead will enable the food service director to be aware of forthcoming situations and do some preparing and cooking ahead of time when storage facilities are available.

Determine Cleanup Procedures

Proper and thorough cleanup is a vital part of any food service program. Decisions about leftover food should be made in advance. Sometimes items can be frozen and used later. A food service director must be just as concerned for cleaning up and putting items in their proper place as any other part of the operation.

Volunteers may be effective in the initial cleanup of the dining area and in bringing the dishes to the dishwashing area, but because of the extra time involved, it will probably be best to pay someone to do the actual washing of dishes, pots, and pans and putting them in the storage areas. Some churches have had good success in employing teenagers for this work.

Adequate provisions will need to be made for getting all garbage to the outside storage area until it can be disposed of properly. Nothing should be left out in the dining or kitchen area that might attract rodents or insects.

Keep Records

A competent food service director or committee will keep records of all activities relating to the program. A list of menus used at regular weekly meals and special banquets is essential. A cost analysis record of all meals helps to keep the program in the black and provides information for establishing the cost for meals. Written instructions to the financial secretary concerning the charges to be made to the proper budget accounts will provide information needed for budget preparation. The development of forms for these purposes helps with the record-keeping process.

Special Food Services Programs

In addition to the regular, weekly meals in which the church may be involved, there are a number of special activities the food services ministry may consider. Each of them will have specific concerns that will have to be dealt with if they are to be successful.

Weddings

Most church weddings have food service needs. The rehearsal dinner may be held at the church, and most likely the wedding reception will be held at the church. The food service director will need to be consulted in these situations unless the church has a separate person who acts as a wedding consultant. Even when this is done, there must be communication about the use of the kitchen and serving equipment.

Policies concerning weddings need to be developed and provided to all persons anticipating a ceremony at the church. These policies should include scheduling the use of facilities, decorations, use of ministers and musicians, premarital counseling, conduct of the wedding party, charges made for the facilities and personnel, photographer and florist requirements, sound system and lighting needs, food service and receptions, use of security, and other matters.[1]

Receptions

In addition to weddings, there will be other types of receptions at the church, such as to honor staff members or others in the church or community. The church may have a committee that helps to plan such occasions. Careful planning with the food services director is necessary for these events.

Banquets

All kinds of banquets may be conducted at the church. Examples would include leadership banquets, Valentine banquets for youth or adults, Christmas banquets, Sunday school class or department banquets, and the like. Decisions will have to be made about the time, the cost (reservations or tickets), the decorations, the need for extra equipment or supplies, and the type of serving to be done. The food services director should always be willing to work with any group that wants to plan a banquet.

Picnics

Many churches use picnics as an informal means of fellowship. Since most of these are held away from church facilities, careful planning has to be done by the food services director. Decisions have to be made about securing the site, facilities available at the site, the food to be furnished by the church or the members, the supplies to be provided (including tables and chairs), and the cleanup.

A Support for Ministry

When properly managed, facilities and food services are valuable assets to the congregation and the work of the church. The wise church will secure competent leadership and provide professional services as necessary to assure lasting and effective support of the church and its purposes.

Figure 9.1

SAMPLE POLICY STATEMENTS

Building Use

1. The philosophy underlying policies for building use is that all church facilities shall be used to carry out the basic purpose and mission of the church. Policies should be kept in the spirit of bringing people to Christ.

2. Use of any facility shall be done in conformity with city fire and safety ordinances. These provide for the prohibiting of smoking and overcrowding in church facilities.

3. Janitors or other building personnel shall be responsible for moving all equipment and furniture when necessary and for replacing it for regular meetings.

4. Regularly scheduled church meetings shall have first priority in building use. Other church-related meetings shall have second priority. Outside non-profit organizations shall be eligible for building use when facilities are not being used by church groups and when their purpose is approved by the pastor and the property committee. Profit-making enterprises shall not use church facilities for any purpose.

Weddings

1. The philosophy underlying policies for weddings is that a Christian emphasis be encouraged and that members relate the ceremony to Christian family commitment.

2. All weddings shall be scheduled on the master church calendar with first priority being given to church members. Nonchurch members shall be allowed to schedule a wedding no earlier than ninety days prior to the event to assure the church member's priority.

3. Counseling of the couple prior to the wedding is essential. The pastor or other minister shall conduct the counseling or be advised as to the person doing so.

4. Church members are encouraged to use the pastor and church organist for the ceremony. Guest ministers shall be approved by the pastor, and guest organists shall be approved by the minister of music.

5. In keeping with the wedding philosophy, church members shall use the facilities without charge. Nonmembers shall pay a fee for facilities a week in advance according to the following schedule:

Sanctuary	$_____	Fellowship Hall	$_____
Chapel	$_____	Kitchen	$_____

6. A minimum fee of $_____ for the services of the janitor (including rehearsal) shall be paid by all (church members and nonmembers) since the work will be extra.

7. In keeping with safety regulations, protective materials shall be used with candles, and rice shall not be used inside or outside the buildings.

8. The church wedding consultant shall work with the couple in developing the wedding plans and implementing policies.

Note: Items 5 and 6 relating to charges will need to be adjusted according to church philosophy (should church members be charged?) and the current charges being made by other churches in the area.

Figure 9.2

ROOM SCHEDULING REQUEST FORM

Submit this form to the church office at least two weeks in advance. A copy of the form will be returned with confirmation.

Meeting Request

Date submitted _____ Requested by _____
Person responsible _____ Phone _____
Date of meeting _____ Organization _____

Type/Purpose of meeting _____
Room(s) needed _____
Room arrangement: Draw a diagram of the room arrangement on the back.
Time of meeting: From _____ to _____
Number expected: _____ *(Diagram room arrangement on back)*
Standing request: Every _____ until _____

Other Services

Equipment needs: _____
Media needs: _____
Food service needs: _____
    (Consult with church hostess after approval.)

For office use:

❏ Approved and scheduled   ❏ Not approved
Reason: _____
Authorized signature _____ Date _____

Figure 9.3

WEDDING REQUEST FORM

(Submit as early as possible. Non-church members may submit no earlier than ninety days before the date requested.)
Date requested _____ Time _____
Bride's name _____ Church member? ❏ yes ❏ no
Address _____
Phone/contact information _____
Groom's name _____ Church member? ❏ yes ❏ no
Address _____
Phone/contact information _____
Minister's name _____
If guest minister: Address _____ Phone _____
Rehearsal date _____ Time _____
Room(s) required _____
Reception time _____ to _____
Room(s) needed for reception _____
Organist's name _____
If guest organist: Address _____ Phone _____
Wedding director/planner, if used _____ Phone _____
Florist _____ Phone _____
Photographer _____ Phone _____
Caterer _____ Phone _____

For office use:

❏ Approved and scheduled
❏ Not approved: Reason _____
Authorized signature _____ Date _____
Church wedding contact assigned _____
Phone _____

Figure 9.4

RECORD OF EQUIPMENT LOANED

Item(s) Borrowed
Description of item(s) _____
Number of items _____ Inventory number(s) _____
_____
Where will item(s) be used/located? _____
Date borrowed: _____ Date to be returned_____

Person Responsible
I agree to be responsible for these items while they are away from the church property. If they are lost or damaged, I will replace them or provide funds to do so.
Signature _____ Date _____

For office use:
Approved/checked-out by: Signature _____
Items returned: Received by _____ Date_____

Figure 9.5

CUSTODIAL DAILY WORK CHECKLIST

Name of custodian _____
Area/Rooms assigned _____ Week of _____

(Initial tasks when completed.)

Duties	M	T	W	T	F
Dust all furniture, equipment, window sills, etc.					
Clean all glass doors					
Pick up and empty trash					
Vacuum carpets					
Clean water fountains					
Damp mop tile floors					
Clean stairwells					
Clean restroom urinals, basins, toilets					
Damp mop restroom floors					
Fill towel and toilet tissue holders					
Special assignments (see below)					
Special assignment:					

Figure 9.6

EQUIPMENT INVENTORY RECORD

Type of equipment _____
Located at _____ Inventory number _____
Description _____
Model no. _____ Cost _____
Serial no. _____ Shipping _____
Date purchased _____ Installation _____
From _____ Taxes _____
Trade-in allowed _____ Total _____
Service contract agreement date to be renewed _____
Warranty _____

Repairs and Maintenance

Date	Description	By	Amount

Figure 9.7

MASTER KEY ASSIGNMENT

Name	Leadership Position	Master Key No.	Issued By	Receiver's Signature	Date Returned	Received By

Figure 9.8

REPORT OF VEHICLE USE

The driver of each vehicle should complete this form at the time the vehicle is returned.

Date(s) of use _____

Group or person responsible _____

Destination _____

Reason for use _____ Acct. no. charged_____

Driver _____ Phone _____

Vehicle used _____

Odometer reading:

    End of trip _____

    Beginning of trip _____

    Total miles _____

Maintenance needs: Please list any repair needs or conditions to be corrected that you observed on the trip.

_____

_____

Driver's signature _____ Date _____

Figure 9.9

INSPECTION/MAINTENANCE REPORT

Property and Building Exterior

Item/Area	Inspected		Location	Condition	Action Needed	Action Performed	
	Date	By				Date	By
Church sign							
Doors/Windows							
Drains							
Exterior walls							
Lawn, shrubs							
Metal flashing, gutters, down spouts							
Walkways							
Parking areas							
Outside equipment							

Figure 9.10

INVENTORY/INSPECTION REPORT

Room no. _____ Made by _____ Date _____

Item	Condition			Repair Needed	Recom-mendations	Number
	Good	Average	Poor			
Ceiling						
Walls						
Floor						
Lights						
Curtains						
Drapes						
Blinds						
Carpet						
Tables						
Chairs						
Piano						
Chalkboard						

Figure 9.11

KITCHEN POLICIES

1. The kitchen and food services operations of the church are to be used primarily by the church and its organizations. Outside nonprofit groups desiring to use the facilities should make a written request thirty days in advance to be considered by the food services committee and director, providing there is no conflict with a scheduled church function.

2. The schedule request form shall be completed by all groups wishing to use the facilities. Written approval must be received before the facility can be used.

3. The food services committee and director shall have supervision of the kitchen at all times. The director or a trained volunteer shall be present whenever the kitchen is used. Food service personnel shall have health or food handler certificates.

4. Agreements for purchasing food and supplies must be made with the director at least one week in advance of the activity to assure adequate financial arrangements are made. The number expected should be estimated and paid for. For church groups the costs will cover the food and supplies. For outside groups the costs will include food, supplies, labor, and an estimated amount to cover utilities and janitorial expense.

5. Keys to the kitchen and storage areas will be issued only to employed food service personnel. These areas will be kept locked when not in use to assure the security of the facilities and the safety of persons in the building.

6. Kitchen and dining room equipment to be loaned for use outside the church building will follow the equipment policy procedure in consultation with the food services director.

7. The organization sponsoring a meal shall arrange for volunteers to assist with serving and shall be responsible for arranging and decorating the dining area.

8. The food services committee and director shall be responsible for maintaining an inventory of equipment and supplies and preparing a budget for additional equipment and supplies as needed.

Figure 9.12

FOOD SERVICE REQUEST FORM

Date received _____ Date of meeting _____
Organization _____
Type of meeting _____ Number expected _____
Time of meeting: From _____ to _____
Person in charge: _____ Phone _____
Area needed: _____
Type of meal service: ❑ cafeteria   ❑ buffet   plates served _____

Menu Suggestions

Meat(s) _____
Vegetables _____
Salads _____
Desserts _____
Drinks _____
Reception _____
Cost desired _____ Budget account # _____

Food Services Office File

Charges: Department/account _____ Amount $ _____
Cleared on church calendar ❑   Menu approved ❑
Personnel assigned _____
Approved by _____ Date _____

Summary

Food cost	$	_____
Supplies	$	_____
Labor	$	_____
Total cost	$	_____
Per plate cost	$	_____

Chapter 10

PLANNING SPECIAL CONGREGATIONAL EVENTS

Robert D. Dale

S pecial congregational events put the minister's management skills, especially planning skills, on public display. These special events are common, high-profile happenings. Three of the most demanding are weddings, funerals, and revival or renewal events. Each of these is spotlighted in this chapter as an example of and model for the administrative care that must support all types of special activities. It's worth noting that a new role has emerged in the hospitality industry, the meeting planner; and that function may inform the special events under discussion here.

Planning Weddings

Weddings are occasions when the minister wants especially to be sure everything goes according to plan. Weddings are so public and so sentimental that the wedding party, the minister, and the plan are all on display. Several aspects of planning for weddings deserve careful attention.

Guiding Premarital Counseling

Ministers often find premarital counseling unfulfilling. They feel frustrated because engaged couples usually want a ceremony, not counsel. One professional counselor friend complains that these couples are "in a state of madness." Consequently, engaged couples usually aren't at a stage of life where they are interested in making decisions; for them the decision is already made.[1] They want a wedding now, and they'll worry about the issues of building a married relationship later. Rather than trying to guide a decision-making process for the already decided, you may want to open a discussion forum for two people who will establish one new family. A forum provides a setting in which a minister can raise basic questions about marriage and husband-wife relationships, and a couple can take advantage of that setting to make sure they have thoughtfully discussed the full range of concerns they will face in marriage.

The minister provides the setting, the questions, an objective listening ear, and some coaching in communication and conflict management processes. The couple responds with frank answers and direct conversation. Most importantly, a relationship is built for later, more substantive conversations.

Whether you prefer more traditional counseling approaches or the forum style of premarital preparation, you may want to use some reading material to introduce issues and to prime the conversational pump. For example, the book by Jerry and Karen Haynes, *Marriage Can Be Meaningful*,[2] is a helpful resource. If the engaged couple reads this or some other mature book a section at a time, even the inexperienced counselor can work with young couples with more confidence.

Many ministers request a minimum number of conversations with the engaged couples whose weddings they have been asked to perform as an integral part of the overall wedding planning process. Discussing the wedding ceremony itself is only one part of premarital counseling.

Rehearsing for the Wedding Ceremony

The wedding rehearsal is a time to clarify what everyone is to do and when he or she is to do it. Rehearsals also are times to calm everyone's anxieties and to reassure them that the plan will work. Therefore, all of the wedding party and all of the officiants need to attend the rehearsal. The exact time and place should be clearly communicated to every person who is expected to take part in the rehearsal.

Some couples enlist the assistance of a bridal consultant. If so, the consultant will also attend the rehearsal and will provide an additional resource to the minister in planning for the wedding. Consultants are generally expert in the etiquette of weddings but have no input into the content of the ceremony.

A variety of customs surround weddings and rehearsals. For example, some brides subscribe to the old superstition that it's bad luck for a bride to take any active part in the rehearsal of her wedding and prefer to use a stand-in during the rehearsal. Additionally, different denominations have varying traditions relating to weddings. The rehearsal provides the occasion for everyone to understand the traditions that apply to this particular wedding.

Before the Wedding Ceremony

The timing of several preceremony events can be crucial. Consider this countdown.

One hour before the ceremony. The ushers arrive, put on their boutonnieres, and seat lady guests by offering their right arms. If designated seating areas are preferred, the bride's section is on the left side (from the rear of the sanctuary), and the groom's section on the right.

Thirty minutes before the ceremony. The organist begins playing music. If candles are used, they are lighted at this time unless the minister instructs otherwise. The groom and best man should arrive and go to the minister's study or another meeting place designated by the officiating minister.

During the final twenty minutes. All final checks of attire should be made. Some churches have facilities for all of the wedding party to use in dressing for the ceremony. If the wedding party dresses away from the church, the timing of several arrivals needs to be considered. The groom's parents arrive at the church at least twenty minutes before the ceremony. The bride's mother arrives at the church at least ten minutes before the scheduled beginning of the ceremony. The bride and her father arrive at the church just minutes before the ceremony and join the bridesmaid(s).

Immediately before the ceremony's beginning, an usher seats the groom's parents on the right front pew. Then the bride's mother is seated on the left front pew where she will later be joined by the bride's father. No one is escorted to a pew after the bride's mother has been seated. Guests who arrive late must either stand or quietly seat themselves in the rear of the sanctuary. If an aisle runner is used, it should be unrolled at this time. If wedding songs are planned, the soloist should sing them just before the processional.

Guiding the Ceremony Itself

The ceremony proper commences with the processional. The minister, groom, and best man take their places at the front of the center aisle. When the organist begins the wedding march, guests should follow the lead of the bride's mother. If she rises, all guests should also stand. The order of the processing group is ushers, bridesmaid(s), maid or matron of honor, ring bearer, flower girl, and (after the organist increases the volume of the march music) the bride and her father.

Most ministers use some version of the traditional Episcopal wedding ceremony.[3] When customized vows are preferred, the minister should guide the writing of the vows closely, be sure the vows are carefully memorized, and make a copy of the vows and have them available during the ceremony itself in case of an embarrassing lapse of memory on someone's part.

What If Someone Objects?

Occasionally a wedding ceremony develops an unexpected glitch. For instance, what are the minister's options if after asking, "If there is anybody present who has any objections to this marriage, let him or her speak up now or forever hold his peace," someone speaks up with an objection? What if an old flame of the bride or the groom chooses the wedding as an occasion for making a public complaint? Or what if future in-laws don't like the prospective mate their child is about to marry? Are these concerns reason enough to stop a wedding? What should you do?

According to justices of the peace, the only valid reason for halting a wedding is when the marriage wouldn't be legal. While the law related to marriages may vary somewhat from state to state, several issues commonly constitute illegal marriages.

- If either the bride or groom has a prior undissolved marriage
- If the parties are related to each other in a manner prohibiting marriage in that state
- If either of the parties is under age
- If either of the parties is judged to be incompetent or insane
- If either of the parties is involuntarily intoxicated or drugged

Consult a justice of the peace or an attorney in your state to see if the instances mentioned above are the law in your state or if additional causes apply also. Review the law and save yourself uncertainty and a wedding party embarrassment.

After the Ceremony

The recessional begins the final element of the ceremony. The order of the recessional is the reverse of the order of the processional with the bride and groom exiting first and the best man escorting the bride's honor attendant. If the guests stand during the recessional, they should be seated following it until after the ushers have returned and escorted the bride's parents and then the groom's parents out of the sanctuary. The aisle runner isn't removed. If the wedding party wishes, the minister may invite the guests to the reception at the close of the ceremony.

Planning Funerals

The Bible notes that there's "a time to die" (Eccl 3:1–2). About one percent of the American population dies each year. On average, residents of the United States experience a bereavement because of a death every six years. Funerals have always been emotionally difficult and structurally challenging services for the minister to lead. No longer, however, is death considered a dirty word in our culture. Americans are more informed about the event of death and the process of grieving.

Why Have a Funeral?

Funerals are changing. Increasingly, families are closing caskets at funerals and even having memorial services after the burial. Do funerals have a purpose any longer?

A funeral is both a family ceremony and a community event.[4] In the first place, funerals demonstrate the strength of our "credit networks." Our families and friends rally around us. Our sense of solidarity with them supports us. Second, funerals provide official farewells. This painful passage in our lives is clearly marked by the ceremony, the body, and the gathering of mourners. And, of course, funerals allow us to share our spiritual values.

The Minister's Role in Funeral Planning

Your role when a death occurs is multifaceted. The family of the deceased, the polity and policies of his or her church, the funeral customs of the local area, the funeral director, and any special military or fraternal groups that may request participation must all be dealt with considerately.

In relationship to the family of the deceased, you extend your most crucial ministry. In most cases you will have known and cared for the deceased previously. When the deceased has suffered some extended terminal illness, you will already have established a pattern of care and may have made some agreements or plans concerning the funeral with the deceased. When a death occurs, make a prompt, generally brief, comforting home visit and offer any assistance needed.

The funeral director generally contacts the minister who will officiate at the funeral, and together they structure the arrangements for the service and burial. In most cases the family of the deceased will leave the details of the funeral service to the minister. If the family requests a favorite Scripture, hymn, or item in the service, consider such appeals carefully and grant them as often as is appropriate.

Your composure at the funeral service is crucial to all of the mourners, especially the family. A brief home visit and prayer before the service, calm demeanor in the conduct of the service, firm handshakes, and sincere efforts to comfort and help will provide emotional structure and practical assistance to the deceased's family. The proof of your care of bereaved families is shown through your ongoing counsel with family members during the difficult and extended period of repairing their social network after the funeral.

No difference in your care of others should be apparent. Prominent church members, marginally participating members, and nonmembers should be treated alike. In fact, nonmembers may be reached for Christ and for church membership because of your, and the church's, thoughtfulness and thorough care during bereavement.

With regard to local customs and congregational policies regarding funeral services, you should be knowledgeable and sensitive. Even if you disagree with some of these customs, don't choose a public funeral to create a test case for your views. Use other congregational settings to discuss issues and clarify church practices. Work to develop policies such as in figure 10.1 that can be used to inform and guide members of your church.

Additionally, you should know and practice consistently the local customs regarding any fees paid to persons who assist with funerals. Be prepared to advise about appropriate fees to pay an organist, soloist, janitor, and others who may assist. Often this information will be requested by the funeral director. In any event ministers should hesitate to ask for a fee for conducting funerals although they may choose to accept travel expenses incurred in fulfillment of their professional responsibilities.

With regard to previous ministers who are asked by grieving families to return to the field and to conduct funerals, the current minister should abide by the family's wishes. Anyone who returns to a previous field of service should be certain the current minister is informed. Invite the current minister to join in conducting the funeral service unless the family prefers otherwise. In any funeral in which more than one minister is officiating, all of the ministers should be fully aware of the responsibilities of each of the other officiants.

In relationship to funeral directors, you should major on spiritual and emotional assistance and leave the physical arrangements to the funeral director. While you may occasionally encounter a difficult person in the funeral home business, you will discover that most funeral directors are sensitive public servants. You may accompany grieving church members to the funeral home to make the final arrangements if members request your assistance in making decisions during difficult times.

With regard to military or fraternal groups, you should acquaint yourself with these groups' prescribed rituals. When conducting funeral services that include these groups, carefully coordinate funeral services and graveside committals with their representatives. The U.S. Department of Defense will, upon request, provide ministers with copies of their pamphlet on conducting military funerals.

Planning for Revival or Renewal Events

Some church leaders suggest that revivals are no longer an effective evangelism approach. This isn't the opinion of the more evangelical groups. While revivalistic methods can become gimmicks and lose their credibility with Christians and non-Christians alike, good planning undergirds wholesome evangelism. A thorough, refreshing treatment on evangelism suggests a framework for prerevival planning.[5] Several planning questions need to be raised by any congregation projecting a revival as an element of its evangelistic witness.

What is the purpose of our revival or renewal event? The pastor and other church leaders in evangelism and ministry should guide the congregation in determining the specific purpose of their revival. Will the meeting concentrate on outreach? On building up the existing Christian fellowship? On both?

When is the revival scheduled? As far in advance as possible, the date of the revival needs to be calendared. The date may need to remain tentative until the preferred preacher and singer can be enlisted. Care should be taken to avoid dates that compete with major community events or holidays.

Who will lead the revival? The pastor and others who may be charged with selecting the revival preacher and singer should carefully enlist leaders who can best help the congregation reach its goal for the meeting. The pastor himself, pastors of neighboring churches, and vocational evangelists provide an array of possibilities for personnel.

How will we organize to reach our goal? The church's evangelism committee (and special groups as needed) can arrange for prayer support, publicity, music, visitation, testimonies, hospitality, finance, ushers, and special emphases. In small churches one person may be able to coordinate each of these activities.

How will we finance our revival? Misunderstandings over finances can tarnish your revival's impact quickly. Several options are used by congregations to underwrite the necessary expenses of revivals. Some churches include an item in their budgets for the total cost of their revival personnel and other expenses. Other churches use only freewill offerings. A few churches cover expenses out of their budgets, then use a love offering to show their appreciation for the preacher and worship leader. Whatever custom a church finds most comfortable, it should pursue its approach openly but without detracting from the revival's primary goal. If revival leaders are required to travel long distances, an advance on their expenses or a prepaid ticket is a thoughtful courtesy.

Are we involving most of our resident members in revival preparation? Prospect visitation, prayer support, and a plan for discipling and assimilating every person who registers a public decision allows every member to contribute more than attendance to a revival's success. Overall involvement and careful preparation can plant the seeds for the Holy Spirit's cultivation and ripening.

Plan, Plan, Plan

Special events deserve the minister's thorough efforts in planning. Special congregational events should be remembered for positive results, not for what went wrong. Planning helps special events unfold in predictable stages. (See figure 10.2 for a special event planning form. Additional forms related to the use of facilities for special events are at the end of chapter 9.)

Figure 10.1

FUNERAL POLICIES FOR OUR CHURCH

The Christian gospel of peace, hope, and triumph is nowhere brought into sharper focus than at the death of Christians. Although we who believe in Christ sorrow at the death of persons we love, we don't grieve "as others do who have no hope. For since we believe that Jesus died and rose again, even so, through Jesus, God will bring with him those who have fallen asleep" (1 Thess 4:13–14 RSV). The plans Christians make to face death are a testimony of faith.

Christians ought to assemble, not to mourn the dead, but to confess our faith in a living Lord. Generally, since the funeral is a service of worship, it should be held in the church building and should itself be a witness to hope and fellowship.

On the basis of this affirmation, the statements below are offered for the guidance of our own members in the matter of funerals.

1. When a death occurs in the church family, the pastor should be called immediately. This call will give you the benefit of the pastor's solace and experience in making funeral arrangements.

2. Since a Christian funeral is a worship service, it is recommended that the funeral service be held in the church; that the congregation join in the singing of hymns of victory, thanksgiving, and fellowship; and that the pastor lead the service, drawing heavily on the comfort of God's Word.

3. The pastor will help the family select the hymns, Scriptures, and other elements of the funeral service to ensure the centrality of the theme of our victory over death through faith in our Savior.

4. When the funeral service is held in the church, with the physical remains present, it is recommended that public viewing of the deceased in the service be discouraged. Private or public viewing of the body may be arranged prior to the funeral service.

5. In order that worshippers may center their thoughts on the comfort and strength God provides, a memorial service may be held without the physical remains of the deceased, which may be committed to the earth prior to the service.

6. A simple casket is as appropriate as an elaborate one since the deceased's worth isn't determined by the cost of the funeral arrangements. Therefore, the church will provide a suitable cloth with which to drape the coffin for services which prefer this courtesy.

7. Families are encouraged to recommend to concerned friends the opportunity of making memorial gifts to the church or designated charities. Members of the church are reminded of the importance of acts of thoughtfulness and practical concern to the living during the grief process.

8. Because the funeral service is regarded as one appropriate function of the body of Christ, no fees of any kind are charged for the use of the church's facilities or its personnel.

Figure 10.2

SPECIAL EVENT PLANNING FORM

1. Event _____ Date _____ Time _____
2. Purpose/for _____ Approx. attendance _____
3. Person in charge _____ Phone _____
4. Facilities needed
   _____ Auditorium (seats XXX)   _____ Nursery (Ages? _____)
   _____ Chapel (seats XXX)   _____ Playground
   _____ Parlor/Bride's Room   _____ Room(s) # _____
   _____ Fellowship Hall   _____ Kitchen (space only)
   _____ Office Reception Area   _____ Parking Lot (East side)
5. Equipment needed
   _____ Sound Equipment   _____ Data or Film Projector
   _____ Piano   _____ White Board/Easel
   _____ # of Tables   _____ Electronic Recorder/
                                            Player
   _____ # of Chairs   _____ Kitchen Equipment
   _____ Lectern   Other _____
   _____ Equipment/supplies will be provided by the following:
   Company/Person _____ Phone _____
6. Preparation and cleanup of facilities
   Janitor needed? _____ (Required for nonchurch function.)
   Payment due, if nonchurch function $_____ Date due _____
   If church function, person in charge _____
7. Arrangement of facilities
   Sketch on the back of this form the room arrangement(s) desired. Show locations of tables, chairs, flower arrangements, and other items that will need to be set up.
8. Schedule and Participants
   Attach to this sheet the schedule/agenda for this event and a list of program participants.

Person requesting _____ Date _____
Address and Contact Information _____
Approved by _____ Date _____

Chapter 11

CHURCH PUBLICATIONS

Bruce P. Powers

To a great extent the personality of a church is conveyed through church publications. There is a direct relationship between how a congregation thinks and feels about its life and the content and quality of its published materials.

For example, look at your church bulletin. What story does it tell about the personality and character of your congregation? Look at the newsletters and other printed materials. Which ones make the church look best? How do they compare with the materials you see from businesses and community organizations in your town?

In this chapter the primary focus is on printed communications; however, you will find that many of the ideas also apply to Web sites and various other media that can be used to communicate with members as well as the general public. Pick out the ones that appeal to you and that have possibilities for your situation.

Following the administrative procedures, there is an idea section containing information on a variety of topics related to enhancing the quality and effectiveness of church publications.

General Considerations

1. *Be clear about your message.* Exactly what is it you are trying to communicate? The best messages are:

- Concise—The writing is tight, direct, and clear.
- Energetic—They are compelling, full of action verbs, and devoid of trite phrases and useless words.
- Respectful—They allow the reader to interpret and make decisions, without overselling or dictating conclusions.

2. *Be clear about your target audience.* Are you speaking to insiders or to outsiders? Are you trying to communicate with an age group or with all ages? Is a message specifically for all persons in a worship service, or is it for those who are members of a Sunday school class?

3. *Follow a planned design.* Publications should not look pieced together. Look at a newsletter or bulletin. What stands out? Is this what you want to emphasize? Look at your church's material through the eyes of a stranger: What are the most important items or activities? Where would you look first, and how would you be guided through the printed messages? What would you remember? Why?

4. *Make basic information prominent.* Look at the title of your newsletter or bulletin and the contact information. Would a stranger be able to:

- tell the full name of the church?
- address a letter to the church?
- call the church office?
- ask for the pastor or other minister by name?
- tell what the various sections or columns are about?

If a stranger would have trouble with any of these, so would many church members.

5. *Use good quality paper.* What type of paper is used, and what does it look like? Is it light colored, clean, and crisp looking? Is it heavy enough so that printing on one side doesn't show through when you read the other side? Is there a good contrast between the printed material and the paper, so that reading, even in dim light, is easy?

6. *Develop editorial skills.* Who decides what goes into and prepares your church publications? Has this person developed skills in church communications, and does the reader feel good about the job being done? Consider providing some helpful resources for this person, such as those listed in the bibliography. And, when possible, encourage participation in a church publications workshop provided by your denomination or other church-related organization.

Administrative Guidelines

The following guidelines will assist you in developing an administrative plan for your church:

1. *One person on the staff should be designated as coordinator of church publications.* Although work might be delegated, this person would plan, organize, direct, and approve all editorial matters.

2. *Develop a policy statement that describes the purpose, content, distribution, and costs for each regular publication.* Have this approved by the appropriate person/group. New publications would be approved in the same way.

3. *Develop a production schedule for each regular publication.* Indicate the dates by which various actions must be completed and the person responsible if other than the editor. See figure 11.1 for a sample production schedule.

4. *Use a planning form, as illustrated in figure 11.2, for each issue of a church publication.* These forms could be prepared ahead of time for each week and maintained on a computer in the church office. Staff members then could easily plan ahead for major emphases and arrange to treat themes over a series of issues. More time could be allowed for important writing assignments, and the editor could give more thought to layout and design. Such planning would enhance publications and help them serve as educational aids as well as promotional tools for church ministry.

5. *Follow the same planning scheme for special brochures, promotional materials, and other related items.* Plan thoroughly and far in advance of the date needed.

6. *Develop a layout form for all regular publications.* This will enable you to visualize materials while still in the planning stage, and it will cut down the time spent in editorial work. This form may be in a graphics design program on a computer or may be a sketch or copy of the actual publication with blanks for all items that change with each issue. In designing an issue, you place new material in the blank areas. For example, a Sunday bulletin form might include spaces for a Scripture passage, hymn titles, the sermon topic, and announcements. When the form is maintained on a computer, previously published information may simply be replaced with current information.

7. *Keep a file copy of every publication.* Place regular items such as bulletins and newsletters together in a binder for quick and easy reference. Occasional items such as brochures can be filed together in a publications folder. When publications are prepared on a computer or by an outside agency, maintain the computer files in a secure location. Back up regularly and record each year's publications on a disk. Label the disk with the name of each publication and year, such as *Sunday Bulletin—20XX.* Three years is probably a good period to keep hard copies of regular publications. Special publications, such as a history of the church or a bulletin honoring a retiring pastor should be kept permanently and securely in the church's historical collection.

8. *Review annually the effectiveness of church publications.* This can be done by the church staff, the church council, or other authorized group of leaders. Guidelines for evaluation and suggested ways of using church publications for outreach and ministry are included in books listed in the bibliography.[1]

Ideas to Enhance Your Publications

1. *Design content based on the target audience.* In publications designed for the total congregation, like a weekly newsletter, focus on general items such as the pastor's message, church family news, program promotion, and people features. Avoid a bunch of personal columns that have to be filled each week.

2. *Space is precious; use it wisely.* Information that applies to a few, such as a report to a committee, might better be sent via e-mail or by mailing photocopies.

3. *Establish a news-gathering system.* Determine what information is needed and how often. Enlist representatives who can gather and perhaps write the needed articles. Determine an appropriate publication schedule, as described earlier in the chapter, and advise assistants of due dates.

4. *Keep freshness in your publications.* Materials that are overly predictable lose their communicating power. Try some of these ideas:

- Study books and Web resources on the layout and design of church publications.
- Take a class or attend a conference on desktop publishing and Web site design.
- Review various design programs that can be used on your office computer.
- Exchange materials with other churches by placing each other's names on your respective mailing lists. Study the Web sites of other churches.
- Collect publications that appeal to you and keep them in an idea file.
- Collect images and artwork that can be inserted in your church's publications. These can be digital pictures taken of your facilities, members, and church activities, as well as images in artwork collections available on computer disks from office supply stores. Some denominations publish artwork collections designed for different seasons of the church year; check with your bookstore or denominational office.
- Attend a church publications workshop.

5. *Become acquainted with proofreading marks.* These are used by printers and professional editors and writers to save time and to indicate specifically what is to be done when preparing a publication. Marks often used in preparing church publications are illustrated in figure 11.3.

6. *Learn the vocabulary used in dealing with church publications.* Many of the words you will use are listed and defined in figure 11.4.

7. *For special publications that require complicated design, layout, and production, churches need professional assistance.* Select a printer, graphic designer, or Web site specialist to handle such publications. Before doing this, determine the types and amounts of items normally produced by

the church during the year; then consult with several firms. Discuss your needs, look at their products, and secure a list of prices and/or quotes. Select a firm that not only has good prices but that can produce what you need within the time frame in which you must operate. Often you can negotiate concerning what layout and design must be done in your office and what will be done by the printer/designer.

8. *Develop a form to use, and learn how to write press releases.* Give facts: *what, who, when, where,* and *why.* Tell the most important information in the first few sentences, then give details. Print double-spaced on one side of 8 1/2 x 11 white paper. A sample form is in figure 11.5.

9. *Contact the local broadcast/cable station(s) and newspaper(s) regarding policies for covering news events and publishing public service information.* Discuss the requirements for submitting information, time schedules, and specific persons to whom you should relate. Discuss the types of information that would be broadcast or printed.

10. *Be dependable.* Get information together on time, in the right form, and to the right person.

11. *Secure a style manual or a secretarial handbook for your office.* Use this for reference whenever you are in doubt about how to communicate in print. Check with your bookstore or denominational office to determine if a specific manual is recommended for your situation.

12. *Proofread, proofread, proofread!* Don't let careless mistakes make a joke of the church's image.

Figure 11.1

WEEKLY NEWSLETTER SAMPLE PRODUCTION SCHEDULE

Thursday
Determine space available and items to be considered.
Meet with staff to plan next week.
Complete a *Publication Planning Form* (see figure 11.2).

Friday
Compile materials.
Write or secure commitments to prepare articles.
Check on supplies, graphics/artwork, and other items needed.

Monday
Secure all materials and complete writing/editing, using information gained from weekend activities.

Tuesday
Prepare copy or submit appropriate material to printer.
Proofread all material!

Wednesday

Print and prepare newsletter for distribution. If published online or sent via e-mail, prepare and send a sample copy to assure that it is transmitted correctly.

Thursday

Label, sort, and package newsletter. Deliver to post office according to local requirements. If distributed electronically, publish at agreed-upon time.

Figure 11.2

PUBLICATION PLANNING FORM

Title _____ Editor _____
Date to be listed on publication _____ Date needed _____

PRODUCTION SCHEDULE

Date   **Action**
_____ Planning meeting(s) with _____
_____ Make assignments for items to be written
_____ Deadline for receipt of all items
_____ Edit copy or send to graphic designer
_____ Print or publish material

GENERAL PLANS FOR THIS ISSUE

Articles or Information to Secure:

What	Person responsible	Due date
1. _____	_____	_____
2. _____	_____	_____
3. _____	_____	_____
4. _____	_____	_____
5. _____	_____	_____
6. _____	_____	_____

Figure 11.3

PROOFREADING MARKS

Proofreading	Mark Meaning
¶ The news is good.	Begin new paragraph
No ¶ The news is good.	No new paragraph
The⌐news is good.	Delete (may be drawn through a letter or may be attached to a circle that encloses material to be deleted)
stet The ~~news~~ is good.	Leave as it was; let stand
Th⌃ᵉ news is good.	Insert item shown
The (is news) good.	Transpose material indicated
The⌃news is good. #	Insert a space
The news i ͡s good.	Take out the space; close-up
bf The news is good.	Print in boldface
The news is good.	Use italic style printing
The Ⱦews is good.	Make the letter lower case
the news is good.	Make the letter a capital
[The news is good.	Move copy to end of box (may be left, right, up, or down)

215

Figure 11.4

CHURCH PUBLICATIONS VOCABULARY

Listed below are words often used in dealing with church publications. Get acquainted with these terms and your ability to communicate in this field will improve greatly.

Artwork, or graphics—all illustrations, pictures, and drawings; the non-written material

Bleed—an illustration that runs off the edge of a page/sheet

Blow-up—an enlargement of an image

Box—a border around text

Bullet—a solid circle of print (•), used for emphasis

Byline—the author's name at the beginning of a story

Caps—capital letters

Center spread—two facing center pages of a publication

Clip art—artwork, digital or printed, that can be used for published materials

Coated paper—type of paper with hard, smooth finish that makes pictures look better

Copy—all written material

Copy desk—where material is edited and given headlines before being published in a newspaper

Cover stock—thick paper suitable for booklet covers

Credit line—information about the source of copy or illustration

Crop—to change the size or proportions of an image

Deadline—the last time to get copy in for publication

Dummy—a made-up model of what the finished version will look like

End—place at the end of a news release (—end—, also —30—)

Filler—short item inserted to fill space in a publication

Flush—even with the margin

Flyer—an inexpensive piece of printed promotional material

Font—a set of type of a particular style or design

Glossy—a shiny-surface photograph

Graphics program—a computer layout and design system for preparing publications

Layout—arrangement of text and artwork on a page

Lead (pronounced like *seed*)—opening paragraph in a news story that gives basic facts

Line drawing—an illustration with solid lines and clear, nonprinted areas; no shading

Master, or camera-ready copy—finished copy ready for duplication as it appears

More—when written at the bottom of a page, information is continued on the next sheet

Point—the unit of measure for the size of type used for printing (12-point type is for average readers)

Proof—an initial image of a publication on which corrections can be made

Trim size—size of printed material after any necessary cutting

Widow—a very short word or part of a word standing alone at the end of a paragraph of printed material

Figure 11.5

INFORMATION RELEASE

Release Date/Time _____

Check one: ❑ For Immediate Release   ❑ Release at Will

Church or Organization _____

Name of Writer _____ Position _____

Local Address _____

City/State/ZIP _____

Telephone _____ E-mail _____ FAX _____

Subject: (state major focus)

Begin information here, using these guidelines:

* Use short paragraphs.
* Do not hyphenate words.
* Use wide margins (at least 1 inch on sides, top, and bottom).
* Double-space all copy.
* If a second sheet is needed, insert "—more—" at the bottom of the sheet before going on.
* After the first sheet, put your name, first three words from the subject, and the page number at the upper left of each sheet.
* At the end of your release, insert "—end—."
* It is not necessary to write a headline for a news release.

Chapter 12

LEGAL MATTERS

William G. Caldwell

One of the most difficult areas for congregations today is the law and its ramifications for the church. Many churches act out of ignorance, a feeling of immunity, or a stance based on the separation idea that says the church has no dealings with the state. Because of increasing litigation and legal accountability among nonprofit institutions, every minister and every church must understand the basic legal matters that apply to the work of the church.

The problem with a general overview, however, is the variance of state and local regulations. A related problem is the continual change in laws and their relationship to churches. This chapter, therefore, seeks to point out areas of concern without giving legal advice. A qualified, local attorney is the best source of detailed information.

Determining Needs for Legal Advice

Every church needs legal advice at some point in its ministry. The need will vary according to the kinds of activities, building programs, and ministries in which the church is involved. A major consideration in this area will involve the ability to know when to seek legal help and the best approach to take when the situation calls for it.

Select an Attorney

A church should seek a reputable, competent attorney who will be sympathetic and understanding of the special legal needs of a church. An attorney who is a member of the congregation may not be the best choice although a Christian is preferable. The need for objectivity in legal matters could be a problem for one who is too closely related to the situation. A church should be willing to pay for the services rendered and not expect discounted or free advice. For a small fee some attorneys will serve on a retainer basis, always ready to provide the service needed. Additional charges would still be made for services rendered.

In selecting an attorney, it is wise to check with other churches to discover if they have found one who has been helpful. State and local bar associations and legal aid societies may be other sources of information. The specialty of the attorney is important. Most churches will not need a person who specializes in criminal law. The more common areas of need would relate to real estate, contracts, employment, liability, and general family law.

The selection process should include an interview to allow the attorney to become familiar with the church, its leadership, and the specific areas of concern relating to legal services. The status of the church as a nonprofit entity would need to be understood by any attorney who would work with a congregation.

The church should feel free to discuss with the attorney the schedule of charges that is used for services rendered. If a retainer fee is to be used, some negotiation of the amount would be in order, based on the expected time involvement and the frequency of advice needed. Once a selection has been made, the church or the attorney should be free to change or terminate the relationship if the need arises.

Situations Requiring Legal Advice

Numerous and rapid changes are taking place in legal matters that may have impact on the local church. At the national level the Internal Revenue Service continues to issue rulings that affect the church. In addition, tax code changes and tax court decisions make it necessary for the church to keep up with those areas that will affect its work.

At the state level, decisions are being made concerning day-care centers and school operations that will affect those churches that offer such services.

At the local level the taxation of properties owned by a church continues to be explored. Many local ordinances also affect a church in its building program and the operation of church activities. Many of these situations will require the church to secure competent legal advice. Ignorance of the law will not be a valid excuse if the church is guilty of failing to abide by its legal responsibilities.

At times the church may be required to go to court to resolve a problem. The church must make several considerations when this happens.

1. *Stewardship.* What is the responsibility of the church from a stewardship standpoint? If a person has attempted to swindle the church, the court may be the only place to deal with the problem. The church must analyze the situation from the perspective of the wise and proper use of its resources.

2. *Safety.* The responsibility of the church to provide adequate safety precautions is sometimes overlooked and may result in a court case. The church must not hide behind any spiritual excuse when its negligence concerning the safety of its members and guests is involved.

3. *Fraud.* In the case of a company that has demonstrated outright fraud, the case may have to be settled in court. The church may have a responsibility to keep that company from treating others in a similar matter.

4. *Public relations.* Going to court should always be the last resort. It will be embarrassing and difficult and may have a negative effect on the church's public image.

The doctrine of charitable immunity no longer protects churches from lawsuits. More and more, the trend is toward close inspection of all non-profit institutions—including churches—as to the ways in which they abide by the rules and regulations of society. Churches must set a good example in all those situations where they are required to do certain things—even going beyond the minimum expectations to do more than is required.

Role of Trustees

The work of trustees in a church will vary according to the structure within which the church operates. In most instances they will be the official group to sign papers and otherwise represent the church in legal matters. They will act as the agent of the church in transacting business.

In some cases, by vote of the congregation, the pastor acts as the agent of the church. It is important that the pastor or the trustees know and have evidence of the authority possessed in acting for the church. Entering into a contract outside that authority could result in personal liability for any loss or damage to the church or any outside party.

When acting for the church, there must be clear indication of the role of the agent on behalf of the church. A resolution passed by the church to this effect will eliminate any personal liability in the case of a dispute. Advice from an attorney can be helpful in this area. The section on incorporation provides additional information regarding this responsibility.

In some organizational structures, trustees may perform additional responsibilities for the church. They may act as the building and grounds or maintenance committee, the personnel committee, or serve in functional areas relating to insurance and like matters. In most cases these structures have evolved over time and work well for the church using them.

Resolving Grievances

A church would do well to establish a procedure for dealing with disputes, disagreements, or grievances that are bound to develop in spite of the best of Christian intentions. It is tragic when such disputes must go to the court system to be resolved. Every effort should be made to settle such matters within the framework of the church structure.

Written procedures for employee grievances should include the following guidelines and be included in the church's policy manual:

1. The immediate supervisor should be the first person involved when an employee has a problem.

2. A written record should be made of the grievance and the attempt to deal with it. Several efforts may have to be made to resolve the issue.

3. If the difficulty cannot be dealt with at this level, then the next level of supervision should be involved. All records of the attempts to solve the problem should be reviewed and additional solutions explored.

4. If supervisors cannot develop a satisfactory solution, the matter should go to a committee (such as personnel, pastor/parish relations) made up of qualified church members who relate to personnel matters. These persons are brought into the discussion to give greater insight into possible solutions. In some organizations they have the final word. In others the congregation becomes involved, or a denominational group is called in as arbiter if the grievance cannot be resolved. Every effort should be made to deal with such matters in the church rather than securing an attorney and going to court.

Using Legal Help in Specific Areas

The church would be wise to secure legal help in a number of specific areas. The extent of the help needed will be determined by the nature of the situations and the degree to which the state or county has gotten involved in the affairs of the church. Each church will have to determine for itself the extent of the need and the legal advice that may be necessary. A word of caution: This is not the time to ignore a situation and hope that it will go away. Issues must be dealt with, and legal help will be necessary in many areas.[1]

Incorporation

The effect of incorporation is to create a legal entity that the law recognizes for purposes of holding title to real estate, executing contracts, and performing all functions necessary in conducting the civil affairs of the church. It does not take away the spiritual nature or purpose of the church. Although the main advantage relates to insulation from liability for individual members, incorporation offers several other advantages.

- Incorporation allows the church to hold property in its own name.
- It restricts the duplication of the church's name.
- It gives the church continued life.
- It protects creditors.
- It offers the church tax benefits in some states.
- It helps the church obtain multirisk insurance.

- It gives the church greater opportunity for obtaining loans.
- It makes the church a separate legal entity.
- It protects church members and trustees.

A church is not required to become incorporated as a nonprofit religious corporation. Each state has its own regulations concerning the status of a church as a nonprofit organization, and some states do not provide for incorporation for a church. The office of the secretary of state is the appropriate place to get information about the incorporation procedure.

The procedure will vary if the church is:

- an *independent* body—a congregational-type church governed solely within itself; or
- a *dependent* body—a church governed by a hierarchical form of government, so that the church itself is a member of a larger organization.

The process usually involves the assembling of members for the specific purpose of approving the documents relating to incorporation. These documents include:

1. The *charter* stating the name and purpose of the organization
2. The *bylaws* that explain the powers and responsibilities of officers, rights and privileges of members, meetings of the body, and provisions for dissolving the body
3. The *minutes* that detail the conduct of the meeting, including the motion and vote to approve the incorporation

All of this information will be filed with the appropriate fee for recording the action. It may be advisable to have an attorney look over the documents to be sure they are in order.

The advantages of incorporation seem to far outweigh the potential problems of remaining a society in the eyes of the state. The advice of an attorney familiar with the laws in your state will help determine the proper procedures for a local church or church-related nonprofit organization to follow.

Liability

The church and the minister are not immune from legal responsibility for their actions because they are in the religion business. Responsibility extends to anyone who is related to the activities of the church in terms of the care and protection of people.

A church may be called upon to provide compensation for *anyone*—members, visitors, employees, or others outside the church—when there is negligence resulting in any loss or damage. The act of negligence may result from doing or not doing something that a reasonable person would do or not do in a similar situation.

The interpretation of what is reasonable has varied from state to state and usually is decided by a judge or jury when the question of negligence reaches the courtroom. Negligence usually requires an injury caused by the defendant's conduct or lack of action. The defendant shows negligence in that the action or lack thereof shows a breach of duty in performing reasonable measures to protect against risks.

Permission forms for trips away from the church are helpful, but they cannot be used as an excuse for negligence. The church should make every effort to keep from being negligent as well as to provide adequate insurance coverage for protection from unforeseen situations. The church should provide *workers compensation insurance* coverage for employees and maintain *public liability insurance* coverage for property and vehicles in significant amounts.

The minister as a professional also has concerns about the proper performance of responsibilities. This is evident not only in those acts as an agent of the church but also in those acts as a professional person, particularly in the area of counseling.

The subject of malpractice by a minister has become one of legal significance. This is due to vague interpretations of a minister's liability when advice given a counselee leads to harmful results. Again, the negligence question is open to interpretation but has become the object of suits that have been filed. Commonsense precautions need to be taken.

Related to this concern is that of privileged communications between a minister and a counselee. The state laws vary as to the extent to which a minister could be required to testify concerning such communications. Almost all states require the reporting of child abuse situations. Some states distinguish formal counseling sessions from informal conversations.

The licensing of counselors by many states is an effort to provide assurance that sufficient training is being done. The minister who is not a licensed counselor should refer persons to someone who is.

Taxation

The subject of taxation of churches is extremely complicated and open to various interpretations. The idea that a church is tax exempt does not remove the responsibility to file certain forms and to pay certain taxes. Federal, state, and local laws have varying requirements relating to churches.

1. *Federal taxes.* A church is usually automatically exempt from federal taxes because it is a church. A relationship with a denominational body helps. Other religious organizations must request exemption from taxes and the right to receive tax deductible contributions as a religious organization defined in Section 501(c)(3) of the Internal Revenue Code. (A church should have a copy of this section and the related publication on applying for exempt status.)

The Internal Revenue Service uses several characteristics to determine if a church qualifies for exemption. Among these are the following:

- A legal existence
- A formal code of doctrine
- A membership not associated with another church
- An established place of worship
- Regular religious services
- An ordained ministry
- Schools for training ministers

A church may have ministry programs that are not separately incorporated and are therefore recognized as units of the church. It may also have separately incorporated ministry programs that are controlled by the church and are therefore recognized as an integrated auxiliary of the church. The key words are *ministry* and *control*. A federal identification number is issued for the church to use in filing forms or other documents with the government.

2. *State taxes.* In many states churches are exempt from paying state sales tax on items purchased for church use. A tax exempt number is required in some states while others issue a refund or simply recognize the name of the church for exemption. The property tax code also varies from state to state concerning what is or is not exempt as church property. A church should investigate what its tax responsibilities are in the state where it is located.

3. *Local taxes.* The same variance in taxation exists at the local level. Local sales taxes and local property taxes are levied against churches in some communities. A church should not assume that all of its properties and purchases are tax exempt but should investigate what is required and what process must be followed to obtain exemptions when they are allowed. Local authorities have attempted to levy taxes on parking lots, parsonages, excessive land, and other church property in an effort to broaden the tax base of their communities.

4. *Employment taxes.* A church is responsible like any other employer to withhold taxes from an employee's wages and to pay those taxes in a timely manner to the proper authority. Income taxes (including state and local where applicable) must be withheld from all employees according to the tax guides provided. The exception to all employees applies to the *ordained* minister (and to the licensed or commissioned minister who performs substantially the same functions as the ordained minister) who is considered *self-employed* for tax purposes and files quarterly returns along with the payment of the self-employed rate of Social Security taxes. The church may withhold amounts from salary for these taxes at the request of the minister.

A newly ordained minister within the second year of ordination may file a request for an exemption (which is irrevocable) from Social Security coverage on religious principles prohibiting acceptance of Social Security benefits (or other public insurance) for services as a minister. Economic considerations for the exemption are not valid.

All other employees, whether paid by the hour, day, week, piecework, or percentage must have tax withheld. The church must keep appropriate records and file the proper forms with the employee and the taxing agencies as instructed.

Rulings on Social Security taxes also require the church to withhold the stated amount from the wages of all employees and to match that amount from church funds when making quarterly payments. Failure to do so can result in tax liens and penalties for failure to comply with regulations. A church should consult with the state to determine if other wage-and-hour laws apply to the church.

5. *Unrelated-business income taxes.* A church may be subject to taxes based on business income that is not directly related to the work of the church or that the church receives from debt-financed property. The income must be from a trade or business activity that is conducted regularly, such as renting parking spaces during the week to an adjacent business. It also must not contribute importantly to accomplishing the exempt purpose of the organization.

If all of the work performed is by volunteers, it would not likely be an unrelated business. A church should carefully examine its receipts in these areas and determine if it should file the proper forms for reporting such income and pay the appropriate taxes required.

6. *Federal excise tax.* In certain cases a church may be exempt from paying federal excise tax that is levied on certain items purchased. This is especially true for church-related schools. The proper form should be secured and filed for the exemption.

7. *Unemployment tax.* A church is usually exempt from federal and state unemployment taxes. An investigation should be made with state authorities to discover the requirement in each state. Some states permit churches to participate voluntarily in these programs.

Employment Practices

A church should establish policies relating to the employment of personnel to ensure consistency in hiring practices. Legal review of these policies may be helpful. Even though churches are not required to follow the government-mandated policies regarding equal opportunity employment, churches should make every effort to assure a nondiscriminatory approach in employment.

A church may want to employ only church members, but that should be a fair and consistent policy and not an excuse used only when it is convenient to keep from hiring someone else. This lack of consistency in hiring practices could result in persons feeling that they had been discriminated against since they were not hired.

Several federal laws relating to employment practices may or may not relate to churches. Some require a certain number of employees for the law to be effective, others apply on the basis of what the church or organization is involved in as a part of its ministry. Each church should look at the laws and, perhaps with legal counsel, make a decision on how they might be affected. Some of the laws to be considered include:

- Title VII, Civil Rights Act of 1964
- Equal Pay Act of 1963
- Family and Medical Leave Act of 1993
- Age Discrimination in Employment Act (1967)
- Americans with Disabilities Act of 1990
- Immigration Reform and Control Act of 1986

Since Congress is continually involved in developing legislation in this area, churches must stay abreast of changes as they occur. In addition, individual states enact legislation that may also apply to churches. There is a continuing need to be aware of how national and state laws may relate to the employment process.

It is also wise to take precautions in case it becomes necessary to terminate an employee. *A supervisor should carefully record any action taken to reprimand an employee and document the effort made to improve performance.* This documented record should be placed in the employee's personnel file. It is helpful if the record also includes a signed statement by the employee acknowledging the agreement to improve performance.

If repeated attempts to rectify the inadequate performance are not successful and termination becomes necessary, the records will provide sufficient information to indicate that the church was justified in its action. If a church does not follow such a process, there is a good possibility that a terminated employee could have legal grounds for a lawsuit.

Wills and Estates

The whole matter of wills and estates represents a significant area of legal concern for the church and the Christian interested in the total concept of stewardship. The advice of those trained in the field is essential for good planning because of the complex nature of government rules and state laws regulating the disposition of an estate.

Many churches have a special committee to promote the concept of making a will or establishing a trust as an act of Christian stewardship. Some churches are fortunate enough to have attorneys, bankers, or accountants who can provide information and assist church members in this area.

The advantages of estate planning must be shared with the congregation. The need to put things in order should be evident to the Christian. The desire to protect one's assets in the way an estate is settled should be of major concern. Good planning will minimize the effect of taxes and other administrative costs relating to settling the estate as well as provide for the efficient and timely distribution of property.

The making of a will is essential to the completion of estate planning. Without a will, state laws specify who benefits from the estate. By making a will, the *individual* specifies who is to benefit. The assistance of an attorney is not required in most states but is highly recommended. The complexity of legal terminology is such that a person may not say what needs to be said unless an attorney assists with the preparation of the will.

A church can and should encourage the inclusion of Christian causes in making a will so that a person who has supported the church while living can reflect that support in the disposition of the assets of the estate. Since a will can be changed anytime prior to the death of the person, it should be reviewed and updated as changes in circumstances should dictate.

General Family Law

There are several areas of legal responsibility that the church will not face directly but in which it may be called upon because of the involvement of church members in these matters. The church that has a day-school or child-care program will more than likely have to make some decisions concerning policies it will follow in its responsibility to children enrolled.

Perhaps the most common area of concern is that of *family violence.* This includes spouse abuse as well as child abuse. Many churches and ministers are being faced with counseling decisions as well as legal decisions relating to the reporting of such activities. Many states and communities now have laws concerning the responsibility of school officials to notify the proper authorities when there is obvious evidence of child abuse. The very nature of church work involves visits into the homes of members and prospective members; you may discover situations where abuse is apparent and must be dealt with. Some of the legal implications of these situations may call for the advice of an attorney.

The increasing occurrence of divorce has created many cases of spousal and child support that may cause difficulties for the church. Since religion is such a vital part of life, some have charged that church involvement has been the cause of alienation and separation. Wise counseling is necessary in such situations.

Several well-publicized cases have presented the need for schools and child-care programs to be extremely cautious in their policies concerning the release of children to relatives or others who may not have the legal right to take the child. A formal procedure for checking children in and out may be necessary. Temporary or permanent restraining orders may have been issued by the court that the church will be involved in enforcing. A church cannot ignore its responsibilities in this area if it desires to be effective in its ministry to the community.

Other areas of family responsibility may affect a church in its work. There have been situations in which court-ordered counseling has been related to the church. The activity of child adoption may involve a minister with families in the church. The problem of court-directed grandparent access may affect the church. It is not necessary that a church or its ministers become experts in these family matters as they relate to legal requirements. It is necessary, however, that a church and its ministers realize that all of these situations can and do affect their work and that legal advice be sought when it is needed.

Contracts

One of the most obvious areas in which legal advice is helpful and necessary is that of making and keeping contracts. A church will have many situations when the services of an attorney will be needed to draw up, interpret, or evaluate a contract. Because a contract represents a legally binding agreement between two or more parties, the document must be accurate, clearly understood, and prepared according to legal requirements. This is necessary for the protection of the church as well as for the other parties involved.

As discussed earlier, the church acts through its authorized agent to enter into a contract. In most cases this agent would be the *trustees*, who have been given the authority to act on behalf of the church. The trustees can only act within the authority given and cannot bind the church to contracts that have not been approved. A pastor or other minister of the church should not assume the role of agent for the church in matters of contract. If this is done outside the minister's authority, personal liability may result. Contract signing should always be indicated as being signed as an agent of the church.

Legal advice is necessary when any real estate purchase is anticipated. In many cases it is helpful to have an attorney who specializes in real estate law. It is never wise to do it yourself no matter how well-meaning church members may be. The need for a title search to assure a clear title to the property, the need to examine the contract to be sure it says what it should, the need to draw up a deed that provides protection for the church, and the need to properly identify any restrictions that may apply—all point to the necessity for legal advice in real estate transactions.

Other contracts that involve major purchases or agreements lasting for more than one year should also be evaluated by an attorney. Any transaction involving an executor or agreements requiring the church to guarantee something should likewise be evaluated. Any expense the church may have to bear for these services may well be savings in the long run if it protects the church from faulty contracts or agreements.

Copyrights

There is no excuse for a church or its ministers to be ignorant of the copyright law and its application to the work of the church. Information about current laws and forms for application for copyright registration are available online at www.copyright.gov, or by writing to U.S. Copyright Office, 101 Independence Avenue, S.E., Washington, D.C. 20559-6000. A church is required to follow the law in its use of material belonging to other persons and organizations.

One of the first things any church should do is to go through files of educational and music materials and dispose of all copied materials that were made without permission. This would provide a good example for church members as well as remove the church from any illegal activity in this area. As the church becomes familiar with the law, it will know what practices it should follow in using copyrighted material.

Generally speaking, a church should not make copies of any material, including music, videos, and computer software programs, when doing so would affect the sales of those materials. Exceptions are allowed for the purposes of criticism, comment, news reporting, teaching (including copies for classroom use), or for research purposes. Copyrighted musical works are also covered, but exemptions are allowed for certain types of nonprofit use. When in doubt, it is usually wise and very simple to request permission for use from the copyright holder.[2]

Churches should be very careful in reprinting copyrighted material from denominational papers or the church paper or bulletin of another church. Even if the other church had received permission to use the material, it would not be right for your church to use it without securing permission from the copyright holder.

Conclusion

In many circumstances in the life and work of the church, legal advice is necessary. The wise church will secure an attorney and seek help when it is needed. The cost involved may be well worth the damages and court costs avoided or the public image preserved if proper legal procedures are followed. Church leaders should use their positions to assure that the church is doing all it can to conduct its business in a legal and ethical manner.

Chapter 13

ETHICAL STANDARDS FOR THE MINISTER
AND THE CONGREGATION

Judy J. Stamey

A minister's ethics are often taken for granted. People mistakenly assume that the calling of a minister and the purpose of a church provide a set of ethics or moral standards that automatically reflect God's standards and cannot be challenged. In reality, reports in the media about immoral and illegal activities by church leaders have focused public attention on ethical standards and legal responsibilities among ministers and churches. From personal morality to corporate responsibility, Christians are increasingly being challenged and held accountable in regard to liability in areas such as tax regulations, financial management, building and safety codes, and employment laws.

Ministers, churches, and church-related agencies are not exempt from complying with pertinent laws, regulations, and reporting rules. Indeed, many ministers and churches have had difficulty understanding and complying with the rules and have found themselves in difficult legal situations. When this occurs, not only are lives affected, but the image of the church is tarnished.

The challenge for the church and its ministers is to return to *covenant thinking*, setting and maintaining high standards or principles that will guide the church and believers in their life and work. Thus, the purpose of this chapter is to challenge ministers and churches to develop personal and business ethics that will mandate the way they do business personally and as a body of believers.

Ethics and the Believer

Ethics is related to human behavior, particularly the standards of conduct and moral judgment, moral philosophy, and rules of conduct. Other terms that could be used for ethics include morality, moral code, decency, integrity, moral conduct, values, standards, code of right and wrong, and honesty.

In *Credibility*, a widely used textbook on leadership traits, James Kouzes and Barry Posner use the word *honesty* to describe ethics. Honesty, they say, is the most-mentioned quality of admired leaders. "In virtually every survey we conducted, honesty was selected more than any other leadership characteristic. Honesty is absolutely essential to leadership."[1] In a similar manner, John C. Maxwell in his book *There's No Such Thing as Business Ethics* clearly proposes that *ethics are ethics*, and that people should live by the same standards in every aspect of their lives.[2] Maxwell emphasizes the critical need for a person to build trust in every relationship.

Believers must examine honesty, trust, and related concepts from a biblical perspective. Consider, for example, the historical significance of the challenge in Proverbs 3:3: "Do not let kindness and truth leave you: Bind them around your neck, Write them on the tablet of your heart" (NASB). Truth is honesty and a mandate from God.

A dictionary may define ethics as "rules of conduct," but something is added for Christians: "So in everything, do to others what you would have them do to you, for this sums up the Law and the Prophets" (Matt 7:12 NIV). Over and over, passages describe the actions of an obedient believer, which in today's language would be defined as a code of ethics.

If these terms validly describe ethics, ministers and the church should not be surprised that Jesus spent much of his life trying to help people understand the differences between right and wrong in order that they could live an obedient life. In addition to the teachings of Jesus, the Bible contains examples that clearly distinguish right from wrong; they were written to encourage believers to honor high standards and values. However, only through the power of God's love and support can we make God's standards our standards.

This is not always an easy thing to do since the development of ethics (values) begins so early in life. When a person becomes a believer, many of his or her values have already taken shape. This is the primary reason that helping a church to determine what the members value becomes a significant challenge.

One of the church's responsibilities is to provide education that will help members grow spiritually, which should include helping them to determine what they value, what their standards are, and what guides them in making daily decisions. Radical changes may have to take place in the life of a new believer because of the relationship with Jesus. Yet many of the changes related to attitudes, values, and knowing how to do the right thing may not be radical at all but will need to be modified to be in keeping with biblical principles.

Many times new members are placed in an orientation class where they learn about the church's history, its various programs and ministries, and how they can participate in the life of the church. This often includes taking a spiritual gifts inventory to help them discover what gifts God has given for them to use. All of this is important, but unless time is given to helping new members understand the values and ethical principles that guide the church in decision making and conducting business affairs, these members may hinder the work of the church because they do not share the same values.

The same standards that guide people in their personal lives will also be the standards that guide them as ministers, members of a committee, Sunday school teachers, and in other places where they will serve. In light of the troubles the church has faced in recent years, it may be time to return to developing a *covenant*, or a *code of ethics*. Churches may not hang a covenant on the wall, as in the past, but they will openly use their ethical guidelines in all decision-making situations.

It is important, also, for the church to use its code of ethics in a positive spirit to train and edify the body of believers. It also should be used to provide direction for enlisting workers as well as a tool in the process of calling a minister to lead the church. These persons should know without question what the church expects from its leaders—what is and what is not acceptable. Therefore, trying to figure out how to avoid complying with a law or making decisions that might hurt people would be less likely to occur. Adhering to the standards of the church could result in better community and business relationships as well as in a higher trust level among members of the congregation.

Ethical Situations That Confront Ministers and the Church

Ministers and lay leaders in conferences, classes, and denominational meetings have reported problems and expressed their deepest concern related to ethics in five areas. It would be helpful to review each of these five to determine if standards have been established and appropriate practices are being followed in your church.

Employment Law

Ethical problems are growing among ministers and the church because many feel that the laws do not apply to them and/or the church. For instance, some church leaders don't think twice about the manner in which they handle personnel matters if they feel the law should not include them or the church. It is important for church members to understand that the church is not exempt from employment law. Laws change rapidly, and churches are not excused for not complying because they were not aware of the law.

One example that continues to be difficult for churches is related to the law regarding *overtime pay*. Many churches continue to pay secretaries or administrative assistants a salary and ignore the fact that if office personnel work over forty hours a week, they must be paid overtime. Often this is ignored because the church and/or ministers feel like the employees are doing the additional work as volunteers or they are allowed to accumulate compensatory time and take off at a later time. The law does not see it that way. The church is not an exception to this law, no matter how much the church ignores it.

One of the newest laws affecting churches is the ruling that a church employee cannot serve in a volunteer position that is related to the position for which one is employed. For example, a youth minister's secretary must be paid the same hourly rate if he/she chaperones a trip or teaches a Bible study class for youth. Although this is a difficult law, the churches are responsible to respect it and abide by its rulings. A strong set of ethics will support doing what is required even when you disagree with it.

To keep the church informed, it would be helpful to assign a staff member responsibility for keeping a file of personnel regulations and attending conferences designed to help the church know and understand the meanings of the law.[3]

Termination Policies

Many churches view church employees as different from those who work in secular businesses, especially as relates to termination. More and more churches neglect performance evaluations, which are necessary for employees to know and understand what is expected in their positions. Instead a supervisor who becomes frustrated with poor performance often asks, "How can I get rid of this person?" This is the wrong question. Instead the supervisor should be asking, "How can I help this employee improve and make a contribution to the church?"

Sometimes a supervisor comforts him or herself by using the "at-will employment law" applicable in many states, without thinking of the consequences for the church or the employee. The "at-will employment law" is often used by a church to fire someone without reason, especially ministers. Churches with established codes of ethics concerning employee relationships are less inclined to fire employees. In addition, the ethics of the supervisor who fires someone should always reflect how he or she would like to be treated.

Financial Policies

Financial problems often result from the attitude of pastors and congregations that church finances should be confidential and that it's nobody's business how funds are being spent or recorded. However, the government holds churches accountable for obeying the laws, even though they are nonprofit organizations.

In recent years church financial ethics have become a major concern for ministers because of dishonesty in reporting correct amounts, especially related to discretionary funds, expense accounts, gifts, and housing allowances. To avoid this, churches should establish policies related to financial expenditures and receipts that reflect honesty and trustworthiness. If a church has a set of ethical guidelines, the task of developing financial polices will become easier.

The following are examples that support the need for developing financial ethics in the church.

Concerning embezzlement. If a survey were taken of full-time church ministers and support staff employees regarding their compensation and benefits, it would not be surprising to discover that many would feel that their compensation is much lower than other professionals who have similar educational backgrounds and experience. This has almost been a given for those in church work.

In recent years, taking or using funds for personal use has been a growing problem. One excuse that has been given is that the church did not pay them enough and employees felt they were deserving of more. Another reason that has been given is that they used the money to help people that the church was not helping. Whatever the reason for embezzling funds, it is clear that the embezzlers did not have or did not apply an ethic of honesty in their work. In addition, the church failed to instill within its staff how important the ethic of honesty is for every employee. In such situations the church should develop financial polices and accounting procedures that will protect the people who handle money and keep the financial records.

Concerning mortgage loans to ministers. In most states churches can make loans to their ministers; however, each church must treat a loan as a business contract, using a credit check and written documents that reflect an interest rate consistent with what other lenders would charge. An ethical problem appears when the church loans money without regard for what is required by law. Although a church may be willing to make such a loan, the minister must exhibit strong ethical standards by helping the church understand what procedures must be applied before a loan can be made.

Concerning gifts from the church to ministers. All gifts for ministers that are solicited by the church or a group of church members require that the value of the gifts must be added to the minister's W-2 form. Whether the amount was included on the donor's giving record or not, the amount must be included on the W-2. This situation involves the ethics of both the ministers and the congregation.

Concerning designated funds. Designated funds are exactly that—designated! If a church receives designated funds for a project, the monies cannot be allocated to another fund, even if the project no longer exists.

It is the responsibility of the church to return the money to the donor. Designated funds must also meet legal requirements to determine whether the gifts are tax deductible. Again this requires the church to understand the ethical responsibility to do the right thing.

Concerning the use and abuse of power. Power is an issue that many ministers and churches struggle with when they experience success, growth, and recognition. It isn't unusual for successful ministers to be invited to share what they and their churches have achieved. In response to invitations to share, a minister should ask the question, "Will the people I share my experiences with know that I give thanks for my experience and want the same or even better for them?"

The need to feel worth and success can be so strong that it may warp a person's thinking, as when one becomes convinced that he or she is more important than others. When this happens, if a minister's ethics regarding ego and power have not been established, the minister may go to extremes to keep up appearances. It may include compromising values in order to stay on top. The hunger for more power and prestige can be subtle and cause ministers to do things that they would not ordinarily do. This is less likely when ministers and churches are guided by a clear set of ethics.

Concerning property management. Buildings and equipment are significant resources for every church. In each of these areas, the church must be concerned with safety, meeting codes, and working with state and city officials when repairing, remodeling, or constructing new buildings. Many times the rules and costs imposed by these governing bodies cause congregational leaders to decide to ignore the rules and convince themselves that churches do not need to let officials know what they are doing. It isn't unusual for a church to do a remodeling project without getting a permit from the city or state. If the congregation has a code of ethics to guide leaders in every business decision, the problem of ignoring building and safety codes should not happen.

Developing a Code of Ethics

Obviously there is a growing need for churches to develop a set of ethics that will guide members in all actions and decisions of life. For this reason, it is vital that the persons God calls to serve as ministers must be individuals who have strong, biblically based ethical standards to guide them personally and as they work with those elected or employed to manage church business. Only a leader who knows and models high ethical standards can lead a congregation to develop a set of ethics that will be meaningful and can be used daily.

Developing a code of ethics, whether personal or for congregational use, involves the same process. Before beginning, however, it is important to determine the purpose the code will fulfill. Will the code of ethics be written to encourage the right behavior or will it be used to inspire people to make the right decisions?

For a congregation, writing a statement of values or a code of conduct may better communicate to the church and personnel what the church expects. When the person or congregation agrees on the purpose for having a code of ethics and is serious about being disciplined to follow the code, the process of determining what to include can begin.

Components of a Code of Ethics

A code of ethics may consist of two parts. One part may contain *goals* that inspire excellence or perfection while another part would consist of *specific rules* that you and/or others would be expected to follow. A code of ethics is designed to promote inspiration and a decision to do the right thing. Although it does not keep you from sinning, it serves as a symbol to remind you when something is questionable or wrong.

Process for Writing Ethical Statements

This process may be followed by an individual or a congregation. Writing individual ethics takes less time because only one person is involved. For a congregation, however, it is a much slower process.

In a church, a team or committee is appointed to do the study. This group then formulates and presents to the congregation a set of ethics that they feel best reflects the values of the church. The more study and discussion among members of the congregation regarding the ethical statements, the greater the likelihood members will adopt the code and consistently follow the guidelines.

The following eight steps can be used by an individual and/or congregation to formulate a code of ethics or statement of values.

1. *Select eight to ten things that you feel strongly about and about which you have already made a decision that these values will guide your life and ministry.* For the church, you will need to decide on the values you expect from those who serve the church as well as the people who make up the church.

2. *Study the Scriptures for affirmation related to your value before you make it one of your ethics.* Too often, a person's ethics come from experiences and/or other role models instead of from the Bible. This step is essential in formulating values that will guide you daily.

3. *Write a draft of the principles you have selected.* These should be scripturally sound and contribute to your life and ministry and/or to the church.

4. *Make each statement active and as simple, concise, and understandable as possible.* For example, one of a pastor's ethics may say, "Administer the ordinances/sacraments and services of the church with integrity and not for financial gain." A business administrator may include one that says,

"Refrain from accepting gifts that may be interpreted as compromising the ministry of the church." A sample code of ethics can be found in figure 1, at the end of the chapter.

5. *Read and ponder your rough draft.* Determine if each statement clearly gives you direction and is a viable tool for your life and/or church.

6. *Share your code of ethics with two or three significant others to get their responses and input.* Although the ethics are for you, it is important that others can clearly understand what values are important to you as a minister and/or leader. For a church code, the committee preparing the document can use leaders from other committees, employees, and other members of the church to react to each statement and suggest any changes or better wording.

7. *Revise, edit, and publish the document.* If it is for the church, present a draft for the congregation to discuss and approve. Following approval, prepare and distribute the document.

8. *Make the code part of your life.* Reflect on its implications and commit to memory its key elements. You could also keep a copy in your Bible and frame a copy to display in your church office.

For a church's code of ethics, copies could be sent to every home. Teachers could lead their classes in studying the code on a special Sunday, and the pastor could use the code of ethics to prepare a series of sermons designed to help members understand and apply their values. The code of ethics should become an important influence in church decisions, business relations, and orientation sessions for prospective/new members, ministers, and other church employees. Periodically review the document and identify any adjustments needed in your life, in the life of the congregation, and/or in the goals and statements.

A Challenge

The headlines of a Texas newspaper said: "Pastor Resigned after Finances Were Reviewed." Many congregations have faced similar situations and discovered that their minister failed to use a code of ethics as a tool when making decisions. In addition, the church discovered that the problem was not entirely the minister's fault because as they reviewed their records, there were not sufficient polices or procedures in place to avoid using funds inappropriately. In cases like this, both the minister *and* the church are to blame.

Every church needs a code of ethics or a statement of conduct as a guide for doing church. People gain strength when they know that others agree with what is important in the Christian life, especially as it relates to right and wrong. When potential employees are interviewed, the code of ethics should be used as a tool to ensure that the person agrees with the things that the church has determined are important in all areas of ministry, especially the business affairs of the church.

For a minister, if you are invited to send a résumé for employment consideration, it would be advantageous to include your personal statement of ethics. This would immediately alert the church that you are serious about being a leader who is committed to being a servant and who is striving to magnify the Lord in every aspect of life.

A code of ethics is a commitment you have made to do your very best to accomplish the standards listed; it is between you and God. Love motivates believers to want to have standards that are pleasing and acceptable to God. Therefore, it is important during our Bible study and devotional times to invite God to help us evaluate our ethical principles in light of our experiences and biblical teachings. John encouraged believers when he said: "And this is love: that we walk in obedience to his commands. As you have heard from the beginning, his command is that you walk in love" (2 John 1:6 NIV).

Figure 13.1

A SAMPLE CODE OF ETHICS

This document was published and distributed under the authority of the General Commission on Ministry of the Christian Church (Disciples of Christ), by Disciples Home Missions, Office of Christian Vocation, published on March 14, 2003. It is used here by permission. A model code of ethics for *congregational conduct* is also available online at: www.discipleshomemissions.org/Ministers/PDFfiles/EthicalGuidelines.pdf/.

My Ministerial Code of Ethics
Christian Church (Disciples of Christ)

In 1944 a ministerial code of ethics for the Christian Church (Disciples of Christ) was published by Disciples Home Missions. That code was developed over a period of several years through the efforts of a widely diverse churchwide committee. It was reviewed and refined as dozens of ministers' associations and fellowships and hundreds of individuals responded to the committee's request for evaluation of the document. The code of ethics has been periodically reviewed by a general committee. Occasionally, editorial changes have been made. The General Commission on Ministry and its predecessor, the General Board Task Force on Ministry, have worked over the past several years with The Disciples Home Missions to update the code of ethics. Proposed changes have been reviewed by regional commissions on ministry as well as by many individuals.

The revised code of ethics maintains much of the language of the original; the principles which guide ministry remain the same from

generation to generation. The ministerial code of ethics has with-
stood the test of time and is commended to be read and followed by
all ministers as a high code of professional conduct.

General Commission on Ministry

My Ministerial Code of Ethics

Believing that Jesus is the Christ, the Son of the living God and
proclaiming him Lord and Savior of the World, I reaffirm my vows as
an ordained or licensed minister. Through dedication and discipline I
will lead and serve with integrity. Relying on the grace of God, I commit myself to the following:

Personal Conduct

- witnessing to the ministry of Jesus Christ;
- dedicating time, strength, vitality and energy for effective
  ministry;
- growing in faith, knowledge and the practice of ministry
  through the spiritual disciplines, study, continuing education
  and service;
- living a life that honors my commitments to my family, including the need for privacy and time together;
- taking time for physical and spiritual renewal, recreation and
  vacation;
- being a faithful steward of God's gifts to me by managing time,
  talents and financial resources responsibly and generously;
- accepting responsibility for all debts which I incur;
- keeping physically and emotionally fit and refraining from
  substance abuse and other abusive behaviors;
- using my position, power and authority in non-exploitive ways;
- maintaining high moral standards in my sexual behavior;
- regarding all persons with equal respect and concern and un-
  dertaking to minister impartially.

Relationships to the Church That I Serve

- nurturing and offering my gifts for ministry to the church;
- calling forth and nurturing the gifts of others in the church
  and joining their gifts with mine for the sake of the mission of
  Jesus Christ and the health of the church;
- preaching and teaching the gospel without fear or favor and
  speaking the truth in love;
- administering the sacraments and services of the church with
  integrity and not for financial gain;

- working cooperatively and collegially with those whom I serve in the particular ministry to which I have been called;
- administering the corporate finances of the church with personal integrity;
- refraining from accepting any gift which would compromise the church's ministry;
- honoring all confidences which come to me in my role as minister and refraining from gossip;
- encouraging and participating in the regular evaluation of my ministry and cooperating with the Region in the periodic review of my ministerial standing;
- seeking the counsel of the Regional Minister should divisive tensions threaten my relationship with those I serve.

Relationships to Ministry Colleagues

- engaging in covenantal relationships with colleagues which involve nurture, discipline, family support, vigorous dialogue, mutual teaching/learning and spiritual formation;
- supporting colleagues in ministry and their families while not exploiting their problems or crises;
- performing pastoral services within another congregation or for a member of another congregation only at the invitation of the pastor of that congregation;
- supporting and at no time speaking maliciously of the ministry of my predecessor or another minister in the congregation in which I hold membership;
- encouraging the ministry of my successor upon my retirement or other departure from a ministry position, without interfering or intruding and by making it clear to former parishioners that I am no longer their pastor.

Relationships to the Community and the Wider Church

- participating responsibly in the life and work of my community, bearing prophetic witness to the Gospel of Jesus Christ, working toward a just and morally responsible society;
- participating faithfully in the life and work of all manifestations of the Christian Church (Disciples of Christ);
- seeking to know, understand and respect the diversity of opinions and people within the Christian Church (Disciples of Christ);
- being a responsible representative of the one Church of Jesus Christ and participating in activities that strengthen its unity, witness and mission.

—Published by the Search and Call Office

Chapter 14

ESTABLISHING A MISSION/STARTING NEW WORK

Bob I. Johnson

T he idea of new work may trigger many images in the minds of today's people of faith. The image of a new congregation rising out of
the dreams and aspirations of concerned church members is probably the first to form. New work images may also take the shape of satellite
ministries, special target groups of persons, and new units of work similar
to or exactly like what the church has already been doing. In one sense,
new work can be anything from beginning a Bible study class for a group
not currently being served to the establishment of a new congregation.

The emphasis in this chapter falls more on new congregation-type ministries; however, you should remember that beginning any new or additional ministry places more demands on a church. Both involve giving up
something and gaining something when a new situation is created.

What New Work Allows

New work allows a church to align itself with a stream of others who,
through vision and purpose, have established new work in their communities and around the world. It helps a church to carry out the command of Christ as found in Matthew 28:18–20, commonly called the Great
Commission.

New work allows a church to have a part in the formation of new communities or new groupings of persons within communities. New work allows the church to experiment with alternative models of congregational
style and to recognize the diversity in the new institutions that may distinguish them from the sponsoring church or churches. Participating in
the development of new work can also help to eliminate racism and tra-
ditionalism within the mother congregation. It also allows, and forces in

some cases, the sponsoring group to relate to other churches within its denomination and even to churches in other denominations.

Creating new work offers the church a fresh and challenging opportunity to express its own Christian faith. It forces the church to rethink its theology and purpose and to provide models for Christian service and ministry. It forces the church to reach out in evangelistic efforts toward persons hitherto unreached by this particular congregation. In short, it allows the church to experience faith as a verb.

Before Beginning New Work

The hopes for good results from many worthwhile projects often turn to frustration due to hasty preparation and decision making by the church. While some ideas germinate quickly and find ready acceptance within a congregation, more often a congregation needs time to mull over significant decisions. People need to raise significant questions and then move together through a studied decision. New work falls into this kind of category. The following are several suggestions for considering new work.

1. *Determine the gifts and inward readiness for new work of the person who will lead the effort.* As the leader, you cannot lead where you are not equipped to go. It has to be in the leader. In other words, determine "who is in here" first, not "who is out there." New works demand that you live out of your center. This calls for the leader to possess and exercise good self-diagnostic skills before looking at the obvious need for new work.

2. *If a congregation is to be involved, determine its true mission interest.* The church may be a heavy contributor to mission offerings and to the denominational plan of unified giving; still, the people may be unwilling to pay the price in time and money to establish a new work on a sound footing. Use formal and informal ways to survey the interest and willingness of church members in becoming new spiritual parents.

3. *Get the congregation to verbalize its story and see the reason for establishing new work.* Often church members are unaware of the verbal and nonverbal cues they are communicating. Perhaps persons who have been members for a longer time and those who have been members a shorter time are not quite sure how to relate to each other in sharing their dreams and aspirations for the congregation.

One example of overcoming this problem is sponsoring one or more informal dialogues among various groups in the church. Perhaps at an evening fellowship the longer-termed members can talk about what it was like in the past, the sacrifices the founders and supporters through the years had to make, and what they need from the church as well as what they are willing to contribute to and through the church.

Newer members could be encouraged to express those things that have benefited them in the past in other churches where they have been members, what they bring in their gifts and attitudes, and what they are willing to commit of themselves to this present congregation.

Summarize some of the history of the church and point out the story the church has been telling the community by both its verbal and nonverbal expressions. Point out how the church was begun and suggest that the church may have come to a time when it needs to consider expressing itself in new and different ways.

At an appropriate point explain to the congregation that new work is being considered informally. Point out the specific needs that have given rise to the possibility of new work. Allow questions and seek to have as much information as possible to give people. Do not make commitments before the church is ready to move deliberately.

Providing for a Healthy Birth

After working through informal discussions and study with the congregation, review all the factors with the church council or, if the church has one, a committee charged with dealing with new work. When there is a strong conviction of God's leadership among the congregation and within the council/committee, draft a formal recommendation that the church proceed to establish new work. Promote this recommendation and advise that it will be considered at a specified church business meeting. At this meeting the church should formally adopt a proposal to sponsor new work and approve procedures to guide the development.

The following steps could be presented as guidelines:

1. *Specify a committee to handle the new work.* This may be a new committee, or it could be an ongoing church missions committee. Regardless, this group requires a mandate from the congregation to give positive and enthusiastic leadership to the implementation of the mission project.

Elect five to seven people who are spiritually mature, positive toward mission outreach, concerned about people, able to relate well with people who may be different from them, and able to analyze situations and make good decisions. Above all, they must be warmhearted, loving people who by faith can see possibilities and act when others may be immobilized.

If possible, have representatives who can give special assistance related to church educational organizations, worship services, and outreach activities. The most competent, mission-minded person should chair the committee. The pastor should, of course, be a member ex officio.

In churches working within a denomination, the committee should consult with someone in the structure charged to strategize new work. If a representative is available in your area, arrange for a consultation so that committee members can be briefed on their duties and receive information concerning possibilities for new work.

2. *Select the geographic area and/or people group to be targeted.* Determine the general area in consultation with appropriate others. Gather data to

pinpoint specific possibilities for location and/or people group(s). From the research, make the selection for which your church will make a commitment.

3. *Prepare the church for the new work.* Develop a strong motivational climate for the new work by sharing information, discussing possibilities, and describing needs that the church will be able to meet. Inform the congregation about the location and type(s) of work that will be developed. Study ways to use gifts of the sponsoring group to energize people in the target area. Begin recruiting volunteers who can assist with surveys (both in person and by telephone), Bible studies, home visitation, worship, and fellowship activities.

4. *Cultivate the mission field.* Take a community survey to locate unchurched and unaffiliated persons of your denomination. Using resources from your denominational missions director, determine who the primary prospects are, where they are located, and possible strategies for establishing a trusting relationship with them.

Be alert to every opportunity for exposure and ministry. Choir concerts, fellowship Bible classes, home visitation, recreational projects, and tutoring classes are some possibilities.

5. *Begin a fellowship group.* This is the first step toward establishing an ongoing mission point. After relationships have been developed and some local support is apparent, the missions committee will determine the best location and target persons with whom to begin a home/office/storefront fellowship mission and/or a fellowship Bible class.

One of the laypersons could be in charge to facilitate a cooperative plan of inreach and outreach for volunteers from the sponsoring church and local participants. They would come together for fellowship, worship, Bible study, prayer, support, and planning. They would reach out into the community to identify and enlist prospects who are unchurched.

When the group is too large for one home or location, an option is to divide into two groups that can meet in different parts of the target area. When at least four such fellowship groups are functioning, a good nucleus for a congregation is underway.

Periodic rallies of the fellowship groups could be used when there are three or four groups. At first, about once a month would be adequate. Work on building fellowship, enthusiasm, and motivation for taking the message of Christ to others.

6. *Start a mission chapel.* If and when the new work is large enough and the expressed need for a central location is strong enough, begin plans for a mission chapel. You might begin with a Bible study and worship service each week at a central location, as well as continue the fellowship groups as a means of growth and community ministry.

Consider using public facilities such as a school building or community meeting hall. Other possibilities are motel conference rooms, a recreation room in someone's home, a vacant store, or even a mobile home.

Before the chapel is established, relationships with the sponsoring church must be carefully defined. Clarify finances, membership, calling of a mission pastor, and other pertinent issues. For sample guidelines, see figure 14.1, "The Church's Relation to Its Mission."

Other items to be completed before beginning include the following:

- Enlist and train leaders for the mission chapel.
- Secure location and gain approval from the church and any other agencies that may be required.
- Publicize the chapel and encourage participation at the first service.
- Mobilize fellowship groups to prepare the location and promote participation.
- Secure needed equipment and supplies. Put out a sign if permissible.

7. *Determine the financial plan for the chapel.* If not determined earlier, specific procedures should be established to handle aid from the parent church, contributions from new-work participants, and the expenditure of funds by the leaders. Financial aid should be carefully considered, with a phaseout planned from the beginning, if possible. Stewardship education should become a part of new-work activities as persons are prepared to assume the responsibilities for their future.

As the mission develops toward maturity, the election of a treasurer and the transfer of funds to the new work account(s) may be a good training step toward constituting the new church.

Another step toward self-direction comes as the new congregation considers calling a full-time pastor to replace the interim provided by the sponsoring church. The usual guideline is that a mission congregation should delay calling someone until at least 50 percent of the pastor's support can be provided from the new congregation's offerings.

8. *Develop building plans.* When the mission has sufficient strength and stability to take on this task and when their growth and ministry require it, if not already determined, the selection of a permanent location begins.

Much time should be devoted to a study of options, raising of funds, and motivation of new-work participants. A modest, attractive, and complete first unit is the goal rather than a large facility designed to hold several times the present number. Note also that in some situations rented quarters for a longer period of several years may be necessary and/or even appropriate.

9. *Constitute the church.* The missions committee of the parent church should be convinced that the mission group is fully committed to the mission of Christ's church and the responsibilities of a local church for carrying out that mission in the world.

When all concerned are sure that the mission congregation is spiritually mature and sufficiently stable to become a constituted church, a date can be set to incorporate the new church.

The preparation of a church constitution and bylaws is most important and should be done two or three months before constituting.

The constituting service is usually held in cooperation with the sponsoring church, sister churches in the area, and the appropriate denominational representative(s). An *organizing council* is usually formed of representatives invited from sister churches. This group meets before the service, examines the group's request, and recommends at the appropriate time in the service that the mission be constituted into a church. A sample outline of such a service, a format for a church constitution and bylaws, and an example of a church covenant appear at the end of this chapter (see figures 14.2 through 14.5).

Working for Effectiveness

The emphasis on church growth has naturally reminded most people of numerical growth. Numerical growth is important; however, effectiveness is more important. Resources abound to help you determine what makes an effective church. The new work should especially pay attention to the research and to the findings to aid the overall health of its existence. New churches can instill principles of effectiveness perhaps more easily than can older congregations. Generally, the distilled wisdom includes the following factors in ensuring effectiveness:

- A set of biblically based values, with a specific mission vision congruent with those values
- An intentionally adequate ministry of pastoral care
- A leadership team that serves to guide the church after the pattern of Jesus Christ and free the member-ministers to fulfill their ministry calling
- Both small and large-group opportunities for worship and study in which God is glorified and human needs are addressed
- Adequate opportunities and encouragement for the members to express their ministries in Jesus' name
- Adequate meeting place with as much parking as possible
- Financial support

The new congregation, and particularly the pastoral team, would do well to study relevant materials on beginning and sustaining ministry for effectiveness. Resources on change are essential, for example.

Intentional ministry will certainly mark an effective new church. The new congregation will understand what it is supposed to do and how it will go about being the people of God who fulfill the divine purpose. As a Christian community, the group will be careful that all its activities contribute to the primary focus of the church. The effective congregation will operate through a planning process that includes goals and ministry plans to reach those goals. These should be evaluated in terms of its overall purpose as reflected in the New Testament.

Winning and discipling new members hold priority in the church's efforts to stay on course during its early years. Effective assimilation of new members into the congregation deserves priority as well. This allows the church to be one in which all members have a part and a stake in its God-blessed success.

The church should develop a clear image of itself. If that happens, the church will know what it is about, and each member will be better able to express and support that picture. The effective church should work to have the strength to face the future in which surprise, excitement, and expectation can be incorporated into its life. The past should only be prologue.

Figure 14.1

THE CHURCH'S RELATION TO ITS MISSION

It is important that a good relationship be maintained between the church and its offspring. This does not just happen: it must be worked for; the lines of communication must always be open.

Communications between the church and the mission will be easier and more effective if they are carried on through the church missions committee representing the whole church and a group, preferably the mission's steering committee. Thus, better understandings will be developed before matters are communicated to the congregations of the church and the mission. Each will receive its communications through its own representatives who can present them in the light of the viewpoints of its people.

In reality, the mission is the church. It is simply the church meeting in a different place or satisfying a special need; it is the church extended.

1. Relationship

An understanding of the relationship between the church and its mission can be stated in an agreement or bylaws.
1. The mission and the church should agree on the pastor of the mission.
2. The mission pastor should be a member of the sponsoring church.
3. Guest speakers for special emphases should be agreed on by the mission pastor and by the pastor of the sponsoring church.

2. Church Membership

All persons who qualify for church membership should be urged to join the sponsoring church. Mission members can be received:
1. *By baptism.* After profession of faith and request for baptism at a mission service, the person's name will be submitted to the sponsoring church for vote. Someone authorized by the church administers baptism.
2. *By letter.* After a request for membership at a mission service, the person's name will be given to the church for vote and for obtaining the church letter.

3. *By statement.* After a request to be accepted by statement at a mission service, the person's name and statement will be presented to the church.

3. Business

The mission meets for business only to recommend items of business to the sponsoring church for its consideration. All items shall be offered as required prior to a regularly scheduled business meeting. (Items that are considered emergencies may be presented anytime.)

1. A written report of the mission should be made to the sponsoring church at the monthly business meeting. The report is to be presented by the church missions committee.
2. The church missions committee and the mission nominate teachers and other leaders to the church for approval.
3. Baptism and the Lord's Supper should be observed according to plans approved by the sponsoring church.
4. The mission should give complaints and correspondence to the church missions committee.

4. Tithes and Offerings

1. All tithes and offerings from the mission shall be kept in a separate fund and handled according to the plan designated by the sponsoring church. The use of the mission fund shall be subject to the approval of the church. The mission fund shall be used for the mission. When the mission is constituted into a church, all funds become the property of the new church.
2. The mission congregation is urged both to give proportionately and regularly through the mission program of its denomination.
3. The mission should consider other opportunities for outreach ministries that fall within its focus and goals.
4. Checks shall be signed and bills paid by the one authorized and in the way designated by the church. All checks written and all bills paid shall be reported and approved by the sponsoring church's guidelines.
5. The mission should use curriculum materials appropriate to its needs and with the approval of the sponsoring church.
6. When both the sponsoring church and the mission feel that the mission is strong enough to organize into a biblically based church, they should express this desire to the church missions committee. After prayer and deliberation the missions committee should present their recommendation to the church for action. If approved, plans should be made for the organizational service.
7. The sponsoring church should do all it can for the mission to enable it to remain focused. Prayer for the mission is essential. The mission should pray for, love, respect, and cooperate with the church for the mutual blessings of both.

5. Property

Property owned by the sponsoring church may be sold or transferred at the discretion of the church. It is suggested that when a mission is ready to constitute as a church, that deeds be in order so that property may be transferred without delay.

Figure 14.2

CONSTITUTING A NEW CHURCH

1. How to Constitute

A church missions committee, after counsel with the pastor of the sponsoring church and with the mission, recommends to the sponsoring church that the mission should be constituted into a church.

The mission and sponsoring church should involve other like-minded churches when the mission is ready to be constituted. Plans should include the following:

A. Set date to constitute.

B. Inform and seek assistance from denominational entities such as associational missions committees, the office of the director of associational missions or the area minister (or the equivalent in your denomination).

C. Invite neighboring churches to send representatives to form a council. Invite the state director of missions or some other denominational representative.

D. Form a council at the meeting to constitute the mission into a church by choosing a moderator and clerk. This meeting can be held before the mass meeting.

E. Council hears reasons for the church being constituted.

2. Service of Constitution

(1) Devotional
Hymn: "The Church's One Foundation"
Scripture: Matt 16:18–19; Acts 2:41–42; 1 Cor 12:27; Eph 4:11–13; Col 1:18
Prayer

(2) The report of the council. The council recommends proceeding with the constituting of the mission into a full-fledged church.

(3) Recommendation from the sponsoring church is read and approved by the mission congregation. The adoption of this recommendation formally constitutes the new church (see figure 14.3).

(4) Election of the officers and committees of the new church.
   a. The moderator of the council may serve as temporary moderator for the further proceedings.
   b. That person should at this time hear the report of the previously appointed nominating committee. The names of church officers and committees may be presented for election.
   c. A pastor should be called according to the plan previously adopted.

(5) If it is advisable to give the new church title to the church property, the transfer should be presented.

(6) Incorporation is desirable and should be acted on at this time.

(7) If the new church desires a constitution and bylaws, a committee should be appointed to draft them (see figure 14.4 for a worksheet).

(8) Worship service.
Hymn: "To God Be the Glory"
Offering
Sermon *(The message should include a charge to the pastor and the people. The universal scope and cooperative privileges should be emphasized.)*
Invitation for charter members

Reception of charter members
Benediction
Charter members are greeted and commended on their new beginning by members of the council and visitors.

NOTE: A new church may want to petition an association of churches to be included in its fellowship. Some such associations provide petitioner letters for such action. Proper preparation and service for the constituting of a new church can mean much to the new fellowship in its getting a good start and in its future ministry.

Figure 14.3

RECOMMENDATION FOR CONSTITUTION

(NOTE: The *sponsoring* church submits for adoption by the new church a recommendation prepared in advance. The following format will serve as a guide.)

Whereas we believe that there is a need for a church in this community, and
Whereas we believe we have found God's divine guidance after prayer, and
Whereas we have consulted with fellow Christians and neighboring churches, and,
Whereas we have called a council to consider this matter and the council has recommended we proceed with the constituting of the new church;
Be it therefore resolved that we do now enter upon the organization of a new church under the direction of the council composed of these members representing these churches:

Council Members   Church Represented

_____

_____

_____

_____

_____

_____

Be it further resolved that we adopt this as our church covenant:

(The covenant should be inserted here.)

Be it further resolved that we adopt the following articles of faith:

(to be inserted)

Be it further resolved that our name shall be the:

(to be inserted)

Be it further resolved that all charter members sign these resolutions and that this document be preserved with the official church records.

Be it further resolved that this church cooperate with these denominational bodies:

(to be inserted)

Be it further resolved that our gratitude is hereby expressed to the sponsoring church and to God for divine guidance.

Witnesses on this date:

(Leave space here for signatures of charter members.)

Figure 14.4

SAMPLE FORMAT FOR CONSTITUTION AND BYLAWS

Constitution

(A constitution reflects the basic truths and accepted patterns of interaction among members of an organization. Write and insert statements about each item.)

1. Preamble

"We declare and establish this constitution to preserve and secure the principles of our faith, and to govern the body in an orderly manner. This constitution will. . . ."

(insert information)

2. Name

"This body shall be known as the _____Church located at _____
_____."

3. Purpose/Objectives

(insert statement of purpose)

4. Statement of Faith

(insert statement of faith)

5. Polity and Relationships

(insert statement of governance and affiliations)

Bylaws

(Bylaws are written guidelines agreed upon by members to direct the activity of the organization. Such statements focus on procedures to be followed and, as such, are more susceptible to modification as needs change than are statements in the constitution. Bylaws are designed to assist the organization in fulfilling its purpose. Items often included are statements regarding each of the following, which should be prepared and added to the document.)

1 *Membership*
2. *Organizational structures/programs of work*
3. *Officers*
4. *Committees*
5. *Meetings/special observances*
6. *Finances/organization operations manual*
7. *Amendments (how to make changes in the constitution and bylaws)*

Figure 14.5

CHURCH COVENANT

Since we have committed ourselves to Jesus Christ and have experienced the acceptance, forgiveness, and redemption of God our Creator, we covenant together as members of this church that with God's help through the guiding presence of the Holy Spirit:

We will walk together in Christian love.

We will show loving care for one another and encourage, counsel, and admonish one another.

We will assemble faithfully for worship and fellowship and will pray earnestly for others as well as for ourselves.

We will endeavor to bring up those under our care "in the nurture and admonition of the Lord."

We will seek, by Christian example and personal effort, to win others to Christ and to encourage their growth toward Christian maturity.

We will share one another's joys and endeavor to bear one another's burdens and sorrows.

We will oppose all conduct that compromises our Christian faith and will uphold high standards of Christian morality.

We will prove the reality of our conversion by living godly, fruitful lives.

We will maintain a faithful ministry of worship, witness, education, fellowship, and service.

We will be faithful stewards of our resources and abilities in sharing the gospel with people of all nations.

As a result of this covenant relationship, we will seek earnestly to live to the glory of God who brought us out of darkness into marvelous light.

(Church Covenant of Immanuel Baptist Church, Nashville, Tennessee)

Chapter 15

COOPERATIVE RELATIONSHIPS

Bruce P. Powers

Churches are not independent bodies. They always function in an environment of mutual support and shared ministry, with primary emphasis on faithfulness to Christ's mission. A church may be related formally to other Christian bodies, as in an association, convention, district, or fellowship, or it may choose to function as an independent unit among Christian churches. Regardless, the commission of Christ requires that all congregations develop the best means possible to function effectively as the people of God and the body of Christ.

Church Polity and Organization

Your church and denomination have a way of working together. The organization you have and the procedures you follow are called *denominational polity*. Polity is a statement of principles and guidelines that determine a Christian institution's form of government and procedures for working together. The same New Testament principles that guide local church government apply as far as possible to the practice of denominational government.

Whether rigid or flexible, clearly defined or vague, there is an expected way of working together for the common good. To the degree that you understand and support these expectations you can guide your congregation in contributing to and drawing from the larger resources God has entrusted to you in support of the church's worldwide mission.

Most major denominations have a basic sourcebook that explains the how and why of church and denominational polity. Such books are used as resources for church leaders and as educational aids for church members. The purpose is to make Christians full participants in church and

253

denominational activities, thereby contributing to order, effectiveness, and harmony.

It is imperative that church leaders grasp the principles by which their denomination functions. In the absence of clarity about purpose, relationships, and procedures, a church inevitably finds itself divided—either within its own house or in opposition to sister churches.

Stewardship of Resources

Effective Christian service depends on a sharing of resources. By combining spiritual and material gifts from God, churches can extend and enrich their witness in ways not possible for a single congregation. For example, most churches cannot publish their own Sunday school materials, provide homes for children or the elderly, establish a college or theological school, provide salary assistance for hundreds of ministers in pioneer missions areas, or send missionaries around the world in an orderly and systematic way.

But, by combining resources, churches can band together in enterprises that would be impossible alone. The people of God and the body of Christ become a reality as we bring ourselves together in an overall purpose and plan.

At the same time, all bodies do not possess the same resources. Consequently, congregations with larger financial resources must contribute a greater share while those less able will give less. And church missions and new congregations that are needy will be assisted by others—for giving and receiving are both part of the stewardship of resources.

How Does This Work?

Most churches follow a plan whereby local resources are shared among the home congregation and the various needs supported by the denominational group(s) with which a church is affiliated. For example, a large portion of church contributions will go toward costs incurred by the local congregation in its activities of worship, education, ministry, and proclamation.

A smaller portion will then be designated to denominational and other church-approved causes beyond the local church. The usual practice is to determine an appropriate percentage of contributions that will go to each denominational group. Then this amount will be deducted periodically from contributions and sent to the designated body. Thus a church supports its own life as well as contributing to the larger mission of the church regionally and throughout the world.

The ways in which decisions are made about channeling contributions to various causes varies widely from denomination to denomination and even among churches.

A denomination in which each church decides for itself what shall be contributed is greatly dependent on an accurate understanding of and commitment to denominational causes. Churches in such situations may give or not give or adjust the amount of their contributions depending on local sentiment regarding denominational activities.

Nevertheless, among denominations that depend on voluntary cooperation, there is a general expectation that at least 10 percent of local contributions will be sent to state/regional and national bodies. An additional 2 to 4 percent will be given to local causes through an association or other organization representing local churches. These contributions are intended for the use of the larger bodies according to the polity of the denomination.

Some denominations assign a share of the cost of cooperative activities to individual congregations. Church leaders then work out a budget that will enable the local group to meet its own needs as well as contribute its proportionate share to the common work.

Benefits of Cooperation

When churches work together, they combine their resources and channel their individual efforts into a united, systematic plan to propagate the gospel regionally, nationally, and throughout the world. Such organized efforts provide practical and efficient ways to conduct a worldwide Christian enterprise on behalf of individual churches.

At the *local/associational/district* level, cooperation enables churches to be involved in these and other activities:

- Starting new churches and mission points
- Sharing Christian fellowship
- Supporting one another in times of need
- Approving persons for ordination to the gospel ministry
- Determining criteria related to denominational recognition
- Assisting one another with leadership training for volunteer workers in church programs

At the *state/regional* level, churches have opportunity to extend the functions of education, proclamation, and Christian service throughout a region. Such activities provide services to participating churches as well as an outreach ministry to unchurched persons. Depending on the availability of resources, state or regional groups might be involved in these activities:

- Developing and promoting methods and resources to assist local churches

- Developing and leading churches in statewide ministry and outreach projects
- Providing leadership training for volunteer church leaders
- Promoting and participating in regional and global mission projects
- Receiving and distributing cooperative offerings from participating churches
- Assisting associations of churches in their work
- Publishing a newspaper to inform church members and to promote denominational causes
- Operating Christian universities, colleges, and schools
- Operating benevolent enterprises such as hospitals and homes for children and the aged
- Operating camps, assemblies, and conference centers

At the *national* level major emphasis is placed on achieving an overall structure and design for the services and ministries required by affiliated churches across the nation. Such activities may be developed and coordinated in one location, or they may be administered from a variety of locations. Regardless of the arrangement, the polity of the body determines policy and organization and tells exactly how decisions are made concerning denominational causes. This information is detailed in the constitution and bylaws of the body.

Activities of a national body might include these items:

- Developing and publishing curriculum materials
- Developing and promoting financial plans to assist churches
- Operating national conference centers
- Providing theological education for ministers
- Administering home mission activities
- Administering foreign mission activities
- Developing and promoting leadership training programs
- Publishing and distributing through public means information related to the emphases and work of the national body

Looking to the Future

The future for Christian work is bright as long as cooperation is acknowledged as a basic New Testament principle. Together churches can more nearly be the body of Christ on mission to the world. James L. Sullivan, who was an astute observer of denominational relationships during the last century, suggested there is no option for a local church. It is the lordship of Christ over the church and its mission to the world that is of utmost importance.

"Even as churches defend their autonomy—their right to self-government—they ought also to defend theonomy, God's authority over them.

A local church cannot remain fully Christian if it stays local in concept and action," said Sullivan. A church must have a burden for the whole world. There must be a delicate balance in which there can be freedom of action and at the same time cooperation in the fulfillment of the Christian mission.[1]

Section Three

HOW A MINISTER DEVELOPS LEADERSHIP AND MINISTRY SKILLS

Chapter 16

EQUIPPING THE SAINTS TO SERVE

Judy J. Stamey

Every believer is gifted to serve God. Every believer is expected to serve God. Every believer must be given opportunities to serve God. Understanding these ideas helps a church begin to develop a theology of service for its members. Throughout the Bible are instructions and challenges to every believer to become a servant. Jesus, using a life of servanthood to show followers what is expected, taught: "But whoever wishes to become great among you shall be your servant, and whoever wishes to be first among you shall be your slave; just as the Son of Man did not come to be served, but to serve, and to give His life a ransom for many" (Matt 20:26–28 NASB).

In another context Jesus provided an example of servanthood that surprised the disciples. Before the Passover Feast, Jesus took a basin and began washing their feet and explained: "I have set you an example that you should do as I have done for you. I tell you the truth, no servant is greater than his master, nor is a messenger greater than the one who sent him. Now that you know these things, you will be blessed if you do them" (John 13:15–17 NIV). Although serving Jesus comes with a promise of blessings, it is important for the believer to understand that serving should be the outward action of a grateful heart. Salvation is God's gift and cannot be earned by good works; however, good works should be a natural expression of Christian discipleship and a witness to God's love.

Developing a Theology of Service

A believer's theology of service must begin with understanding the essentials in the life of Jesus and the love that motivated him to a life of service, leading eventually to the cross. When this understanding is clear, believers can live a full and meaningful Christian life that will reflect the

261

lordship of Jesus and inspire others to seek to know how Jesus can change their lives.

A church leader's theology of service should include a strong desire to help new believers experience growth in and understanding of their commitment that will lead to a life of service motivated by their love for God. Ephesians 4:12 (NASB) clearly communicates the responsibility of "equipping the saints for the work of service, to the building up of the body of Christ."

Too often churches see themselves as nonprofit organizations that depend upon a core group of volunteers to accomplish their goals. However, a church has much greater potential than any other organization because God has said that every follower is gifted and has a responsibility to serve. If the church truly believes this, a great deal of energy must be spent in helping individuals discover and develop their gifts that can be used in Christian service.

Church leaders must decide that their job is not to motivate lay members to serve but rather to help them grow in understanding why they must serve and the joy that comes from serving. The theology of servanthood is clearly defined in Ephesians 2:10 (NASB) when Paul says, "We are His workmanship, created in Christ Jesus for good works." In James 1:22 (NASB), the challenge is for believers to prove themselves as "doers of the word, and not merely hearers"; and in 2:14: "If someone says he has faith but he has no works . . . can that faith save him?" Church staff members often become so excited about sharing the gift of salvation that they fail to communicate that work and service are expected and natural responses for every believer.

Helping someone to make the decision to follow Jesus is probably the most rewarding experience a believer can have. Closely related, however, is helping a new believer to understand that serving God is an expression of thanksgiving for the gift of salvation. Never forget that leading people to Christ also includes teaching about discipleship and helping them to find a place of service. The joy of the Christian life begins with salvation and finds expression in service, thus a theology of service can be defined as love for God in action.

Discovering Spiritual Gifts Is Essential to Service

The Holy Spirit endows the members of Christ's body with the gifts required for healthy life and service in the world.

The Bible clearly says that God has given gifts to each. First Peter 4:10 (NASB) says, "As each one has received a special gift, employ it in serving one another as good stewards of the manifold grace of God." Ephesians 4:16 (NASB) says, "The whole body, being fitted and held together by that which every joint supplies, according to the proper working of each individual part, causes the growth of the body for the building up of itself in love." Other passages in 1 Cor 12:4–7 describe varied gifts and how they all are given to manifest the spirit for the common good; in 1 Cor 1:6–7

(NASB) there is assurance that "the testimony concerning Christ was confirmed in you, so that you are not lacking in any gift, awaiting eagerly the revelation of our Lord Jesus Christ."

The church is blessed because God has given every believer a gift that can be used to help the church to be healthy and accomplish its mission. It is God's plan that everyone should become a volunteer—a servant. Therefore, it is vital that church leaders seek to provide opportunities for the membership to discover the gifts with which God has so richly blessed them. In most churches this would need to be an ongoing activity that invites members and new members to participate and experience the joy of discovering where they are best able to contribute to the life and work of the church.

Many resources available in Christian bookstores address spiritual gifts. Some are designed for groups while others are designed for a one-on-one teaching and discovery time. Resources have been designed to help church leaders do a better job and to lead a congregation to actualize its mission by putting a greater emphasis on helping every member to find a place of service.[1]

Another way to build awareness is occasionally to provide devotions or have testimonies at church meetings about the gifts that God has given to us and how the church can provide each of us a place to use those gifts. Leaders can also encourage members to complete an interest survey that has been designed to point members to service possibilities in the church. A sample Service Interest Form is shown in figure 16.1.

A church leader must continue to dream of serving a church where every member senses a call to use his or her gifts to serve the Lord and build up the body of Christ. This dream may never become a reality, but church leaders must never lose sight of the accountability for being faithful to provide opportunities for every believer to discover gifts and use them in service.

Establishing Qualifications for Service

How do you know that a person is right for the job? The only measuring stick for knowing this is the list of qualifications that the church has endorsed and clearly expects from every person who serves. The following qualifications are examples of what a church may expect from people who serve the church.

Relationship to God and the Church

This is probably the most significant qualification for enlisting someone to serve in the church. When a person works because he or she wants to serve and please the Lord, that person will be much more effective than one who serves just to receive personal satisfaction or to fill an ego need. This means that the person in charge of enlisting will need to spend adequate time with potential volunteers to learn about their desires and commitment level. This qualification often requires more time than one is willing to give. But if patience is exercised and we allow God to give an affirmation that this person is right for the job, the results will provide greater success and longer tenure among workers.

It is important to remember that when someone says, "I am called" to do a job, the one in charge of enlisting also needs to believe that the volunteer is called to do the job. Sometimes the wrong people are enlisted because those enlisting fail to spend enough time discovering what is *motivating* people to volunteer.

Questions to ask. What does their life say to the church? Are they faithful in attendance in the programs of the church? Are they faithful in worship attendance? Do they contribute to the financial support of the church? How long have they been members of the church? These are only a few questions that can help the leader determine if persons have the foundation needed to do a particular job.

Good Reputation

Many times people will say, using Scripture, "By their fruits you shall know them!" when they are trying to point out that a person says one thing and does another. The Bible does teach that we are known by our fruits, and it is the fruits we bear that create a person's reputation. Many times a person will not be able to serve in certain positions until the reputation problems have been resolved.

First Timothy 3 emphasizes that one who serves should be a person "above reproach." This is just another way of saying the person's reputation should be as good on the inside of the church as on the outside. You can trust this person explicitly.

Cooperative Attitude and Team Player

This qualification means that a person has the ability to relate to and work well with others. When a woman tells you that she would rather work alone, this may be a red flag to mean that this person does not work well on a team. If this is the case, you would need to evaluate how important it is for the person in this position to be a team player and to cooperate with a group of fellow workers. Attitudes are often difficult to change; therefore, it is important before enlisting a person to know the feelings related to authority, schedules, and evaluations.

Team spirit is vital in most areas of service, which means that members must become interdependent and share the overall success of the work. When team members are committed to the idea that working together is important, more effective decisions will be made. When persons work together on a team, no one is left out. Everyone is there to share the victory or the loss. Support is felt because all are members of a team.

A Willing Learner

Every position requires training. Recruitment is not the end but the beginning. The volunteer must understand how each position fits into the overall purpose of the church. The provision of training may involve many approaches, and the potential worker needs to be made aware of the expectations of the church.

When these qualifications are used as a guideline to understanding an individual, you will have a much keener awareness of whether this is a person who could serve with you as an effective volunteer. In some cases you may see potential in persons but feel that they need to be involved in additional discipleship training, such as doctrinal or denominational studies. It is important that you work with them to provide the necessary attention and training for future positions of service. Members can also be encouraged to serve as apprentices in areas where they are interested in working.

Other qualifications may need to be developed as they relate directly to the job being considered: Is there a minimum age for serving in the preschool area? Does a person need experience to do this job? Can a husband and wife work in the same department? These and other qualifications may need to be discussed before beginning the enlistment process.

Enlisting for Service

Enlistment procedures vary from church to church; therefore it is important to know how people are enlisted in each organization. The most important question to ask is, "What guidelines are used to consider who is qualified to serve?" The answer to this question may lead to a training session to formulate guidelines that will aid the church in enlisting the right persons in all areas of service. The main principle is this: *When a person is properly enlisted, performance will be at a much higher level.* Another benefit from proper enlistment is that the person will most likely take personal pride in doing a good job.

Proper enlistment begins with the person doing the enlisting. This person must understand the need for the position, the goals, the tasks, and how the job is to be evaluated. The leader will then be ready to make an appointment with the person being considered to discuss the position.

It is important that this be a face-to-face meeting in a place where there will be little or no interruptions. The setting for the interview is important. The first part of the meeting should focus on the service opportunity that is available. The leader's attitude should convey to the person that the position is important and that it contributes to the ongoing work of the church.

During the course of the discussion, the leader should go over the *job description*, pointing out the specific assignments and how one is evaluated. Every service opportunity must include a written job description that can be given to the individual being considered.

If you do not have job descriptions for all volunteer positions, it would be wise to prepare them before contacting any new workers. (See figure 16.2 for a worksheet.) When positions are the same, as on committees, the same job description can be used for all members. The important part of writing a job description is to tailor it to meet the requirements of your church. Samples of what other churches use can assist in the writing, but your church's job descriptions should reflect what your church expects. This will help members understand the job being considered and the helps that are available to assist volunteers in achieving the assigned tasks.

It is not unusual for persons to turn down a position after a quick look at the job description. They recognize immediately that they will not be able to perform the tasks in an acceptable manner. The person enlisting should respond with appreciation for considering the position and feel blessed that someone did not take a job without the desire and/or skill to do it.

If someone being interviewed appears hesitant when reviewing the expectations in the job description, it would be appropriate to ask, "Do you believe that you would be able to give the time and effort needed to do the tasks listed on the job description?" If the answer is positive, you will be able to continue the interview process. If it is negative or "I don't know," it may be best to thank the person for his or her time and encourage the person to let you know if interest develops later.

If both parties feel positive at this point, continue the interview by discussing expectations related to training. The leader needs to explain what has been planned for the year and how important it is for the volunteer to be involved. There needs to be an agreement from the potential worker that participation in these planned training activities will be a priority.

Training may include explaining to those who serve in the preschool, children, youth, and special education departments that the church requires all workers in these areas to read a set of guidelines adopted by the church and sign an agreement to observe the safeguards listed. These guidelines are in addition to the job descriptions reviewed earlier.

In light of new employment laws regarding background checks for persons who work with babies through eighteen years of age, many churches are implementing the same requirements for all volunteers who work in these age groups. This information should be included as one of the safeguards and, also, as a significant part of the enlisting process.

Even though asking a worker to sign an agreement to observe guidelines may not be required by law, a church would be wise to consider such as part of the training process since many child-abuse cases are being reported in schools, day care ministries, and churches. The sample set of guidelines in figure 16.3 may be adapted and used by your church.

Following the job-description review and discussion, and the completion of agreement forms, the next important part of the interview is the presentation of the available resources. It is important to point out required resources, such as a curriculum that must be used in a teaching program of the church. The leader must not assume that the one being enlisted knows these special requirements. Other resources that must be reviewed are budget allocations, budget procedures, room assignments, and supplies. These items are important because they enable the worker to do a much better job.

Providing Training for Those Who Serve

Every worker must be given an opportunity to learn how service in a position contributes to the work of the church. When one has been trained to understand the importance of the job and has committed to it, the specific tasks will make much better sense. A well-planned training program can reduce conflict and misunderstandings in the organization.

The purpose of training is to help the person succeed. Each position will dictate what should be required to accomplish this. Training may range from a brief orientation to involvement in many training events throughout the year. The important thing is to decide what you need to provide to keep the worker focused, motivated, and productive.

Leaders must think of training as an ongoing responsibility that begins when the person agrees to do the job. This means giving new workers an opportunity to talk about the specific tasks on the job description and how they intend to accomplish them. Ask them if they have any questions about expectations, scheduling, deadlines, or any other matters that tell you how they plan to begin the new assignment.

Listen carefully to what newly enlisted workers are saying. If you hear comments about their intentions to do something differently from what has been done before, it is important that you affirm their intended changes or guide them back to the current practice, explaining why the job is done a particular way. This informal aspect of training helps the worker to understand that while there is freedom to do a job, there is also responsibility to discuss possible changes.

Formal training is also important and should be planned well in advance of the enlistment time. This gives the leader an opportunity to discuss what is being planned and how it will help workers do a better job. It is important that people know ahead of time what training is expected so their commitment to the job includes a commitment to training.

The schedule of training must also fit people's needs. Whether it is set for a weeknight, a Sunday afternoon, or a weekend should be determined by what time is best for the workers.

Every training tool a leader provides should be thoroughly examined and evaluated before asking a worker to invest time in it. Too often people have attended a conference, watched a video, or read a book that was supposed to help them do a better job, and felt that the activity was a complete waste of time. When this occurs, workers quickly develop the attitude that training is not important. One bad experience for workers will require a lot of encouragement from the leader for them to be motivated to participate in future training events.

Leaders have many tools available to train workers in their specific areas of service such as those listed in figure 16.4. Again the key to selecting the best training tools is to determine how they will make a contribution to each person's job. With more options than ever, you should choose the training tools that you know can be used most effectively in your church. The leader is responsible to select the tools that will effectively train workers and also make them feel that the time invested was worthwhile.

Evaluating Workers

When a person accepts a position of service, the leader's responsibility increases. The leader is called to equip workers to become effective and enjoy their contribution of service. When a worker fails to serve in an acceptable manner, the leader may also feel a sense of failure. Before the worker can be evaluated, the leader's role must be evaluated. A leader can expect a favorable worker evaluation if the answers to the following questions can be answered in a positive manner:

1. *Was the worker properly enlisted?* This includes meeting personally with the worker, discussing job-description requirements, and clarifying expectations about training opportunities and accountability. And don't overlook the importance of praying together.

2. *Is the job description current?* Can a person understand what is expected and how to do it in an acceptable manner? Job descriptions should be reviewed annually, making changes or deletions, to assure the worker of a reliable guide.

3. *Have training opportunities been provided throughout the year?* Were the commitments met that were discussed in the enlistment interview? Many times problems of performance arise because of failure to provide adequate training.

4. *Have regular follow-up meetings been provided for the worker and leader?* Time for meeting together is vital to developing workers. These meetings reflect the accountability relationship that was discussed in the enlistment time.

If the leader feels that certain areas of weakness are related to any of these areas, you should discuss them with the worker in order to decide what corrections can and will be made. Many times workers do a good job regardless of how well the leader enlisted them; however, when a worker's performance is poor because the leader did not do a good job of enlisting, these issues should be discussed thoroughly before a worker is allowed to resign.

A worker evaluation provides a time to discuss the assigned tasks, how well the worker is accomplishing the tasks, and what improvements can be made. The written job description should be used as a guide for discussion and evaluation. It gives the worker and leader an opportunity to work out and agree upon goals for improvement. If tasks need to be modified, deleted, or added, this is a perfect time to make the changes. An evaluation helps the worker know how important the job is in relationship to the work of the whole church. It also is a time for the leader to express appreciation for specific things that the worker has done exceptionally well. The leader should always conclude the meeting with words of encouragement and prayer.

Occasionally a leader enlists someone who does not do the job he or she was enlisted to do. This is disappointing for the leader and many times creates problems because the work needs to be done. The leader must address this question: *Is replacement worth the cost?*

Answering this question will depend on the leader's experience during the evaluation. Did the worker express hostility, complacency, or a negative attitude? If this person is terminated, how much will it hinder the work of the church? Do you sense that replacing this person will damage the person's spiritual development? How many people will be affected? Will the person leave the church?

If the leader believes that replacing this person will have a long-lasting negative response, it may be more beneficial to wait until the next time the church nominates and elects people to serve in various positions. If this approach is not possible, the leader may have to decide that it is best to ask for the person's resignation. When a person for some reason—such as stubbornness—refuses to resign, your only option may be to begin the steps of termination. This is probably one of the most difficult tasks for a leader. Use these steps if termination is necessary.

Step 1: Prepare for a meeting with the individual. Prayer is vital. It will give the leader strength to do what must be done and, hopefully, give understanding to the one who must be terminated. In addition to prayer, the leader must write down specific reasons and dates that indicate poor performance. The meeting will be very weak without proper documentation.

Step 2: Inform the pastor and proper screening committee. Every case will be unique. The leader will need to decide if the pastor or a member of the screening committee should be present when the worker is confronted about the problems. In either case it is very important to make these people aware of the situation. Occasionally the worker will become upset and feel a need to go to the pastor or the proper committee. If they are aware of the problems and are supportive of what you have done, then they will support and affirm your decision.

Step 3: Arrange to meet in a place of few or no interruptions. The environment is important for a meeting of this nature. In most cases it would probably be best to meet at the church in an office or conference room. A controlled environment helps prevent possible embarrassment that you or the person might experience if interrupted by others.

Step 4: Clear your mind about what is to take place. Face-to-face encounters like this are the most difficult and require the leader to be prepared to address the problem directly. Begin the session by stating the purpose—to discuss the contribution of the worker. A time of prayer will be helpful as the leader and worker ask God to guide them in this meeting to enhance the work of the Lord and of the church. The leader is then ready to present to the worker the problems that have been documented. It is important to allow the worker to respond to each one as it is presented.

The leader should listen well in order to respond in a caring way. If the individual gets offtrack by discussing the work of others or another unrelated issue, quickly move the discussion back to the issue at hand. The task of terminating the worker has not changed. Be sure to affirm the worker by pointing out the positive qualities that you believe will lead to a better and happier place of service.

If the worker does not resign, be prepared to indicate that the committee or council in charge feels that it will be best for the organization to terminate the worker from the position of service. Explain that this decision was made after much prayer and evaluation, and they, along with you, feel that it is best for the individual and the church.

Conclude by thanking the person for meeting with you and then, if appropriate, pray again. If the person has potential in another area of work, you could suggest the possibility of seeking God's leadership about other opportunities for service.

Step 5: After the meeting, check on the individual periodically. Only in caring genuinely for people can we effectively terminate an individual who is not doing the job. This kind of respect for people will enable the leader to continue building a relationship that helps the person discover and commit to another place of service. The spiritual challenge for the leader is to follow the example of Jesus, who never gave up on people.

There are no easy answers to dealing with ineffective workers. Because equipping believers to grow spiritually and serve the Lord is at the heart of our calling, terminating someone is probably the most difficult duty we face. The task will not be easy and hopefully will rarely be necessary. However, leaders must always stay focused on the understanding that God will provide the strength, wisdom, and courage required to do what is best for an individual and for the church.

Supporting Those Who Serve

Support means:

- Someone cares.
- Someone is there to help you when the going gets tough.

- Someone is praying for you.
- Someone appreciates your contribution to the church and the Lord's work.

Support strengths and encourages those who are trying to do their very best to serve. When or if support is neglected, those serving may feel that their contribution is being taken for granted. The only way to avoid this is for every leader to make the responsibility of affirming as much a part of his or her job as enlisting, training, and evaluating.

Support from the leader does more than give recognition. It affirms that the job is important; it offers motivation to the worker to continue to do a good job. Most of all, it helps the worker to know that the work and the workers are appreciated.

Support means having a listening ear. Workers must be given the opportunity to talk about their work and discuss the various concerns related to their jobs. The leader must develop sensitivity to knowing when this is a need for a worker. Often, when a worker is talking, there is an underlying need to hear how the leader feels things are going.

Support means taking the time to affirm those who serve. There are many ways to do this. Figures 16.5 and 16.6 give ways a leader may affirm and guide the work of others. It is important to choose ways of affirmation that will be most meaningful to the individual. A leader who is a strong advocate for and supporter of workers is usually one who is also appreciated; people feel good about being on the same team.

Support means the leader prays for and with workers. It is so important for every person to know that the work he or she is doing is for the glory of the Lord and that prayer is essential to doing an effective job.

Support from the leader is vital, but the leader should never neglect to remind workers that they are a team and that their ultimate goal is to serve God in such a manner that someday they will hear the words from Matthew 25:21 (RSV): "Well done, good and faithful servant; . . . enter into the joy of your master."

Figure 16.1

SERVICE INTEREST FORM

Name _____   Please list educational experience:
Address (home) _____
Address (bus.) _____
Phone (home)_____ (bus.) _____   What kind of service would you be
                                                interested in?

Employer _____
Type of business _____
Position in company_____
Age: 17–25 ☐ 26–35 ☐ 36–55 ☐ Over 55 ☐   Hours available to serve:
Birthday _____   Monday ___   Friday ___
Marital status _____   Tuesday ___   Saturday ___
Spouse's name_____   Wednesday ___   Sunday___
Formerly served as an ___elder?___ deacon? Thursday ___

PLEASE CHECK INTERESTS/SKILLS/HOBBIES

___ Acting	___ Food Services/Cooking	___ Public Speaking
___ Animals	___ Fund-Raising	___ Puppetry
___ Artwork	___ Graphic Arts	___ Radio/Television/Film
___ Bible Studies	___ Greeter	___ Reading
___ Bridge	___ Handbells	___ Receptionist
___ Budgeting	___ Horticulture/Gardening	___ Recreation
___ Calligraphy	___ Hunting/Fishing	___ Research/Archives
___ Child Care	___ Instrumentalist	___ Scouting
___ Choir	___ Interior Design	___ Senior Citizens
___ Clowns	___ Job Placement	___ Set Design
___ Community Ministries	___ Languages:	___ Sewing
___ Computers	___ French	___ Singing
___ Construction	___ German	___ Small-Group Leader
___ Costume Design	___ Spanish	___ Song Leader
___ Counseling	___ Other_____	___ Stage Lighting
___ Crafts	___ Library	___ Statistical Analysis
___ CPR/First Aid	___ Mail-outs	___ Surveying/Polling
___ Dance	___ Mechanic	___ Telephoning
___ Education	___ Misc. Repairs	___ Tellers
___ Adult	___ Organist	___ Transportation/Driving
___ Preschool	___ Narration	___ Travel
___ Children	___ Photography	___ Tutoring
___ Youth	___ Pianist	___ Typing/Secretarial
___ Day School	___ Prayer Room	___ Ushers
___ Vacation Bible School	___ Printing/Typesetting	___ Visitation
___ Electrician	___ Prison Ministries	___ Woodworking/Carpentry
___ Exercise/Aerobics	___ Public Address Systems	___ Writing
___ Financial/Estate Planning	___ Programs for Disabled	___ Public Speaking
___ Flower Arranging	___ Public Relations	

Figure 16.2

WORK SHEET FOR JOB DESCRIPTIONS FOR VOLUNTEERS

Title of Position _____

Supervisor _____

Purpose _____

Duties

1. _____
2. _____
3. _____
4. _____

Expectations

1. _____
2. _____
3. _____
4. _____

Figure 16.3

SAMPLE GUIDELINES FOR PRESCHOOL, CHILDREN, YOUTH, AND SPECIAL EDUCATION WORKERS

Purpose

The disturbing and traumatic rise of physical and sexual abuse of children has claimed the attention of our nation and society. Unfortunately, churches that have children's programs are not insulated from this alarming trend. The following policies have been established in response to this trend and reflect our commitment to provide protective care of all preschoolers, children, youth, and special education pupils attending any sessions at the church or any church-sponsored programs or activities.

General

1. Individuals who have been convicted of either sexual or physical abuse should not volunteer to serve or seek employment in any church-sponsored activity or program for preschoolers, children, youth, or special education pupils.

2. Adult survivors of childhood sexual or physical abuse need the love and acceptance of this church family. Individuals who have such a history should discuss their desire to work with preschoolers, children, youth, or special education pupils with one of the pastoral staff before engaging in any volunteer service.

3. Volunteers in the preschool, children, youth, or special education areas are required to be members of this church and must be approved by appropriate church personnel before they may begin working directly with pupils in these areas.

4. Workers will be expected to observe the "two-person" rule. This means that when working in the preschool, children, youth, or special education areas, workers should avoid one-on-one situations with pupils.

5. All paid and volunteer workers should immediately report to the age-appropriate minister, church administrator, minister of education, or minister of music any behaviors or other incidents that seem abusive or inappropriate. The age-appropriate minister, church administrator, minister of education, or minister of music is responsible for making sure that appropriate actions are taken.

6. From time to time, opportunities for training in the prevention and recognition of the sexual abuse of children will be provided by the various ministry areas of our church. Paid and volunteer workers in these areas are expected to participate in the sessions.

7. A criminal-records check will be run on all new preschool, children, youth, and special education paid and volunteer workers. The criminal-records check may also be run on all current paid and volunteer workers in these areas. Criminal-records checks may be rerun periodically.

8. Have you ever been arrested for, charged with, under probation for, convicted of, or pleaded guilty, or no contest to (a) any sexual or physical abuse, (b) molestation, or (c) any felony crime or any action prohibited by state law (or similar code or statute in any state)?

___ Yes (Please describe on a separate sheet of paper.)
___ No

9. If you were personally a victim of child abuse, we require that you make this information known before your beginning service to the minister under whose leadership you will serve (if you prefer, you may discuss this with the pastor, minister of youth, minister of children, minister of preschool, minister of education, minister of music, or church counselor). You understand and agree that this information is being provided for the purpose of determining the suitability of those who will be allowed to work with the church's preschoolers, children, youth, or disabled. Admitting you were a victim will not automatically disqualify you from service. This information may be discussed with the pastor or one or more ministers but will be kept confidential.

I have read the above policy and agree to observe the safeguards listed.

Signature _____ Date _____

Please print name _____

Figure 16.4

CHOOSING THE BEST TRAINING TOOL

1. Meetings. Time should be well planned with a written agenda. It is important to communicate to the worker in advance the purpose of the meeting and how long it will last. Every meeting should begin on time, follow an agenda, and end on time.

2. Books. Choose books that are up-to-date and will help the person understand the role of a position and how the position enhances the work of the church. Point out specific chapters that will be most beneficial to their position.

3. Videos and Online Seminars. More and more videos and online seminars are being published for training. Check your denominational office to see what may be available to you with a small purchase or rental cost. Be sure to review it before giving it to the worker for training. You may develop a written guide for workers to use while viewing the video or doing an online study.

4. Conventions and Retreat Centers. Request conference schedules many months in advance to determine what may be available for your workers. Give the workers a copy of the schedule with your comments about what sessions would be helpful in their job. When a leader encourages workers to attend, there should be a strong feeling about what the conference has to offer to help the workers do a better job.

5. Guest Lecturers. Choose carefully. If you have not heard a person speak before, take the time to interview others who have. When you extend an invitation to a speaker, write down what you are hoping to accomplish and go over it with the person and ask if he/she feels comfortable with the challenge. Give the speaker a schedule and emphasize how important it is to honor it. People's time is valuable, and if they receive good information and the schedule is kept, they are more likely to attend future training events.

6. Observation. Many times it is better for someone to see how another person is doing the same job. The leader should choose a class or situation that best models the position of the worker and work out a period of observation for the new worker with the one being observed. An observation questionnaire for the person to complete during each session is a good tool to use for follow-up discussion between the leader and the worker.

Figure 16.5

25 WAYS TO RECOGNIZE WORKERS

1. Smile.
2. Be open to suggestions.
3. Reimburse assignment-related expenses.
4. Ask for a report.
5. Send a birthday card.
6. Recognize personal needs and problems.
7. Keep challenging workers.
8. Provide good preservice training.
9. Help develop self-confidence.
10. Take time to explain fully.
11. Enable workers to grow on the job.
12. Create pleasant surroundings.
13. Take time to talk.
14. Provide expenses for special training conferences or workshops.
15. Write thank-you notes.
16. Invite participation in formulating policies.
17. Celebrate outstanding projects and achievements.
18. Provide useful equipment in good working condition.
19. Plan social events.
20. Provide opportunities for conferences and evaluation.
21. Plan a recognition edition of the church newsletter.
22. Provide adequate orientation.
23. Be familiar with the details of assignments.
24. Say, "Thank you."
25. Greet by name.

Figure 16.6

WORKERS WILL DO BETTER WORK WHEN THEY KNOW

1. They will be given regular supervision.
2. What is expected of them.
3. To whom they are responsible.
4. They are making a contribution to the cause of Christ and their church.
5. They will be furnished the needed physical resources.
6. There will be opportunities for training.
7. There are standards for measuring performance.
8. There will be support and affirmation.

Chapter 17

STAFF RELATIONSHIPS

William G. Caldwell

Developing good staff relationships should be of primary concern when a church has several people working together in staff leadership. These relationships will involve all paid staff members to some extent. This is especially true when a team approach is taken. In addition, those who provide ministerial leadership will desire closer relationships with one another as a means of becoming more effective in their work.

Many staff members will have certain feelings about their relationships with others, whether in reference to a specific staff member or to the group as a whole. These feelings should indicate that things are good and getting better rather than bad and getting worse. However, it is necessary to work on relationships. They don't just get better by themselves. The following suggestions are provided to help staff members work on relationships.

Improving Church-Staff Relationships

A church staff may be defined as: *(1) a group of Christian persons called by God who (2) willingly agree with God, a local congregation, and one another to (3) live out their vocational calling as they (4) guide a church in its mission.* On a church staff as defined here, feelings about staff relationships become extremely important. All staff members must be committed to improving relationships.

Concepts

There are four highly significant concepts about *building relationships* among staff members:

- Relationship building is a mandatory activity.

- It is a continuing activity.
- It is to be done with God, with a church, and with other staff members.
- It involves shared responsibility and shared authority.

Each of these concepts also has a significant corollary for all staff members:

- It should be both encouraged and engaged in by all.
- It should begin during one's prestaff experiences and continue throughout one's time in a position.
- It should encompass all three parties—God, church, other staff members.
- It should include both dimensions—responsibility and authority.

The choice is not whether to have relationships. The choice is what kind of relationships we will have!

Commitments

Commitment on the part of all staff members helps good relationships develop. It is imperative, at the beginning of their work together, that staff members are clear about their working relationships with one another and their agreements with the church about their work. If staff members do not work at the task of clearly defining their commitments and expectations with one another and the church, then significant misunderstandings, conflicts, and unhappiness will develop.

Developing Expectations

Staff ministers quickly become aware that the expectations held by church members, other staff members, and they themselves about their role and function are numerous, varied, and often conflicting. While some expectations are apparent to everyone—perhaps even specified in writing—and others may be evident enough to be sensed by a perceptive staff minister, many may be unknown (or hidden) to a particular staff minister. When expectations clash or are not met, problems arise in staff relationships.

For the optimal potential in staff relationships to be realized, there must be clear agreement between a staff member's personal expectations, the expectations of church members, and the expectations of other staff members. The testimony of scores of staff ministers is that where there is not a clear understanding by all parties of the expectations of each party, there is apt to be misunderstanding. This is especially true when inadequate effort is made by a staff member to clarify these expectations during the process of joining a staff as well as during the period of service.

Because clarity of expectations among all parties is prerequisite to healthy staff relationships, each party should ask the question, *"What are the common understandings that we must have in order to work together most redemptively?"*

Common Expectations

Although a church staff is likely to have access to many documents that provide information on how the staff is to work together, it would help if every church provided for its staff at least one document in which the general expectations of staff work are clearly stated. It should be the standard agreement common to all staff members and should list the primary expectations that guide them in their work together.

The following information, which covers basic principles for working together, is presented as it might appear in such a document. You could adapt this for your church and use it as a staff manual.

Principles to Guide a Staff in Planning and Working Together

Spiritual Principles

1. All staff members love the Lord, love the church, love one another, and behave like Christians.
2. All staff members are predisposed to joy.
3. There is among all staff members a spirit of humility and submission.
4. All staff members maintain a daily devotional time when they intercede in prayer for all other staff members.

The Scripture on which these spiritual principles are based is Galatians 5:22–23 (KJV), which speaks of the "fruit" of the Spirit rather than the "fruits" of the Spirit: "The fruit of the Spirit is love" as manifested in "joy, peace, longsuffering, gentleness, goodness, faith, meekness, temperance." For the church staff, *joy* is love's strength; *peace* is love's security; *long-suffering* is love's patience; *gentleness* is love's conduct; *goodness* is love's character; *faith* is love's confidence; *meekness* is love's humility; and *temperance* is love's victory. Every staff member, without exception, should be committed without reservation to faithfully practicing these spiritual guidelines.

Administrative Principles

1. The staff is a shared-ministry leadership team; however, there can be only one chief of staff.

2. Ongoing attention is given to building relationships in order to ensure clarity in policies and guidelines.
3. There are regular staff meetings with adequate time devoted to both short-range and long-range planning.

These guidelines affirm the validity and necessity of the ministry of each staff member. Ministry that is united in effort and objective but divided in responsibility is to be expected. The pastor is acknowledged as having the church-assigned responsibility of leading the team. While diversity of function among staff members is recognized and accepted, unity in the ministries of all staff members is affirmed. There is a commitment to expending whatever time and energy it takes to ensure that all staff members have clear understandings of expectations and ample opportunity to participate in all planning processes affecting their work and ministries.

Practical Principles
1. Each staff member is loyal to the Lord and one another, and all are loyal to the church.
2. Each is encouraged to think and function as a full minister and a team member.
3. There is good communication, especially when there is a problem.
4. Relationships are also built on a personal level.

An understanding must develop concerning the practical ways in which expectations are worked out with each staff member. This requires that each staff member must have a good self-image and be able to relate well to others who are equal in their team responsibilities. Personal involvement with one another and family members outside of work assignments is essential to this understanding.

These guidelines provide for great latitude in the responsible use of freedom in exercising one's ministry to the fullest extent possible. A high level of trust, openness, relationship, interdependence, and maturity among staff members is assumed.

Special Expectations
In contrast to standard expectations that all staff members and the congregation hold in common, there is a need to clarify the agreements, understandings, and expectations that are unique for each staff member. These special expectations include:

- How you will be supported
- What your job will be
- How you will work with others

Although these will vary from situation to situation, each will be developed in some form. In the simplest form they will be informal working agreements, determined primarily by tradition and the ways in which various people mesh in their personality and work styles.

In more developed forms, there will be church-approved statements concerning how the congregation expects staff members to work together and specific job descriptions for each position. (These were presented earlier in chapter 5.) Staff members will learn to work intentionally on the issues that will bring them together into an effective ministry team.

How Will You Be Supported?

An agreement that specifies the resources provided by a church for maintaining a minister's services should be written. Its purpose is to (1) clarify the church's personnel policies relating to a specific staff minister and to (2) clarify the financial resources provided by a church for that minister.

This agreement is usually negotiated with the personnel committee, the finance committee, and/or a search committee, and approved by the church. Churches without these committees will develop their own process for establishing this agreement.

Thorough negotiation should take place at the outset of one's ministry in a church. There will never be a better time to negotiate this agreement. A staff minister should use this opportunity wisely to ensure that an equitable salary (including housing), benefits, and other provisions are made for adequate support. There should be an annual opportunity to discuss selected contents in the agreement with the personnel committee and/or the finance committee.

Information about any or all of the following may be included in the agreement: employment policies and procedures (interviewing, calling, moving expenses); salary (arrangements, administration, review); office and equipment; travel reimbursement; basic work schedule; vacations; holidays; sick leave; time off for personal reasons; personal/professional development; sabbatical/study leave; advancement; grievances; insurance; retirement plan/pension; dismissal policy and procedures; release/resignation.

A checklist (figure 17.1) may be used for clarity. Details of agreements regarding employment (figure 17.2) should be provided to help avoid misunderstanding. Ministers and churches will have to decide what happens if there is a disagreement about the provisions being made.

What Will Be Your Job?

A written agreement specifies the functional responsibilities assigned by a church to a specific staff minister. The purpose of such an agreement is to clarify what the church expects a specific staff minister to do. It answers the question, What is my work responsibility? It focuses almost exclusively on the relationship a staff minister has with the church. Such an agreement is typically called a job description.

The channels for negotiating a job description are usually the same as the ones mentioned earlier. However, for certain staff members, such as a minister of music, additional opportunities may be available through a specialized group or committee. Staff ministers with multiple responsibilities because of combined jobs will need to have clear information concerning how the duties will be handled.

A job description should be discussed at the outset of one's acceptance of a position. Schedule adequate time for this discussion. Many sessions with various persons/groups may be necessary. An opportunity for review of a staff member's job description with a church should be provided annually through the personnel evaluation process.

A staff member's job description should be much more than an organized list of duties and responsibilities, as important as that is. It should be based on the vision that a staff minister and the church have for that person's overall ministry. Sample descriptions of the duties usually expected of staff ministers are included in chapter 5.

How Will You Work with Others?

Staff members must understand how they are involved with other staff members. The focus is more on knowing how one functions in a team relationship than on what one does; it is more on knowing how one does the work than on what is achieved. Its purpose is to clarify the quality of relationship that now exists; the perceptions each minister has about how to work with every other person on the staff; and how, as staff members work together, the quality of relationship between and among them can be significantly strengthened.

As with the other types of agreements, much attention should be given at the outset of one's ministry to understanding relationships with colleagues. This understanding, however, requires continuing work on a regular basis. Rule of thumb: Touch base with other staff ministers as often as possible—not because you have to but because you want to! When staff members both solemnly and joyfully enter into a relationship with one another, the outcome is a better relationship and a clearer understanding of how they can most effectively work together and enjoy the Lord's work.

Each person's understanding of self and others in the areas of value system; self-image; the goal, nature, and work of staff ministry; church expectations of staff members; leadership style; and church personnel policies and procedures must be dealt with for effective ministry results. These and other issues considered significant by staff ministers should be a part of the content to be discussed. It is unlikely that all of these issues will ever be discussed fully, and they need not be discussed in any particular sequence. However, none of them should be avoided or ignored in building relationships with staff members.

Evaluating Ministry Relationships

Each minister must accept personal responsibility for ministry by taking the initiative in purposefully directing one's life as much as possible rather than simply allowing it to be determined by past and present pressures. It is a proactive—in contrast to a reactive—ministry stance. But ministers who work together must also develop processes for evaluating how they are working together. The use of some instruments that have been designed for relating to others may be helpful. Staff groups may want to consider Life Orientations (communication styles), Myers-Briggs (personality inventory), Taylor-Johnson Temperament Analysis, or other such instruments for this purpose.

Using Staff Meetings Productively

The most effective approach to evaluating relationships can come as part of a regular, weekly staff meeting. Amid the time allowed for prayer and Bible study, calendar coordination, problem solving, and reporting, time should be allowed for evaluating and building relationships. Any discussion of conflicts over scheduling, finances, or use of volunteers should include a frank evaluation of relationships that exist among and between staff members. Only as relationships improve can there possibly be any effective and productive resolution of conflicts.

All staff members must be involved in the regular staff meetings. They should remain as long as the agenda calls for their participation. This procedure will usually mean that support staff members will return to their work after the first several agenda items. It is possible that some time may be given to relationship building before they are dismissed. Of necessity, the ministerial leadership staff members who remain for program and ministry planning and evaluation will want to be involved in strengthening their relationships with one another.

Using Retreat Settings

The logical expansion of the staff meeting for relationship building is a staff retreat. Three main differences in the two allow for this to happen. One is the time factor—much more time is available in a retreat setting. The second is the location—being away from the office reduces the possibility of interruptions and distractions. The third is fellowship—the possibility for increased fellowship is provided on a retreat. Scheduling a retreat every six months would be helpful.

A retreat setting does not require an expensive property. It will help if recreational opportunities are available and time allows. The main need is to get away and to have sufficient time to work on relationships. This might be accomplished in a meeting room at a neighboring church, in a conference room at a local hotel, or at a church member's vacation home. Each staff member will need to make a commitment to use the time provided to strengthen relationships with other staff members.

Evaluating Constantly

Meetings are not enough. It is essential that regular evaluation of relationships takes place. There must be one-to-one involvement among staff members including honest communication about facts and feelings. Potential and actual conflicts must be dealt with in seeking to improve relationships. The importance of ministries and turf protection must be discussed in light of how the staff works together to accomplish the mission of the church. One purpose of performance analysis is to determine how effectively staff members work with one another—the peer group.

The results of evaluating relationships will be seen in more satisfied, joyful staff members who remain in a position for a longer period of time; but more importantly, much more effective work will be done in leading the church toward its vision and the accomplishment of its mission.

Figure 17.1

CHECKLIST FOR CLARITY IN A CALL

		YES	NO
1.	Church moves/provides moving expenses?	____	____
2.	Church provides housing?	____	____

If yes, in what form?

Church-owned house _____

Housing allowance _____

		YES	NO
3.	Church provides utilities or allowance?	____	____
4.	Church assists in purchasing home?	____	____

If yes, indicate the following: Provides down payment as gift or loan in the amount of $_____ at an interest rate of ___% to be repaid at $_____ days of termination. (Any gift or loan amount forgiven must be treated as added income.)

		YES	NO
5.	Monthly salary to begin $_____ with review for increase at the end of ___months.	____	____
	Recommendation for increase to be made by committee.	____	____
6.	Monthly travel expenses reimbursed?	____	____

If yes, in the amount of ___cents per mile for travel on church business.

		YES	NO
7.	Church provides insurance coverage?	____	____

If yes, how much? _____

Health $_____

Life $_____

		YES	NO
8.	Church provides reimbursement for ministry expenses?	____	____

If yes, up to what annual amount $___

		YES	NO
9.	Church provides weekly days off?	____	____

If yes, number of days _____

		YES	NO
10.	Church provides annual paid vacation?	____	____

If yes, _____ number of weeks first year;

second year and thereafter _____

		YES	NO
11.	Is necessary supply paid by church for vacation absences?	____	____
12.	Church provides time off to assist other churches with meetings?	____	____

How many weeks? _____

		YES	NO
13.	Church provides time and expenses to attend denominational conventions?	____	____
	How much? _____		
14.	Is necessary supply paid by church for these absences?	____	____
15.	Church provides time off for death of family members?	____	____
	If yes, how much time? _____		
16.	Church provides time off for illness?	____	____
	If yes, amount of time annually _____		
17.	Are salary and benefits paid during time of illness?	____	____
	For how long? _____		
18.	Necessary supply paid by church?	____	____
	For how long? _____		
19.	Church provides annual physical examination?	____	____
20.	Pastor is designated as supervisor of other staff?	____	____
	If no, who is designated and for which staff members? _____		
21.	Time off is provided for study leave and professional development?	____	____
	If yes, how much time annually? _____		
22.	Does church pay cost of job-related training?	____	____
23.	Does church provide retirement benefit?	____	____
	If yes, what amount? _____		
24.	_____	____	____
25.	_____	____	____

Figure 17.2

SPECIFIC AGREEMENTS
(These Will Vary from Church to Church)

Annual Financial Arrangements

1. **VOCATIONAL COMPENSATION**
   Basic Salary: to be paid $
   Housing Allowance $
   Utilities Allowance $
                                          Total $

2. **PROTECTION COVERAGES**
   Retirement Plans _____ % of
      Vocational Compensation
   Family Health Insurance $
   Life Insurance
   Disability Insurance
   Worker's Compensation
                                          Total $

3. **REIMBURSEMENT OF PROFESSIONAL EXPENSES**
   Travel _____ cents a mile
   Conventions and Meetings $
   Professional Dues
   Entertainment/Hospitality
   Books
   Other ministry expenses
                                          Total $

4. **ANY OTHER CONSIDERATIONS***
   Christmas Bonus or Cash Gift $
   Social Security Tax Allowance
                                          Total $

5. **RELOCATION COSTS***
   Commercial mover $
   Transportation
   Motel/Meals
   House down payment
                                          Total $

*Will be added to W-2 Form.

Annual Time Arrangement

The church acknowledges that a minister's work cannot be rigidly regulated because of the nature of ministry. Crisis situations and emergencies along with meetings and a heavy schedule may alter the schedule and sometimes necessitate arranging work and leisure at different hours.

Despite weekend work and evening obligations, a minister must find some time to spend with the family and for personal needs.

1. Day(s) a week off _____
2. Weeks for vacation _____
3. List holidays _____
4. Study-leave time _____
5. Sunday absences _____
6. Total number of Sundays for church-paid supplies _____
   Vacation time _____
   Conventions or conferences _____
   Study leave _____
   Other engagements _____
7. Sick leave arrangements _____
8. Any other arrangements _____

287

Chapter 18

THE MINISTER'S PERSONAL LIFE

Robert D. Dale

What does it take to live happily and healthily in our hectic world? One formula for effective functioning includes a family that loves you, a job that challenges you, and five friends whose faces light up when they meet you. Add your personal faith in Christ to these three factors and you have the raw materials for managing the personal dimensions of your life and ministry.

Effective ministry requires effective support-system management. Why? Because ministry is a stressful, wear-and-tear calling and because ministry is a vocation of attrition for ministers and their families. The give, give, give of caring for others causes some ministers to give out and others to give up.

We who minister must receive in order to give to others. Thankfully, the Christian faith has rich resources for ministerial support: prayer, the Holy Spirit, and the fellowship of other believers.

This chapter highlights three major aspects of managing personal dimensions of ministry: marriage and family relationships, career development, and the general elements of a well-balanced ministry support system. Overall, managing your personal life as a minister involves a variety of concerns:

- Enriching family relationships
- Handling stress
- Charting your career span
- Planning for career growth
- Discovering the stages in a minister's career cycle
- Balancing your support network
- Managing personal and professional stress
- Avoiding burnout

Enriching Family Relationships

Ministers are reminded by biblical instruction to be responsible in marriage and family relationships. Whether married or single, all live as part of a multigenerational family system that requires nurturing and supportive relationships.

When family living is viewed as a lifelong process, managing relationships becomes an ongoing practice of updating our promises and vows to our family members. For those who are married, consider the stages of a nuclear family and the recommitments that are basic for each phase.[1]

1. *The happily-ever-after family*. Newlyweds view family life simply: we love each other. Life is a romantic fantasy of rainbows, roses, and rendezvous.

Then we begin to discover the "I never knews." New and disappointing revelations come to light: the early morning grouch, the inability to balance a checkbook, the irritating habits. The "I never knews" reveal the double-edged nature of relational growth and raise up several occasions for renewing promises:

- Building a new family unit separate from the two families of origin
- Developing a mutual partnership
- Learning to disagree agreeably
- Accepting personality differences as growth opportunities, not as threats, flaws, or faults

2. *The making-ends-meet family*. Two-paycheck families make up the majority of American households. In fact, for many families, two incomes are a necessity rather than a career option. Ministers increasingly are finding making ends meet is a state of family living instead of a passing stage. Several important promises need to be considered for these families:

- Keeping work from driving a wedge between family relationships
- Not letting job talk dominate at-home conversation
- Developing a joint plan for managing both incomes

3. *The bundle-of-joy family*. Parenthood creates family in its fullest sense. Especially when the child has been planned and prayed for, births are really blessed events. Even so, the introduction of new babies into the family circle creates strains—loss of schedule flexibility, added expenses, care responsibilities, and potential neglect of the primary husband-wife relationship. These challenges suggest some additional updating of vows.

- Seeing children as unique persons, not rivals or substitutes
- Developing a parenting style appropriate to your current family situation
- Keeping the husband-wife relationship strong as a base for family health and effective parenting

4. *The expanding-world family*. This is a blossoming phase for both parents and children. Adults are putting down roots and investing in their careers. Many husbands are feeling more independent; some wives are returning to school or entering the work world again. Children are entering school and developing a circle of friends beyond the family. New commitments also confront this family:

- Facing power struggles as the family's interests diversify
- Resisting the child-centered family that neglects the fundamental husband-wife relationship
- Coping with deadening routines

5. *The breaking-away family*. Teenagers have a habit of storming the family fortress in their attempts to grow up and develop their own personalities. At this stage of family life, a double bind often develops between children's adolescent search for identity and direction and parents' "middlescent" search for identity and direction. Both generations face similar struggles simultaneously. A range of renewed promises present themselves to this family:

- Admitting that some tension is natural in families
- Adjusting discipline approaches as teens become more responsible decision makers
- Resisting the temptation to become pals with children and go through a second childhood
- Creating family boundaries that are flexible enough to provide children with both protection and freedom
- Preparing the husband-wife relationship for the empty-nest stage

6. *The untying-the-apron-strings family*. Launching children into their own independent lives is both exciting and frightening. Excitement arises from watching our parental influences and emotional investment in our children being tested in others' lives. Fright frequently emerges in the discomfort of letting children go and seeing the family circle shrink. Mothers who have focused exclusively in child-rearing feel the trauma of losing their identity when they launch their children. Becoming obsolete looms large on these families' horizons. Crucial new promises face these families too:

- Passing the torch to younger generations gracefully
- Coping with the loss of children's dependency and facing the evidences of aging
- Seeing children as only one aspect of our legacy to the world

7. *The empty-nest family*. This is a husband-and-wife family again. The real test of this family stage is the health of the spouses' relationship. Grandparenthood opens a new, and generally more relaxed, dimension of parenting. Painfully, the empty nest can refill as children lose jobs or divorce and as aged parents become dependent on their adult children.

Three generations are learning to relate to one another in new ways during this stage. A number of recommitment opportunities emerge at this stage:

- Concentrating on spouse rather than children
- Becoming in-laws
- Nurturing another generation as grandparents
- Assisting aging parents

8. *The three-generations family.* Most families experience intergenerational relationships involving at least three generations. In reality, Grandma is the third generation in many families. Grandmothers who have lived traditional lifestyles are confronted with an unfamiliar role—putting themselves first. Another rare role some members of the third generation face is great-grandparenthood, especially as another life stage beyond eighty-five is now emerging. Several decisions call for updating promises for three-generation families:

- Affirming the present when you have so much past
- Freeing and encouraging children and grandchildren to live their own lives
- Identifying with grandchildren without isolating the generation in between

Each stage of family living takes on its own texture and challenges. The test of healthy families is how well they recognize the stage they're in and how completely they update their faith and actions to their stage.

Handling Stress

The minister's family is both a great resource and a heavy responsibility. Parenting is an increasingly demanding role, not only for those who have children but also for those who care for aging parents and grandparents. Some family counselors refer to "parent burnout," the condition of trying to be superdad or supermom with only ordinary resources. Burned-out parents feel tired, depleted, numb, angry, and blue. Stressed families are not fun for either parents or children. Mothers are a bit more apt to burn out than fathers, especially if teens are in the home.

Parents are waking up to the magnitude of stress modern teens face. Suicide has become the second highest cause of death among teenagers (following accidents). What are the primary teen stresses?

- Peer pressure
- Personal appearance
- Parental expectations
- College and career decisions

Being Adolescent: Conflict and Growth in the Teenage Years, a study of teenagers' activities, private thoughts, and emotional ups and downs, yields some interesting findings. Teens use forty-two hours weekly in leisure activities and thirty-eight hours in schooling. Teens spend 19 percent of their time with other family members; less than 5 percent of their time is spent alone with one or both parents. Dramatic mood swings of only fifteen minutes in duration are common. Contemporary parents apparently need to devote more time and patience in their parenting efforts.[2]

Preteen children also experience stress. These stresses arise from a variety of primary sources and frequently affect children's health:

- School performance
- Too little playtime
- Parental unemployment
- Minimal contact with grandparents and extended family
- Peer pressure
- Too much responsibility too soon
- Lack of discipline
- Excessive television viewing

Warning signs of stress in children are similar to many normal ailments. However, physicians agree that when at least five of the symptoms listed below persist for an extended period, a child is showing high levels of stress:[3]

- Bed-wetting
- Chronic complaining
- Compulsive ear tugging or hair pulling
- Cruel behavior toward people or pets
- Poor grades
- Feeling afraid or upset without being able to identify the source
- Depression
- Aches or pains
- Sudden crying
- Extreme nervousness and worrying
- Listlessness or loss of interest
- Poor eating and sleeping habits
- Difficulty getting along with friends, siblings
- Alcohol or drug use
- Nightmares
- Nervous tics, twitches, or muscles spasms
- Lying

Steps can be taken to help your family cope with its stressors. For example, you can:

- Talk about pressures. After all, two (or more) heads are better than one when families face their stresses.
- Escape for a while. Everyone needs a break from togetherness occasionally, particularly when relationships are already strained

and nerves frayed. Get some space and read a book or take a walk.

- Exercise away some pent-up energy and frustration. Jog, swim, or enjoy a family outing.
- Talk to someone outside your family circle. Friends, ministry colleagues, or a counselor can help put pressures into healthier perspective.
- Serve others. Get your mind off yourself.
- Create a private place for yourself. Prayer and meditation are recognized methods for reducing stress.
- Use figure 18.2 as a measuring stick to see how much change and stress have accumulated.

Charting Your Career Span

Just as there are seasons of life for individuals and stages through which families move, so your calling of ministry can be charted and examined as a developmental process.[4] Think of ministry as a career span of five steps.

1. *Entrance into Ministry.* Industrial psychologists claim that a worker's first professional job has long-term career implications. It helps shape the workers' outlook about that particular vocation, about success and failure, and about their fit with that type of job. The same is apparently true for ministry as vocation too. For some the work is exciting. For others it is overwhelming and bewildering. The first three or four years of full-time ministry mold our feelings about working with people.

2. *Advancement and Stabilization.* Now committed to ministry, the still-novice minister faces the "make or break" element of career spans. Identity and skills begin to mesh comfortably.

3. *Maintenance.* Thoroughly into the career of ministry by this time, ministers might begin to feel some pressure not to rock the career boat.

4. *Decline.* The point of no return in work has likely been reached by now. The minister must resist the attitude of "a job is a job is a job."

5. *Retirement.* Giving up work is difficult for most workers. But this transition is even more traumatic for many ministers who lose professional identity as well as vocational status.

Planning for Career Growth

The calling of ministry is a dynamic career; it grows and stretches the minister as God opens new frontiers to us. Some of the new opportunities are positive and exciting. Other situations are more uncomfortable and crisis oriented.

Three predictable crises in a minister's career have been identified.[5] The first predictable crisis in ministry tends to occur three to five years out of seminary or divinity school. In this crisis the realities of congregational leadership collide with idealism and the protection of academic life. To overstate the issue, the fledgling minister feels the internal tension between a headful of theology and a bellyful of people. Application of biblical insights to the real world of caring for people is the challenge facing the beginner minister.

A second crisis emerges about midlife. Typically, young adults invest their energies in a variety of enterprises: work, family, advancement, and individual concerns. Life and ministry begin to feel frazzled around the edges. The challenge of midlife is to put all of our career eggs into one basket and regain a focus in our professional lives. As the apostle Paul said about refocusing at midlife, "This one thing I do" (Phil 3:13 KJV).

Predictably, a third crisis develops as retirement nears. Many ministers find laying down the mantle of pastoral ministry more difficult than it was to take up at our experience of calling. Older ministers are overlooked for new ministry opportunities. As an energetic minister friend reported to me, "A pastor search committee visited my church, heard me preach, and enjoyed an animated luncheon conversation with my wife and me. They spoke of a visit to their church field so we could get acquainted with their ministry opportunities. Then they asked me how old I am. When I replied, '62,' the conversation tailed off. They said their good-byes. I haven't heard a word from them since." Preretirement and retirement are a difficult emotional, financial, and leadership transition to face.

These crises are prime times to consider career assessment. Contact your denominational office for minister support or a theological school in your area to secure information and recommendations.

Discovering the Stages in a Minister's Career Cycle

Life and our careers move through a series of important stages. Each new stage builds on the former stages, profiting from the lessons learned earlier or being blocked by other lessons that haven't been incorporated. These stages, while natural and fairly predictable, are fueled primarily by our decisions.[6]

Novice adults enter the work world from their late teens to about age thirty. Novices experience some suspension of expectations. Five basic issues confront the novice: (1) What dream or life goal will I structure my life around? (2) Which career will I pursue? (3) Who will become my mate? (4) Who will become my mentor? (5) Who will become my lasting friends? Vocational issues underlie and color all five of these concerns.

Novice adults in ministry can take several positive steps to meet the challenge of this stage of ministry.

- Study the life of Christ as a model—especially His vision of the kingdom of God.

- Allow your sense of calling to grow. Ministry directions often require some time and experience before they emerge clearly and finally. Jesus, Paul, Luther, and Wesley were all mature persons before they launched the ministries we remember them for.
- Recognize that ministry involves "paying the rent" of varied expectations. Some members will expect what's within your power to perform. Others will expect the magical and unrealistic of you.
- Accept the guidance of experienced adults. Mentors can often sense our best potential even before we see it ourselves.
- Cultivate professional relationships from seminary and early ministry experiences. These friendships are apt to sustain you personally and professionally during the rest of your ministry.
- Choose a ministry style that's comfortable to you. Let your own unique approach emerge over time rather than adopting someone else's style wholesale.

Junior adults settle down as they enter their thirties. Junior adults begin to stand on their own two feet; they aren't still novices, but they aren't senior adults either. They are junior adults—in between.

Junior adults face four challenges. (1) Junior adults put down roots. During the late twenties or about thirty, adults examine their life structure and, if it has served well, they get serious about life. (2) Junior adults focus on career advancement. They pursue a dream and try to become craftsmen. (3) Junior adults recognize and concentrate on meeting real needs. They begin to take some time to cultivate emotional and spiritual gardens. (4) Junior adults grow more independent. They put away the childish ways of earlier days (1 Cor 13:11) and ready themselves to become mentors in their own right.

A number of actions can be taken by junior adults to move them purposefully forward.

- Develop a strong ministry-support system. You can find several strategies to consider in strengthening your support network later in this chapter.
- Renew your family relationships and those with lifelong friends. Keep in mind that no relationship flourishes on autopilot. Don't neglect these precious relationships; heed the suggestions mentioned earlier in this chapter.
- Plan for continuing education. Reading plans, seminars, advanced degrees, professional certifications, and similar resources help us keep our ministry skills sharp.
- Cultivate your devotional life.
- Guard your physical and mental health. Discipline in diet, exercise, and stress management are wise actions.

- Establish family financial planning practices now. Saving now for college and retirement keeps more of your options open for the future.

Midlife adults slow down for a major life and career evaluation sometime after age thirty-five. They sense they are "old" for the first time. They discover that aging is rarely fun—especially in a youth-worshipping culture.

1. Midlife adults examine the structures of their lives. This "time out" to review life's progress is often referred to as a midlife crisis.

2. Midlife adults often revise their life dream. "Middlescence," midlife's echo of adolescence, raises two old questions again: Who am I? What will I do with my life? These issues are raised when we feel plateaued and stuck, feel that we peaked too soon, or feel that we've failed in some significant way.

3. Midlife adults are threatened by obsolescence. The deadline decade, ages thirty-five to forty-five, causes them to feel a sense of urgency and to ask, "If not now, when?"

4. Midlife adults try to create a personal and professional legacy. Symbolically, they work to make themselves immortal by living on through children, church building programs, and books.

5. Midlife adults watch the home nest empty and parents/grandparents grow feeble.

6. Midlife adults face obvious physical and emotional changes.

7. Midlife adults move toward senior status.

Numerous possibilities are open to ministers at the midlife stage:

- Maintain supportive relationships. Our friends often sustain us during difficult days.
- Continue to be involved in family enrichment activities. If you are single, keep involved with family members and those who are like family to you.
- Research midlife issues to lessen the anxiety of the unknown.
- Consider career assessment if you seriously question your fitness or ability to serve effectively in ministry posts.
- Stay fresh devotionally.
- Get regular exercise.
- Become a mentor for the next generation of ministers.
- Clarify your ministry priorities.
- Recommit yourself to lifelong learning. Many midlife ministers investigate doctor of ministry programs as a structured approach to continuing education.

Senior adults approach their sixties feeling the double-edged nature of aging: mellowing because purpose and meaning in life have been discovered or becoming more brittle, bitter, and angry about growing older. Senior adults are approaching membership in America's largest minority—retirees.

Thus, senior adults deal with several basic life and career transitions. (1) Senior adults transfer hope to the younger generation. To illustrate, aged Elijah gave his mantle to the younger Elisha. (2) Senior adults cope with fixed income. This situation is made even more difficult because fewer than one-half of Americans under fifty-five have made any financial plans for retirement. (3) Senior adults face the erosion of health and vigor. (4) Senior adults accept "followership." (5) Senior adults may accept an expanded mission in life.

Numerous strategies are available to senior adults for moving through the transition to retirement:

- Plan for retirement. Some psychologists claim that vacations are miniretirements; our reactions to vacationing provide clues to how we'll retire.
- Stay "green above the ears." Keep on learning.
- Exercise. Medical doctors prescribe walking because they describe our thigh muscles as substitute hearts.
- Take the risks of new ministries. Now may be the time in your life to start a new church or write a book. You've done so much else that the risks are low.
- Don't become angry that churches tend to value energy more than experience. The greying of America is working in the direction of raising the status of older ministers.
- Work smarter, not harder. You know some shortcuts now. Use them and save energy.
- Remember the difference between self-concern, a necessity for us as we age, and self-absorption, an unattractive trait in persons of any generation.
- Keep in perspective that ministry is an attitude as well as a role. Caleb at eighty-five asked for the toughest task in the conquest of the promised land; he was aging, but he retained an exciting can-do attitude about life and work (Josh 14).
- Families and career opportunities are important aspects of managing our personal lives. Basic to guiding our own lives, additionally, is the strength of our support network.

Balancing Your Support Network

Support networks generally contain at least five ingredients: soul mates, lifelong learning, spiritual coaching, mentoring, and physical fitness. Each of these five ingredients suggests ways ministers have arranged for ministry support. Each ingredient is crucial; none is complete by itself. Some ministers, however, rely on one or two ingredients to the virtual exclusion of the others. All five ingredients, when balanced according to personal and professional needs, provide resourceful support for your ministry.[7]

The first ingredient in an effective support system is your network of friends. Ministry support is people-to-people relating. That's where our friends in Christ fit in. Friendly soul mates believe in us, pray for us, provide listening ears, share objective feedback amid our questions and struggles, and lend us a shoulder to cry on. Soul mates help us repair the frazzled edges of our lives. Intimate encouragers from our family and friendship circle help us recharge our spiritual and emotional batteries after we drain ourselves by constant caring for others, helping in crisis situations, and standing with others amid the general wear and tear of ministry.

Jesus, our Savior and model, chose twelve persons to minister with Him and *to be with Him* (Mark 3:14). Our network of friends provides us with similar vital assistance:

- Offsetting isolation
- Learning to be a "helpee"
- Encouraging us
- Exploring problems
- Helping face our weaknesses and owning our gifts

The second ingredient in your support network is a portable seminary or divinity school. Support for ministry is fresh ideas and lifelong learning.

Some ministers take a "union card" approach to education and assume that a theological degree provides all of the information and training the minister will ever need. That mind-set cuts the minister off from new insights and overlooks what professional education means. The term *seminary* literally means "seedbed." Seminaries are greenhouses where seeds are sprouted before they are transplanted into the world. A seminary is a starting point, not a finishing school. A plan of continuing education and ongoing growth, therefore, keeps us "green above the ears."

Our portable theological school lends us support in deepening our convictions and expanding our ideas. Book clubs, loan libraries of ministry-related books and tapes, and idea-sharing groups are basic learning resources. Idea groups help us trade, test, and organize our thoughts. Some groups structure themselves to review books and read formal papers on topics of mutual interest. Most are less formal in their organization.

Because two (or more) heads are better than one, our portable seminary allows us several possibilities:

- Brainstorming ideas
- Exchanging newsletters, clippings, and resource lists
- Evaluating new approaches
- Analyzing books, literature, and programs

The third ingredient in your balanced support system is your spiritual coach. Ministry calls for the constant growth of faith. One way many Christian groups have traditionally encouraged spiritual development is through the enlistment of a spiritual coach.

A spiritual coach is a person who helps you set, evaluate, and celebrate the milestones in your spiritual development. Almost always a one-to-one relationship, spiritual coaching requires maturity from the coach and commitment by the novice.

Disciplined spiritual growth takes advantage of a variety of resources. A spiritual coach helps us use all the avenues of development available to us:

- Bible studying
- Praying and confessing our sins
- Contemplating and using silence
- Reading the devotional classics and biographies of spiritual giants
- Fasting and other forms of self-discipline
- Fellowshipping with other Christian pilgrims

The fourth ingredient in your support network is mentoring. A mentor in ministry is a model, sponsor, advisor, and ally. Our mentors believe in us. They are ordinarily older ministers who have already reached some goal in ministry to which we still aspire. Our mentors see our potential and nurture the promise they see in us.

Mentor relationships are common in the pages of the Bible: Abraham for Lot. Elijah for Elisha. Saul for David. Barnabas for Paul and John Mark. Paul for Silas and Timothy. These biblical mentorships, like modern instances of mentoring, are intense and sometimes, therefore, end painfully. Good mentoring is as important to adults as good parenting is to children. Being effectively mentored strengthens us for solid ministry now and for becoming a mentor for others in the future.

Mentoring brings us a range of valuable resources:

- Apprenticing in our craft
- Evaluating professional progress
- "Learning the ropes" of ministry
- Modeling how-to-do acts of ministry
- Mapping a route of advancement

Ministry is an on-the-job-training vocation for the most part. A mentor provides a key link in our ministry-support network by placing a mantle of confidence on us.

The fifth ingredient in your support system is your physical health. The apostle Paul described our bodies as temples of God (1 Cor 3:16). And ministry can clearly stress our physical systems. For example, public speaking is considered the most fearsome activity humans indulge in. Someone has estimated that a twenty-minute sermon is as physically taxing as eight hours of moderate labor. Vigorous health provides us the energy reserve to engage in strenuous ministry.

Regular exercise and dietary discipline yields several important dividends:

- Maintaining health
- Looking fit
- Feeling good
- Increasing energy levels

Balancing Your Support Network

Balanced support is necessary for healthy and effective ministry. Emotional support is aided by our network of friends. Practical ideas for ministry grow out of our portable seminary. Development of our religious life is assisted by our spiritual coach. Professional growth is encouraged by our mentors. Physical fitness occurs when we treat our bodies like God's temples.

When one or two elements of support are stressed primarily or exclusively, our support network becomes somewhat unbalanced. A complete system of support can be visualized as a wheel (figure 18.1). Like a wheel, symmetry is essential for balance in our ministry-support resources. And balance is a critical clue to the strength of our support networks.

Managing Personal and Professional Stress

Stress accounts for the best-selling prescription drugs in the United States. According to family physicians, two of every three office visits are stress related. Ironically, our lifestyles are making us sick.[8]

Stress is the "wear and tear of life," according to Hans Selye, the father of some of the best early stress studies.[9] Stress is triggered by life changes that demand we adapt. A "ready response" is created by stress: adrenaline pumps, blood sugar levels soar, circulation to our extremities lessens to reduce blood loss in case of injury. (The last phenomenon explains why our hands and feet feel cold and clammy when we get nervous.) The ready response is vital when we're

Figure 18.1

BALANCED SUPPORT SYSTEM

PHYSICAL

EMOTIONAL

PROFESSIONAL

INTELLECTUAL

SPIRITUAL

in a real emergency situation. But if our lifestyle keeps us revved up too much of the time, and we catch "hurry up sickness," we wear out too fast. Then stress becomes distress, or bad stress. Interestingly, some folks react especially well to stress and are described as "hardy personalities."

Stress-free living is both impossible and unattractive. In fact, the complete lack of stress is death. Studies suggest that life needs some stress to spice it up. Moderate stress, then, becomes *eustress*, or good stress.

Several clues serve as early warnings of stress. This range of detection symptoms provide helpful signals for our self-care:

- Physical—fatigue, headaches, backaches, sleep disorders, chronic illness, hypertension, ulcers
- Psychological—boredom, irritability, defensive behaviors, anxiety, depression
- Behavioral—overeating, compulsive use of prescription or illicit drugs, drinking and/or smoking, temper tantrums, withdrawal from social contacts, escapist behaviors.
- Occupational—job dissatisfaction, decreased work productivity, tardiness and absenteeism, sloppy decision making, a sense of helplessness

Our natural "fight-flight" response, when constantly switched on, supercharges us and keeps us stuck in overdrive. The powerful chemicals triggered by stress combine to place unrelenting strain on our weakest organs. Our "reward" may be heart attacks, ulcers, diabetes, cancer, high blood pressure, suicide, and other physical or emotional breakdowns.

Some jobs are more stressful than others. Traditionally, we've thought policemen, surgeons, coaches, and air traffic controllers occupied the most stressing work position. However, two factors combine in the most stressful jobs: high demands from people and low control over those demands. In reality the toughest jobs belong to cooks, waiters, cashiers, telephone operators, and assembly-line workers. And ministers? Yes, when high demand and low control factors become prominent in our work.

Two mental health researchers, Thomas H. Holmes and Richard H. Rahe, have devised and refined a widely used instrument, the social readjustment rating scale, to measure stress. These researchers have listed and ranked the forty-two common life changes they discovered to be precursors of illness. Strangely enough, an outstanding achievement was found to be as stressful as some dreaded catastrophe. Their basic finding was clear: *change causes stress*. For an indication of your personal level of accumulated stress, see figure 18.2.

Stress management has grown into a multimillion-dollar-a-year industry in America. Professional help, while useful, isn't always required. Some personal strategies for coping with stress make our lives more manageable.

Figure 18.2

HOLMES AND RAHE STRESS CHART

Think back over the past year. How many of the events have occurred in your life? Check them on the list below.

RANK EVENT	VALUE YOUR SCORE

RANK EVENT			VALUE YOUR SCORE		
1.	Death of spouse	100 ___	24.	Outstanding personal achievement	28 ___
2.	Divorce	73 ___	25.	Spouse begins or starts work	26 ___
3.	Marital separation	65 ___			
4.	Jail term	63 ___	26.	Starting or finishing school	26 ___
5.	Death of close family member	63 ___	27.	Change in living conditions	25 ___
6.	Personal injury or illness	53 ___	28.	Revision of personal habits	24 ___
7.	Marriage	50 ___	29.	Trouble with boss	23 ___
8.	Fired from work	47 ___	30.	Change in work hours, conditions	20 ___
9.	Marital reconciliation	45 ___			
10.	Retirement	45 ___	31.	Change in residence	20 ___
11.	Change in family member's health	44 ___	32.	Change in schools	20 ___
12.	Pregnancy	40 ___	33.	Change in recreational habits	19 ___
13.	Sex difficulties	39 ___	34.	Change in church activities	19 ___
14.	Addition to family	39 ___			
15.	Business readjustment	39 ___	35.	Change in social activities	18 ___
16.	Change in financial status	38 ___	36.	Mortgage or loan under $10,000	16 ___
17.	Death of close friend	37 ___			
18.	Change in number of marital arguments	35 ___	37.	Change in sleeping habits	16 ___
19.	Morgage or loan over $10,000	31 ___	38.	Change in number of family gatherings	15 ___
20.	Foreclosure of mortgage or loan	30 ___	39.	Change in eating habits	15 ___
21.	Change in work responsibilities	29 ___	40.	Vacation	13 ___
22.	Son or daughter leaving home	29 ___	41.	Christmas season	12 ___
23.	Trouble with in-laws	29 ___	42.	Minor violation of the law	11 ___
				TOTAL	___

Add up your total score. (Be sure to multiply individual event values by the number of their occurrences.)

Here's how to understand your score. A total of 150 or less gives you a 37 percent susceptibility to disease during the next two years, 150 to 300 points a 51 percent chance, and over 300 points an 80 percent possibility of health difficulties.

Practicing preventive or management measures can help you deal with your stress level.

- Read up on stress and stress management. Understand the problem.
- Exercise. Change pace. Rest.
- Adjust diet. Eat balanced meals. Stop drinking caffeine and other stimulants. Lose weight. Reduce sugar and salt intake.
- Slow the pace of change. Approach decisions, career moves, and major projects deliberately. When large-scale events are completed, don't stop all activity abruptly. Live life as a process, not a series of sudden starts and stops.
- Cultivate your social support network. All of us need encouragers. Families and friends are particularly crucial in managing stress.

Avoiding Burnout

When ministers worship their work, work at their play, and play at their worship, they burn out personally and professionally. Misplaced priorities trigger burnout. Satisfaction in ministry wanes when we become messianic. Inflexible overresponsibleness opens the door to disillusionment in ministry.[10]

The minister who is "most likely to succeed" in the burnout process is the idealist who pursues an unattainable goal, like setting out to single-handedly bring in the kingdom by Thursday. Their good intentions, verve, and extreme optimism can consume them and leave them spiritually arid and psychologically depleted. Godly persons don't have to carry their burdens alone like the godless do.

Remember that the most likely candidates for burning out (1) work with people, and (2) have a low degree of control over their jobs. As a career, ministry may be more stressful than medicine, law enforcement, coaching, and air traffic control. Why? Because ministers deal with many situations in which their degree of control is low.

Four career stages track the process of dampening idealism. The burnout cycle repeats itself but can be recognized and successfully confronted.

1. *Enthusiasm is stage one.* Most ministers zero in on new tasks with fervor, hope, and tunnel vision. Typically, we overinvest in the new—jobs, relationships, and challenges. When idealism collides with reality, we may find ourselves blue, disillusioned, and unsure of our resources for coping.

2. *Stagnation is stage two.* The thrill of the job is dulled. Idealism tilts toward concern for days off, income, and evaluating performance. Dealing with isolation and intangible results wears on us. We still do the job, but the job does less for us.

3. *Frustration is stage three.* Powerlessness, red tape, and little leverage for change causes us to feel fatigued, irritable, and pessimistic. Because we wonder if we have any say in our own life's direction, we allow our frustration to set off a cycle of questioning our own effectiveness.

4. *Apathy is stage four*. We feel trapped. We must work, so we adopt a job-is-a-job-is-a-job attitude. We withdraw from our tasks emotionally and do only what's absolutely necessary. Security becomes our goal. Otherwise, we just go through the motions. Apathy is the bottom of the barrel but isn't the end of the story. We can light the fire again after burning out.

Self-care for the caregiver is the key to recovering from burnout. Although churches and other Christian institutions help ministers cope with depletion and disillusionment, the recovery and preventive processes are set in motion by ministers themselves. Four families of growth strategies are available.

1. *Boundary marking*. Creating clear boundaries deflects burnout in ministry. Several boundaries need to be marked off and contrasted: call to ministry and basic identity, personal life and professional life, self and others, work and play, and possible goals and unrealistic expectations.

2. *Monitoring*. Tracking our feelings, patterns of ailments, and sense of spiritual depletion helps us confront the burnout process. Ministry is a vocation of attrition. When we give, give, give without renewal, we may give out and give up. Keeping tabs on where we are helps us avoid burnout.

3. *Replenishing*. Ministers need a backlog of encouraging relationships and accessible resources to offset burnout. Visualize your support system for replenishment as a cube. The cube's front face is your devotional disciplines and sense of relationship to God. The back face of the cube represents your family's encouragement. The cube's top face is your denomination's available relationships and continuing education resources. The bottom face of the cube symbolizes your congregation or institution's atmosphere of encouragement. The cube's right face points to your network of peers in ministry. Finally, the left face of the support cube notes the link ministers have with other helping professionals in the community and their insights into and resources for refreshing our vocational batteries. All six aspects of encouragement are needed for full and balanced support.

4. *Providing safety valves*. In spite of our best efforts, burnout can still sneak up on us. Real friends, spiritual revitalization, a healthy sense of humor, physical exercise routines, and medical assistance provide primary backup resources for recouping from burnout.

When response and reward remain at a minimum after idealism and effort have been kept at a maximum, burnout is a likely possibility. Ministers can begin the rebuilding process by taking some self-care actions. Then, we can minister effectively and give freely.

Self-Management: A Key Issue

Managing your personal life is crucial. In fact, it's commanded for the Christian. Jesus' great commandment reminds us to love God totally and to love our neighbor as we love ourselves (Matt 22:36–40). By implication, if we're to care for others, we must take care of ourselves.

Chapter 19

LEADERSHIP IN SMALL AND
RURAL CONGREGATIONS

Bob I. Johnson

M ost churches have only one paid staff minister. Such a church calls and/or receives you as pastor because they feel you can lead the church to be the kind of church they think they ought to be. A vital question is then, How do I lead the church not only so that the people sense fulfillment but also so that God is pleased? This chapter is intended to help answer that question.

Getting Started

Although it is not possible here to provide comprehensive coverage on how to lead a small congregation with limited resources, it is possible to say some things that will make life for you and the congregation more fulfilling. Every congregation exhibits unique characteristics; however, common factors do exist in most if not all such situations. One obvious fact is that there are always starting points as an opportunity to impact ministry for good. When your tenure begins as pastor is one of those times.

One approach is to make as many needed changes as possible in the first year, or during the honeymoon time. However, this isn't recommended in most cases. Most situations call for the steady, long-term process of change—the exception being a church with a history of failure and/or turmoil that calls a pastor specifically to make rapid changes. Even then, be on guard. What "they" say they want to do might not be what "they" actually want to do.

Assess the Situation

Ask questions. Is it a newer parish? Is it an older congregation? What is its context: rural, urban, or other? Does it have a history of destructive conflict (not all conflict is bad)? Have pastors served long or short tenures? What was the nature of the interim period? Did the church go through a self-study and determine before they called you what their focus would be over the next five to seven years? How does the church view and how do you view authority for pastoral leadership? What are the capabilities and commitment of lay leaders? What resources are available? What is the capacity of the congregation to dream and follow through on their dreams? Does it appear the church needs to remodel existing buildings and/or provide new space? What are other congregations in the area like, and how effective are their ministries?

How does the church make decisions, budget its resources, nominate and choose its official leaders? Who are the power brokers? Are they among the elected leaders? And after you ask yourself these and other questions, ask, "Who am I? Can I be the person to lead this congregation, with all that implies, to be the people of God on mission for God?"

Get Your Bearings

Usually, to begin a formal planning agenda immediately is not the next step to take. Take advantage of the informality of the smaller congregation and talk to people and groups about what the church is like and what it ought to be doing to fulfill its calling from God. Emphasize that as pastor you want to lead the church to be the church God wants it to be and to help its members grow. Remember that the church has chosen you because they believed you were right for the church. Ask for suggestions on how to be the most effective pastor you can be.

Take a Basic Approach

As people make suggestions for your leadership, listen without comment. There will be time for you to respond. When meeting with a small group or the entire congregation, set up a chalkboard or attach large sheets of paper to the wall and write the suggestions in brief form. At this point receive each one as though it has equal value with all the others. This will encourage people to believe that you want to hear what they have to say.

When suggestions cease, you may want to mention any items omitted that you think are important for consideration. Then look at the list and say something like, "Thank you. It looks like we have several things that you feel are important . . . more than we can get done anytime soon. We will need to decide which one(s) we do first."

Point out how the items relate to the church's ministry. It may be appropriate to ask the group to choose the top two or three items for priority attention. Or it may be better to determine one need or emphasis that seems to have stronger support to serve as a lead ministry emphasis. An example is the children's ministry. To lead with one emphasis doesn't mean that others will not get attention. It simply means that the church will address other ministries as they relate to the lead ministry. This approach may be especially helpful where unhealthy conflict or other troubles have prevailed by focusing on something where there is strong agreement.

Within the context of such an exercise, it is appropriate to introduce the concept of *dreaming*. The people should be encouraged to think back to the original dream of the founders if it is an older church and to re-dream that dream in the context of today's ministry.

With this basic approach to planning, you may be able to take members a step at a time toward longer-range planning. In the beginning stages of this effort, the leader can focus on the church's self-image. One way to do this is to ask the people to respond to questions such as these:

- What does our church do well?
- What are our strengths?
- What good things about our church are on the community grapevine?
- What things about our church would you like to be on the community grapevine?

It is not suggested here that you focus on *strengths versus weakness* assessment. People too easily know the weaknesses. Focus on the strengths, and the weaknesses will be addressed. When a congregation expands its strengths, the church becomes more effective in mission. The companion truth is that when a church becomes taken up with weaknesses, the church begins to lose the strengths it has.

Retain the information you have gathered for future use. Allow this information to come alive and help tell the story of the church. Use it to help determine what steps should be taken next. Use it in preaching to show the strengths and challenges of the church.

Moving Ahead

Moving ahead implies, among other things, staying connected to the church's past. Indeed, in many single-staff churches, people are more attached to the past than pointed to the future. Ignoring or fighting this attachment always means trouble for a pastoral leader. To overcome a pre-occupation with the past and to use it for good, celebrate it and learn to tie new ministries to the helpful aspects of that past. Where possible, show how changes are true to these traditions of the church.

Use a Leadership Group

If the church already has a council or cabinet consisting of leaders of programs and major committees, use it as the base of planning and support of the overall ministry. If no such group exists, either formally organize one with church approval (or permission) or simply meet with such people on an informal basis.

In a small church where few qualified people are available for council and committee assignments, consider the following suggestion. Form one task team. Decide on the major areas of ministry such as worship, Bible study, youth ministry, stewardship, and outreach and missions. Bring together a leader from each of these areas to form a group. The leadership of the group depends on the matters to be discussed. When Bible study is the focus, then the Bible study leader is the chairperson of the group, and everyone else serves on the Bible study committee. The same would be true for the other major areas. This group, under the leadership of the pastor, could serve as a *church council* to coordinate the entire ministry of the church.

Choose the Curriculum Resources

Remember, the *curriculum* of the church is all that the church does to carry out its commission to be the church. *Curriculum resources* are the Bible, lesson guides, audiovisual materials, and other items used to assist the church in fulfilling its commission.

As the pastoral leader, you will need to be involved in selecting curriculum resources, even as you are involved in helping the church determine its curriculum. Study what the church says it wants to be and do. Gather information from denominational offices and other desirable sources about curriculum materials that fit your church. Ask for samples for this study.

Use the *leadership group* mentioned above or another appropriate group to assess current curriculum materials that are being used. Make recommendations for the church decision-making process to act upon if changes are desired. Once adopted for use, provide interpretation sessions on how to use curriculum materials. Keep reading the materials on a regular basis after adoption to assure their relevance to the church's needs.

Mobilize the Workers

The minister must remember the pithy words of the person who said, "Pastor, we will do anything you can get us to do." Like it or not, this statement places the burden of leadership on the single-staff minister. It also implies that there are people who will share ministry responsibilities if they are properly recruited, trained, and supported.

People want to know where they are being led. A leader should know what is to be accomplished and how to accomplish it. Once these issues are established, it is time to recruit persons for ministry positions.

Recruiting. In some cases the pastor is the person best suited to recruit workers. Recruiting requires special skills as well as prayer and patience. Be sensitive to each person's needs. Some nominees need all the facts about the potential ministry you are asking them to consider. Others are interested mostly in how it will help those involved. Still others like to be part of a team effort and provide and receive support from team members. Also, some are attracted by the challenge of the task. Be sensitive to personal preferences.

With appropriate sensitivity to personal preferences, refer to the following suggestions for face-to-face contact with persons to be recruited:

1. *Schedule a time that is convenient to the person.* Avoid asking someone to make a serious decision hurriedly or in a place that is not conducive to thoughtful consideration of your request.

2. *Recruit in the atmosphere of prayer.* Pray for the person to be asked to serve and for yourself, especially for yourself if the person does not respond positively.

3. *Explain clearly the ministry task you are asking the person to accept.* Include what is expected, the potential joys and heartaches, the resources available, the names of others with whom the person will work closely, and the potential for personal growth.

4. *Furnish printed information to leave with the person.* This may include a brief list of things he or she is expected to do, resources available, copies of helpful materials, and any pertinent church document(s).

5. *Allow the person adequate time to think and pray before giving a decision.* Ask the potential leader if a week is enough time to make a decision. Suggest that you will call in a few days to make another appointment to receive the decision.

6. Complete the task as promised. Call in a few days to see if additional information is needed and to make an appointment to receive the decision. If the answer is negative, thank the person for his or her consideration and leave open the possibility of other service. If the person responds positively, provide any further information needed and review information already provided.

Developing workers. The pastor may get some help from outside sources, such as denominational training events, but most of the development of volunteer workers will be the responsibility of the pastor. This is a biblical role as indicated in Eph 4:11–13: *Pastors and teachers are to equip the saints for the work of ministry.*

First Peter 2:9 describes all Christians as ministers, or priests. Every member of the faith family through Jesus Christ is to do the work of the church. A primary task for the equipping pastor is to ingrain this biblical role of ministry in the minds of the people. First Peter 4:10 reminds us that all spiritual gifts are to be used in serving one another and not to be exploited for self. Remember that for many people, the best use of their gifts does not always parallel the way they earn their paychecks. The most creative expression of their gifts may be in and through volunteer ministry.

As pastoral leader, you probably have more Bible knowledge than do the volunteers with whom you work. Helping them grow in such knowledge can be one of your most challenging and rewarding tasks. Provide systematic Bible study for spiritual enrichment, but also periodically help members deal with the knotty theological and biblical problems. If such study is led by someone the workers trust, they can handle more than one might suppose. Make sure you are trustworthy, and then go for it!

Workers need someone to walk with them and be available to provide guidance as they do their tasks. As the pastor, you may even have to take the leadership in a ministry for a time while providing in-service training for a newly recruited worker and potential leader.

Take the younger student ministry as an example. As a minister you may have served as a youth leader and can offer expertise no one else in the church possesses. You may find that the best way you can spend some of your time is to work with this age group until you can train someone to take the leadership.

Workers need to know how to handle problems and conflict. You can offer classes or seminars on how to minister at such times before those times come. People need to know that problems will arise and conflict will occur. Teach them that not all conflict is bad and that it may occur because of a difference over how the church can best do its work. When people care deeply about something, they will disagree about what is best. Sharpen your own skills and knowledge about problem solving and conflict management. Then teach volunteers about them.

Volunteers want to know how they are doing with their work. Provide some specific time for workers to tell how they are feeling about it. Encourage questions. Ask questions. Offer assistance and give encouragement. Watch for signs of stress and/or dropout. Do prevention. Show that you genuinely care for them. A follow-up note in which you can give substantive evaluation as well as encouragement is always fitting.

Celebrating Success. As the team of workers becomes more effective and ministry becomes a function of many rather than the task of a few, there must be *recognition* and *celebration*.

How do you show recognition? Handwritten notes are effective. Praise in front of others, when possible, is also appropriate. Recognize achievement and service during a worship service or at another gathering. For example, you could (1) plan a service to recognize and express appreciation to church leaders and (2) work with the church council to host a covered dish meal to honor the teachers.

Be abundant with two phrases: (1) *Thank you so much for the contributions you make to our church,* and (2) *I am very proud of you.* Be consistent, factual, and Christian in the practice of public praise.

Memorable accomplishments, both small and large, can be celebrated with great profit for the entire church as well as for individual workers. You and your church should know how best to celebrate. Decide specific criteria about celebration at the same time you plan for ministry with the church council or committee. However you decide to celebrate, let it be intentional and consistent but not superficial.

Concluding a Ministry

Concluding a ministry depends to a large extent on the conditions present. In the usual closure, celebration and a focus on the future can be mixed with the tears of departure to help strengthen all involved. If conditions are unpleasant, however, negotiation may be the best approach.

As the departing minister, you seek to leave the church poised for life and ministry without you. That means you either do not start ministries that cannot survive without you, or you make sure new ministries have leaders in place and can succeed after you are gone (this usually requires a few years).

Seek to leave all the aspects of the church in a healthier state than when you arrived. Discuss with them the options they should explore as to the interim period. Remember that the church belongs to God, and you are a steward of the local expression of that divinely ordained institution.

Notes for the Journey

Certain matters are vital all along the way. Remember, people do not want to be managed; they want to be led. *If you want to manage someone, manage yourself.* You must manage your time and resources. Use a pocket calendar or notebook. Record major events first, such as church meetings, conferences, and family commitments; then schedule other events and appointments according to priority. Jotting down specifics is a vital behavior. A Chinese proverb says, "The faintest ink endures longer than the strongest memory." Learning to impose a disciplined approach to memoranda will offend few people and accomplish more.

Here are basic guidelines to enhance your ministry, particularly when serving small and rural congregations:

1. Communicate clearly and persistently.
2. Learn what needs to be accomplished and pursue that.
3. Make your agenda decent and open.
4. Own the willingness to take risks because success is not assured.
5. Keep a calendar and publicize events well ahead.
6. Follow good business practices consistent with Christian principles.
7. Know the difference between leading and pushing.
8. Cultivate the ability and willingness to share the power.
9. Develop your own personal ministry so as to be more than just a "professional" minister.

10. Learn and use good telephone and computer manners.
11. Guard study and prayer times, and let the people know when those times are.
12. Guard and practice quality family time, even if you are a family of one.
13. Visit members, comfort the sick and disabled, and participate in community affairs.
14. Relate to fellow ministers in a mutually helpful way. Consider forming a support group for study and mutual counsel.
15. View every person as one for whom Christ died and, therefore, as the object of the church's ministry.
16. Ask for specific help from people who can provide it.
17. Make prayer, Bible study, and spiritual direction priorities in your ministry.
18. Discover, reinforce, and practice the importance of Christian education in the life of your congregation.
19. Learn good writing skills and practice them.
20. Be a loving and caring human being.
21. Keep your promises.
22. Make a lifetime goal of being a skilled servant leader, after the pattern of Jesus Christ.

Be secure in your calling. The calling to be the only paid staff person (and perhaps also bivocational) is indeed a challenging one. It isn't impossible, however. Success depends on many things. Be as wise as a serpent and as harmless as a dove. Remember, that according to Rom 8:28, God is at work in everything, both good and bad (though God doesn't author the bad) to bring about good for those who are called for God's purpose. You are linked with a powerful partner in your ministry, and that ensures the foundation for successful ministry

Chapter 20

GETTING STARTED IN A NEW MINISTRY

Bruce P. Powers

Getting started in a new position is not difficult. However, getting off to a good start that will forge a productive partnership requires effort by the new minister and by a knowledgeable person or small committee in the church.

There are three phases to getting started: *making the transition* (four to eight weeks before arriving), *getting oriented* (about one week of intense orientation and four weeks followup), and *developing a data base* (about three months).

Phase 1: Making the Transition

The first phase requires four to eight weeks before moving to a new position. This time is used for the new person and for the church to get all their affairs in order so that from the first day both parties can give themselves unreservedly to each other.

For the Church. This phase allows time for getting the person's office ready; approving financial arrangements; agreeing on housing matters; and making plans for welcoming, orientation, and so forth.

For the New Minister. All your responsibilities to a previous congregation or job must be terminated or clearly agreed upon with the new church. All personal business needing to be resolved should be cleared prior to the move. You should study information from the new church such as church history, constitution and bylaws, and organizational structure. You should acquaint yourself with information about staff members and key volunteer leaders. Then write brief notes to these people expressing your anticipation in working with them. And don't forget those professional colleagues who care for you; send them a note about your move and give your new address.

Make all arrangements regarding the move, particularly of your household and office items. Close local accounts and arrange to transfer or open new personal and business accounts. Send change-of-address notifications to all individuals, businesses, and organizations with which you wish to maintain contact. Make plans for housing and your personal and family needs.

Keep your contact person apprised of your progress and maintain regular contact in regard to arrangements the new church is making for your move and the first few weeks as their new minister. Work on messages, worship services, and special presentations for which you will be responsible. At the same time, remember to give of your best to the church family you are leaving. Work diligently to say good-bye in appropriate ways so that they (and you) will remember the wonderful season during which you served among them.

Phase 2: Getting Oriented

The purpose of this phase is to get the new person acquainted with the persons, facilities, procedures, and ministries of the new church and with the leaders and resources of the community. This requires about one week of intense orientation and three to four weeks of follow-up activities.

For the Church. The responsibility for orienting new staff members definitely belongs to the church. Usually orientation can be conducted by persons closely involved with various areas of the church's life, but the overall schedule should be planned and directed by the supervisor of the new person. In the case of a new pastor, the orientation would be planned and offered by an appropriate lay leader, such as the chairperson of the personnel committee or of the deacons. Although much of this information will have been discussed during interviews, it is helpful to make a complete review.

Here are things that should be included. Naturally, adjustments would be necessary depending on the level of experience and the background of the new minister.

- Introduce staff members and tour the facilities.
- Tell how the staff is organized and how the various programs and ministries are administered. Review and answer questions about primary documents such as the constitution and bylaws, personnel manual, and church directory.
- Review how the church operates through its deacons, church council, committees, teams, and so on.
- Describe the church's programs, ministries, calendar of events, and schedule of services; interpret the personality of the congregation; review the church's history.

- Explain employee benefits, personnel policies, salary plan, pay dates, work hours, holidays, and other pertinent items.
- Review and discuss job expectations and office protocol.
- Tour the community. Introduce the new person to other local ministers and denominational representatives as well as to important business contacts with whom he or she will work such as the postmaster, bank officials, funeral home director, and social service representatives. Visit the church's mission(s), if any. Have an informal staff luncheon to allow the new person to get better acquainted with coworkers.

The intense orientation of the first week gradually subsides as the new person settles into a daily work routine. The orientation continues, however, at the initiative of the new staff person. For example, get-acquainted and orientation meetings with church program leaders, committees, and appearances at church functions should have high priority.

For the New Minister. Check signals once a week with the person(s) responsible for your initial orientation. Clarify any impressions about the work and expectations of the church. Ask if you are missing anything. Look ahead to other responsibilities that might slip up on you such as Vacation Bible School, budget projections for a new church year, or an annual revival. Find out what has been done in the past, what has been planned (if anything), and suggestions about what must be done and when.

Plan a schedule for visiting church families. Ask if there are some priorities for these initial visits, the reasons, and what might be expected. For example, a key leader may not have been favorably impressed with your coming to the church and may need reassuring.

You will see many needs, but don't try to remake the church into an ideal situation during these early months. Rather, find what is good and affirm the people. Get acquainted with them and how this unique congregation lives and functions. Withhold for a while your judgments and your ideas for significant changes.

Right now you must earn the congregation's trust and come to understand and appreciate the people, the organization, the facilities, and the community as they are. Once you truly love and have become a part of them, you will be in a much better position to help the congregation deal with shortcomings.

Phase 3: Developing a Data Base

The third phase of getting started is an extension of the basic orientation begun in phase 2. During this time the new minister develops the knowledge and secures the information that will guide his or her planning and strategy for this place of service. This phase requires about three months.

For the Church. As the new minister develops a data base, more information may be needed than was obtained during orientation. Cooperate by furnishing pertinent data and/or referring the minister to persons knowledgeable about the needed information.

For the New Minister. This third phase is a professional way of equipping yourself to provide the most effective ministry in a church. The database you assemble informs every decision in your ministry and becomes the foundation for effective church administration. In the absence of such information, decisions for planning, organizing, staffing, budgeting, and evaluating will be based on emotion and personal opinion—an approach to leadership that tends to create conflict.

Use the following items to guide the collection and development of information that will assist you and your congregation in making good decisions about your future together.

Church Ministry Database

I. General

1. Name and address of church
2. Constitution and bylaws
3. Incorporation and other legal data

II. History

1. The church's history: its beginnings, major developments, and changes
2. Significant events and personalities

III. The Church's Community

1. The church's location, history, socioeconomic situation, population trends, business and industry, educational resources, civic and social life, and such
2. The church's immediate community
3. How has the community situation affected the church's programs and ministry?
4. How is the church seeking to meet the challenge of its community?

IV. Membership

1. Active membership in church and in organizations
2. Inactive membership in church and in organizations
3. How has church and organizational membership varied numerically each year for the last fifteen years?
4. Demographic data on church membership (including age profile, location of residences, etc.)
5. The church's targeted area(s) for outreach

V. Grouping and Grading
1. How are organizations set up and graded (age, sex, etc.)?
2. How are decisions made to start new units/classes/groups?
3. How are decisions made to merge or disband organizations or units?

VI. Curriculum

1. How does the church select organizational resources and curriculum materials?
2. What resources and curriculum materials are approved or recommended for use in the various organizations/units?
3. What process is used to coordinate selecting, purchasing, and distributing church materials?

VII. Cooperative Ministries

1. How does the church participate in the work of the association? the state and regional groups? national and international bodies?
2. How does the church cooperate with secular community organizations (such as schools and clubs) and with other local religious organizations?

VIII. Building and Equipment

1. Survey of church property
2. Architectural drawing of facilities
3. Appraised value of church property and outstanding debts
4. Inventory of equipment available for church use
5. Plan for supervision/servicing of building and equipment
6. Floor plan of church facilities, with dimensions of each room, furniture and equipment in each, current assignment, and schedule for use

IX. Finance

1. Church budget
2. Stewardship plan (planning and supporting the budget)
3. Total annual income and expenditures for the last ten years
4. Administrative plan for receipt and disbursement of funds

X. Records and Reports

1. What kinds of records (membership, attendance, activities, etc.) are kept? Who keeps them? Where? For how long?
2. What information is reported? To whom? When?

XI. Communications

1. Administrative plan for church communications
2. How is the church's ministry interpreted to the public?

XII. Outreach and Ministry

1. How are members being trained and motivated to share their witness on the job and in the community?
2. What are the general attitudes related to evangelism? to missions? to Christian service projects?
3. What specific approaches are used (or have been used) to reach non-Christians in the community? church visitors?
4. How does the church receive and assimilate new members?
5. How are benevolence funds received and distributed?

XIII. Leadership and Administration

1. What style of leadership does the congregation expect?
2. What are the principles, policies, and procedures that guide church administration?
3. How are volunteer leaders recruited, trained, nominated, and elected?

XIV. Organization

1. Diagram each program and organization (show the relation of each group to the overall program and the lines of responsibility and authority now in operation).
2. What are the reporting and coordinating responsibilities for each member of the ministerial staff?
3. What informal working relationships are important? With whom? Under what conditions?

XV. Planning, Coordinating, and Evaluating

1. By whom and when are planning, coordinating, and evaluating done for the church? for church programs? for the staff?
2. How is the work of the church evaluated? the work of church programs? the work of staff members?
3. What are the appeal procedures in case of disagreement among groups or persons in the congregation or on the church staff?

Building a Ministry Team

Shared ministry is more than a concept; it is a biblical imperative. Simply going through the steps described in phases 1, 2, and 3 will not ensure an effective start. These activities must be undergirded by an intense desire to become part of a ministry team. This approach includes developing a work-family commitment to caring about, sharing with, and supporting one another in common tasks.

In addition to calendar-work and regular planning, staff meetings should include time specifically for (1) reviewing personal needs and job pressures, (2) clarifying perceptions of how staff members are relating to one another, and (3) sharing in fellowship and worship. This approach will enhance the team concept and will make routine work more enjoyable.

These ideas for getting started are a way to move into an effective and personally satisfying ministry. By following these suggestions, you will have the knowledge, skills, and support system that will prepare you, your staff colleagues, and the congregation for exciting years together!

Chapter 21

FINDING FULFILLMENT IN MINISTRY

Bruce P. Powers

T he best approach to getting and keeping a ministry position—and enjoying it—is twofold: (1) perform job responsibilities at a level acceptable in your church, and (2) meet your personal needs at a level acceptable to you and your loved ones. One approach cannot be emphasized to the neglect of the other! The way job responsibilities and personal needs mesh is the clearest indicator of future job success.

Paying the Rent

The starting point is effective job performance. Life is made up of a lot of things you have to do. I call this "paying the rent."[1] For example, in keeping myself fit to live and work with, there are certain things I must do. I must bathe, brush my teeth, keep my body healthy and my mind reasonably alert, and maintain a wholesome outlook on life.

Look at your job. What are the minimum job expectations that will make you and others feel good about your work? This list of expectations is what I mean by things you have to do to pay the rent. To whom are you responsible? the deacons? personnel committee? pastor or other minister? church business administrator? Their expectations are a large part of paying the rent.

Paying the rent is a two-dimensional activity; that is, you can approach the same work in two entirely different ways. One leads to satisfaction, and the other leads to dissatisfaction.

As shown in figure 21.1, the reaction to any dimension of life begins with a choice between an *active response* or a *passive response*. From that point the direction is set. We may progress slowly or rapidly, but the potential is limited by the choice of an active or passive response.

One way of viewing this concept is that each route begins with the way we respond to paying the rent. An active response puts me in control of my life. A passive response is "surrender."

"But isn't the minister to give away his or her life?" you ask. Yes, if that is the *active* choice to achieve the desired results of your life. But, no, if it is a *passive* surrender because you are immobilized and cannot deal with the pressures and tugs of priorities in your life. Results are achieved by *active* ministers.

But beware! There often is a major misunderstanding about paying the rent. Some active persons get trapped by paying the rent and paying the rent and *paying the rent*. They never stop to calculate what is appropriate in light of their personal needs; they overpay in one area while draining themselves in other areas.

The appropriate choice is to *calculate* the rent (something many of us never do), then pay the rent perhaps 110 percent. Beyond that, channel your energy and resources into other areas that are important to you. After calculating the rent, if you have difficulties with paying the cost, or if you are unwilling to pay the cost, you have four options![2]

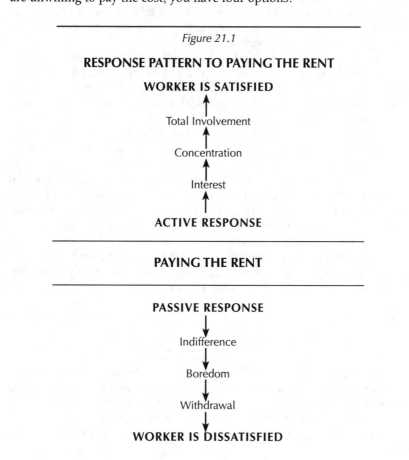

Figure 21.1

RESPONSE PATTERN TO PAYING THE RENT

WORKER IS SATISFIED

↑

Total Involvement

↑

Concentration

↑

Interest

↑

ACTIVE RESPONSE

PAYING THE RENT

PASSIVE RESPONSE

↓

Indifference

↓

Boredom

↓

Withdrawal

↓

WORKER IS DISSATISFIED

Four Options for Getting and Keeping a Position

When matching personal needs and job potential, you always have at least *four options* for a job and even for your profession:

1. Stay and accept the situation.
2. Leave or get out of the situation.
3. Change yourself.
4. Change the situation/organization.

The first option is the grin-and-bear-it approach. This approach sometimes is a conscious choice, but more often it is the result of a passive ministry stance. We gradually lose drive, and survival becomes the primary concern. The grin-and-bear-it approach is a yielding, no-decision stance, halfway between retreating and advancing.

The second option—leave—is always a viable choice. Whenever one's basic values are threatened and alternatives are exhausted, resigning may be the only route that preserves personal integrity. This option must be distinguished from forced termination, which might be a consequence of the first option. Leaving by your choice is an aggressive action designed to assist you in meeting personal needs and values.

The third option—change yourself—is designed to help you bring your values and skills more in line with the needs of others. This option assumes that you have some areas in your life in which you can become more tolerant and harmonious; and, as situations change, you can make your share of adjustments related to common tasks.

The fourth option is to change the situation or the organization. Under certain circumstances you might choose to implement change in order to accommodate better your needs and values. This choice must be made based on the cost to you personally as well as to the church. This option assumes that you will make changes that improve your status while helping or at least not harming the institution. So, in the face of any problem, you always have these *four options*. Each is acceptable if you look logically and sincerely for the best answer for all involved.

My particular bias is a combination of the third and fourth options—a combination of changing myself and the situation. This, in my judgment, is the basis for an effective, long-term relationship with a church or other employer.

Choosing a Strategy

Option 1. Grin and bear it. If this strategy is preferred, such as surviving in a position until retirement, do not take major initiatives. Rather, focus on maintaining existing work and good interpersonal relationships.

Determine what has to be done and at what performance level. Then do your best to meet these minimum expectations. When asked to do something, make no promises unless you will follow through. Work out a schedule for the time you are able and willing to give, then try to maintain it.

Maintain supportive relationships wherever possible. Expand the time you are with people of the congregation, going with them and being with them in as many church activities as possible. Do not respond directly to criticism. Counsel with a trusted friend, spouse, or mentor.

Option 2. Leave. In many ways this decision is the most difficult to make. It involves leaving a known situation for the unknown, which may turn out to be worse. Yet this option may be the best choice under intolerable circumstances.

This option should include an accurate assessment of the issues leading to separation. If you have not made a thorough assessment before you decided to leave, do this before moving to a new situation. Try to answer these questions: What are my values? What are the job possibilities? What are my life circumstances? What changes must be made?

When facing a change, plan ahead. If you are convinced that a move is necessary, negotiate with the person(s) to whom you are responsible for a phaseout period. This phaseout period is a time, usually three to six months, during which you fulfill your job duties while seeking another position. The church avoids conflict, and you have a support system while seeking new work.

Consult with your family, trusted friends, and a mentor or denominational leader who helps with ministry transitions. Then contact your school's placement office, a state or regional placement consultant, and professional colleagues who might recommend you. Prepare a résumé that accurately tells the benefits you could provide a church.

If you have been fired abruptly or have been out of work for some time, consider attending a vocational guidance workshop, a career assessment program, or seeking personal counseling. Ask the persons mentioned above for advice about vocational assessment.

Follow-through is essential for this option, so focus on personal assessment concerning your job skills and personal needs. What was out of balance that caused the termination? Searching and redirection are necessary; otherwise, termination may happen again.

Option 3. Change yourself. This choice requires knowing job requirements and developing and/or improving needed skills. How do you do this? Review basic textbooks such as this one and resources available from the Alban Institute. Consider attending conferences or classes offered by your denomination or by a seminary or divinity school. If your denomination has a minister support office, request information about resources and recommendations.[3] Seek feedback about your job performance and interpersonal skills. Find areas of weakness and make plans to improve.

Option 4. Change the situation/organization. Although a person some-times seeks to change a situation for selfish reasons, most are sincerely seeking to help the church become more effective.

If you believe your motives are pure and the job and working relation-ships are the problem, you may seek to change the situation to make it more compatible with your perception of what is needed. This approach involves a high degree of risk and an assumption that if it is good for you it is good for the congregation (which may not be so!). If you are not suc-cessful, you will need to switch to one of the previous options.

Guiding Principles

1. *Remember, you always have four options.* The best way is to assess who you are and what a position requires; then make your own decisions about the future. The most harmful situation for you and for a church is for them to make the decision.

2. *The pastor may not always be right, but the pastor is the person to whom the congregation looks for overall leadership.* If you are not the pastor, you always are subject to the pastor's perception of whether you are pay-ing the rent. If you are the pastor, remember that the congregation and/or the official representatives of your church or denomination will make the judgment. If you disagree, you must negotiate, keeping in mind your four options.

3. *Before accepting a new position, explore all facets of the situation.* Know to whom you will report, and get a clear understanding of the expectations for the job as listed in the position description and as interpreted by those who would evaluate your work.

4. *Don't oversell yourself.* When considering a job, we too often say, "Yes, I can do this; I can do that!" as the people name off all the high ex-pectations they have. The church also can oversell itself to you. The result often is discouragement and disillusionment for them and for you. Be real-istic, set achievable goals, and make good decisions that will serve you and the church well, not only now but also in the future.

5. *Maintain your anchor points.* Amid change and increasing pressure, try to keep some points stable. Maintain your recreation times with family and friends, keep your body healthy, and protect your worship and study time.

6. *Make a plan and follow it.* Where or what do you want to be five years from now? Describe these goals on the right-third of a large sheet of paper. On the left-third, list where or what you are now. In the middle, list the steps that you need to take to achieve your goal(s). This step is the begin-ning of your plan for the future. Now look at your present situation and evaluate your *four options.* Make plans for tomorrow!

NOTES

Chapter 1

* Material related to the nature and purpose of the church is adapted from Daniel Aleshire, "Christian Education and Theology," *Christian Education Handbook*, Bruce P. Powers, ed., (Nashville: Broadman & Holman, 1996), 14–18.

1. These principles were developed by Bruce P. Powers and first published in Bruce P. Powers, *Covenant Ministry* (Cary, NC: Baptist State Convention of North Carolina, 1999).

2. From mid to late twentieth century, a developing theology of lay ministry and an emphasis on *every believer a minister* resulted in a blurring of the distinctions between clergy and laity in regard to authority and responsibility. Today leadership is largely shared among believers based on calling, giftedness, spiritual maturity, and faithfulness to Christ and the church. Although ministers provide primary direction for ecclesiastical matters, laity in many traditions take the lead in dealing with finances, buildings, property, and various programs and ministries offered in the church and community.

3. Patricia Cranton has helped adult educators focus on ways their lives are changed and how they can assist others in life-changing learning experiences. Her insights in *Professional Development as Transformative Learning* (San Francisco: Jossey-Bass, 1996) and *Understanding and Promoting Transformative Learning* (San Francisco: Jossey-Bass, 1994) provide a frame work that can be adapted in a church-related context by substituting "ministry professional" and "ministers" in place of "teaching professional" and "educators."

4. For those in ministry, theological reflection is central to personal and organizational renewal. Theological reflection is a major component in the formation components of theological education, particularly in doctor of ministry programs.

5. Jack Mezirow, *Transformative Dimensions of Adult Learning* (San Francisco: Jossey-Bass, 1991), 42.

6. Cranton, *Professional Development*, 96.

7. Mezirow, *Transformative Dimensions*.

8. Cranton, *Professional Development*, 20.

9. Mezirow, *Transformative Dimensions*, 145.

10. Ibid.

11. Lee G. Bolman and Terrence E. Deal, *Reframing Organizations: Artistry, Choice, and Leadership* (San Francisco: Jossey-Bass, 2003).

12. James McGregor Burns, *Leadership* (New York: Harper & Row, 1978).

13 Definition by James T. Roberson Jr.

Chapter 2

1. The obvious differences among denominations in which some ministers are *called* and others *appointed* require some adjustments in a minister's start-up work.

2. Also see chapter 20, "Getting Started in a New Position."

3. For help crafting ministry strategy, see items in "Resources for Church Administration." Also see Robert D. Dale, *Leading Edge* (Nashville: Abingdon, 1996) for a biblical perspective on ministry strategies.

4. Robert D. Dale, *To Dream Again* (Eugene OR: Wipf & Stock, 2004).

5. For more information, see chapter 8, "Planning and Budgeting."

6. See chapter 4 for information on working with volunteers.

Chapter 4

1. Committees and teams are the terms most often used for various work groups in churches and related organizations. Whenever committees are referenced in this book, the information applies also to teams and other work groups with similar duties. Organizational details are given in chapter 3.

2. Marlene Wilson, *How to Mobilize Church Volunteers* (Minneapolis: Augsburg, 1983), 28–36.

3. For a full discussion of the "synectic" problem-solving method, see George Prince, *The Practice of Creativity* (New York: Harper & Row, 1970).

4. For a more complete exploration of managing meetings, see Robert D. Dale, *Ministers as Leaders* (Nashville: Broadman, 1984), especially chapter 8.

5. For helpful information on parliamentary rule and its applications, see Henry M. Robert III and others, *Robert's Rules of Order Newly Revised in Brief* (Cambridge, MA: Da Capo, 2004), or go to www.robertsrules.com.

6. Here's a formula for specifying the number of relational bonds in a work group: (the number of staffers) times (the number of staffers minus one) divided by two equals the total bonds. For example, a staff of two contains only 1 bond, a staff of four has 6 bonds, a staff of ten involves 45 bonds, and a staff of fifty consists of 1,225 bonds.

7. For a complete discussion of how controlling actions impact congregations negatively, see Robert D. Dale, *Surviving Difficult Church Members* (Nashville: Abingdon, 1984).

8. For discussions of organizational climate, see Robert D. Dale, *To Dream Again* (Nashville: Broadman, 1981), 83–85, 91–95; Robert F. Allen and Charlotte Kraft, *The Organizational Unconscious* (Englewood Cliffs, NJ: Prentice-Hall, 1982); and Dale, *Ministers as Leaders*, especially chapter 9.

9. Edwin L. Baker, "Managing Organizational Culture," *Management Review*, July 1980, 8.

Chapter 5

1. Legal and ethical issues change rapidly. Current information may be secured from the National Association of Church Business Administrators (www.nacba.net), from publications recommended by a professor of administration at a divinity school or seminary, or from the director of church relations at your denominational office. Portions of this section have been adapted from the previous editions, prepared by Mark Short and compiled by Bruce P. Powers.

2. If you are unsure about the specific procedures for your church, consult the denominational office in your state/association/district.

3. This practice varies from denomination to denomination. The focus in this chapter is on churches with a congregational-style polity.

4. Mark Short, a contributor to the first edition, suggested this analogy and the characteristics that follow.

Chapter 7

1. This chapter is designed to assist church leaders with the specifics of fiscal responsibility, which usually are handled through the church office. The material included supplements the information in chapter 6 and provides background information for planning and budgeting presented in chapter 8. Information in this chapter has been adapted from material in the original edition prepared by Mark Short and compiled by Bruce P. Powers, editor.

2. Request information from your denominational office, religious bookstore, or a theological school.

Chapter 9

1. Chapters 9 and 10 have information and forms related to weddings and other specialized activities held in church facilities.

Chapter 10

1. For a useful classic book and a more recent resource on ministering to premarried, see Russell L. Dicks, *Premarital Guidance* (Philadelphia: Fortress, 1963) and Bobbye and Britton Wood, *Marriage Readiness* (Nashville: Broadman, 1983).

2. Jerry and Karen Hayner, *Marriage Can Be Meaningful* (Nashville: Broadman, 1983).

3. For an extremely helpful resource for planning wedding ceremonies, see Marion D. Aldridge, *The Pastor's Guidebook: A Manual for Worship* (Nashville: Broadman, 1984), 72–97.

4. Bill G. Bruster and Robert D. Dale, *How to Encourage Others: A Resource for Preaching and Caring* (Nashville: Broadman, 1983), 69.

5. Delos Miles, *Introduction to Evangelism* (Nashville: Broadman, 1983), 287–99.

Chapter 11

1. Resources in the bibliography and those available in book stores and libraries are usually in the categories of *church communications* or *church marketing* and include these terms in the title or subtitle. Denominational offices and theological schools often maintain a list of recommended resources and information about workshops and conferences for church leaders.

Chapter 12

1. The bibliography includes several helpful resources dealing with the issues discussed in this chapter. One that has been developed by a lawyer at the Campbell University Law School and widely used in North Carolina is Lynn R. Buzzard, *Church Policy Manual: A Legal and Practical Guide for Developing Church Policies* (Cary, NC: Baptist State Convention of North Carolina, 2004).

2. For an annual license fee, there are organizations that handle permission and royalty arrangements. One such organization that is widely used by religious organizations is CCLI (Christian Copyright Licensing International). Information is available online at www.ccli.com/US, or by writing CCLI, 17201 N.E. Sacramento Street, Portland, OR 97230.

Chapter 13

1. James M. Kouzes and Barry Z. Posner, *Credibility* (San Francisco: Jossey-Bass, 2003), 14.

2. John C. Maxwell, *There's No Such Thing as "Business" Ethics* (New York: Warner, 2003), 21ff.

3. Several resources that would be helpful are listed in the bibliography. For a manual that also includes a computer disk with forms and recommended guidelines, see the book by

Lynn Buzzard, *Church Policy Manual Guidebook*. This manual is published by and available from Church Administration Ministries, Baptist State Convention of North Carolina, 205 Convention Drive, Cary, NC 27511. Information is available online at http://www.ncbaptist.org/index.php?id=170.

Chapter 15

1. James L. Sullivan, *Rope of Sand with Strength of Steel* (Nashville: Convention Press, 1974), 119. See also, James L. Sullivan, "Nature and Importance of a Local Church," in *Baptist Polity* (Nashville: Broadman, 1983), 17–27.

Chapter 16

1. It is imperative that the persons who lead spiritual gift classes and/or inventories be careful not to lead a believer to feel that his or her gifts are less important than another's. As already pointed out in Scripture, gifts vary, but each is equally important in God's eyes.

Chapter 18

1. Robert and Carrie L. Dale, *Marriage: Partnership of the Committed* (Nashville: Sunday School Board of the Southern Baptist Convention, 1983).
2. "Teens' Private Moments Studied" (Raleigh, NC) *News and Observer*, 17 June 1984, 7C.
3. Steven Findlay and Gina Rogers-Gould, "The Pressure Is Starting to Get to Our Children," *USA Today*, 8 July 1983, 4D.
4. Charles William Stewart, *Person and Profession* (Nashville: Abingdon, 1974), 75–78.
5. James D. Glasse, *Putting It Together in the Parish* (Nashville, Abingdon, 1972), 40ff.
6. Many helpful resources are available on career development. A basic beginning book is Daniel J. Levinson and others, *The Seasons of a Man's Life* (New York: Knopf, 1978). The career framework used in this chapter draws heavily on Levinson's research.
7. For a complete discussion of this ministry support model, see Robert D. Dale, "The Minister of Youth: Developing a System of Support," in *The Work of the Minister of Youth*, comp. Bob R. Taylor (Nashville: Convention Press, 1982), 95–107.
8. This was observed as early as the 1980s, as noted in "Stress: Can We Cope?" *Time*, 6 June 1983, 48.
9. Hans Selye, *Stress without Distress* (New York: Signet, 1974), 11–51.
10. For an overview of burnout symptoms and causes, see Fred Lehr, *Clergy Burnout* (Minneapolis: Augsburg Fortress, 2006).

Chapter 21

1. I recall first using this term after reading James D. Glasse, *Putting It Together in the Parish* (Nashville: Abingdon, 1972).
2. I was helped in understanding these options when I read the process of vocational guidance presented in Len Sperry, and others, *You Can Make It Happen* (Reading, MA: Addison-Wesley, 1977). Most current career assessment processes include an assessment of one's gifts and calling and the relevance for various ministerial duties and contexts. Making good, informed decisions is the objective.
3. Some combination of career assessment resources, including materials, workshops, and counseling would be helpful. Additional information about the process of career assessment is included in chapter 18, "The Minister's Personal Life."

RESOURCES FOR CHURCH ADMINISTRATION

The items below are provided as references for additional information and study. This list includes resources from religious and secular publishers relating to the three sections of the book. Readers will need to determine the appropriate applications consistent with the Christian leadership and biblical guidelines presented in this text.

Section 1: How a Minister Relates to Organizations and to People

Ashhenas, Ron. *The Boundaryless Organization.* San Francisco: Jossey-Bass, 1995.

Barna, George. *The Power of Vision.* Ventura, CA: Regal, 2003.

Bass, Richard, ed. *Leadership in Congregations.* Herndon, VA: Alban, 2006.

Bolman, Lee G., and Terrance Deal. *Reframing Organizations.* San Francisco: Jossey-Bass, 1991.

Bolton, Robert, and Dorothy G. Bolton. *Social Style/Management Style.* New York: AMACOM, 1984.

Burns, James McGregor. *Leadership.* New York: Harper & Row, 1978.

Cranton, Patricia. *Professional Development as Transformative Learning.* San Francisco: Jossey-Bass, 1996.

Dale, Robert D. *Leading Edge: Leadership Strategies from the New Testament.* Nashville: Abingdon, 1996.

_____. *Ministers as Leaders.* Nashville: Broadman, 1984.

_____. *Surviving Difficult Church Members.* Nashville: Abingdon, 1984.

_____. *To Dream Again.* Nashville: Broadman, 1981.

Drucker, Peter F. *Managing in a Time of Great Change.* New York: Truman Talley/Dutton, 1995.

Granade, Nelson. *Lending Your Leadership: How Pastors Are Redefining Their Role in Community Life.* Herndon, VA: Alban, 2006.

Jones, O. Garfield. *Parliamentary Procedure at a Glance.* New York: Hawthorn Books, 1971.

330

Kouzes, James M., and Barry Posner. *The Leadership Challenge*. San Francisco: Jossey-Bass, 1995.

Laubach, David. *12 Steps to Congregational Transformation*. Valley Forge, PA: Judson, 2006.

Massey, Floyd, and Samuel B. McKinney. *Church Administration in the Black Perspective*. Valley Forge, PA: Judson, 2003.

Mezirow, Jack. *Learning as Transformation*. San Francisco: Jossey-Bass, 2000.

Oswald, Roy M. *New Beginnings: A Pastorate Start Up Workbook*. Herndon, VA: Alban, 1989.

Ott, E. Stanley. *Transform Your Church with Ministry Teams*. Grand Rapids, MI: Eerdmans, 2005.

Powers, Bruce P. *Growing Faith*. Eugene, OR: Wipf & Stock, 2003.

_____, ed. *Christian Education Handbook, Revised*. Nashville: Broadman & Holman, 1996.

Schaller, Lyle E. *Strategies for Change*. Nashville: Abingdon, 1993.

Smith, Douglas K. *Taking Charge of Change*. Reading, MA: Addison-Wesley, 1996.

Tapscott, Don. *The Digital Economy*. New York: McGraw-Hill, 1996.

Wilson, Marlene. *How to Mobilize Church Volunteers*. Minneapolis: Augsburg, 1983.

Section 2: How a Minister Performs Administrative Responsibilities

Allison, Michael, and Jude Kaye. *Strategic Planning for Nonprofit Organizations*. Hoboken, NJ: Wiley, 2003.

Bloss, Julie. *The Church Guide to Employment Law*. Matthews, NC: Christian Ministry Resources, 1999.

Buzzard, Lynn R. *Church Policy Manual Guidebook*. Cary, NC: Baptist State Convention of North Carolina, 2004.

Cadenhead, Al, Jr. *The Minister's Manual for Funerals*. Nashville: Broadman, 1988.

Flake, Floyd H., and others. *African American Church Management Handbook*. Valley Forge, PA: Judson, 2005.

Gonnerman, Frederick H. *Getting the Word Out*. Herdon, VA: Alban, 2003.

Henry, Jack A. *Basic Budgeting for Churches*. Nashville: Broadman & Holman, 1995.

Klann, Gene. *Crisis Leadership*. Greensboro, NC: Center for Creative Leadership, 2003.

Klopp, Henry. *The Ministry Playbook: Strategic Planning for Effective Churches*. Grand Rapids: Baker, 2002

Kouzes, James M., and Barry Posner. *Credibility*. San Francisco: Jossey-Bass, 1993.

Mallory, Sue *The Equipping Church*. Grand Rapids, MI: Zondervan, 2001

Malphurs, Aubrey. *Advanced Strategic Planning*. 2nd ed. Grand Rapids: Baker Books, 2005

Maxwell, John C. *There's No Such Thing as Business Ethics*. New York: Warner Business, 2003.

Pappas, Anthony G. *Entering the World of the Small Church*. Washington, DC: Alban, 1988.

Pollock, David R. *Business Management in the Local Church*. Chicago: Moody, 1996.

Powers, Bruce P., ed. *Christian Education Handbook, Revised*. Nashville: Broadman & Holman, 1996.

Rendle, Gilbert R. *Leading Change in the Congregation*. Herndon, VA: Alban, 1998.

Schaller, Lyle E. *The Interventionist*. Nashville: Abingdon, 2006.

Stewart, Carlyle Fielding, III. *African American Church Growth*. Nashville: Abingdon, 1994.

Stroman, James, et al. *Administrative Assistant's and Secretary's Handbook*. New York: AMACOM, 2003.

Vassallo, Wanda. *Church Communications Handbook*. Grand Rapids: Kregel, 1998.

Welch, Robert H. *Church Administration: Creating Efficiency for Effective Ministry*. Broadman & Holman, 2005.

————. *The Church Organization Manual*. Fort Worth: NACBA, 1993.

Section 3: How a Minister Develops Leadership and Ministry Skills

Burt, Steve. *The Little Church That Could: Raising Small Church Esteem*. Valley Forge: Judson, 2000.

Callahan, Kennon. *Small, Strong Congregations*. San Francisco: Josey-Bass, 2000.

Dale, Robert D. *Leading Edge: Leadership Strategies from the New Testament*. Nashville: Abingdon, 1996.

————. *Seeds for the Future: Growing Organic Leaders for Living Churches*. Atlanta: Chalice, 2005.

————. *Surviving Difficult Church Members*. Nashville: Abingdon, 1984.

Halaas, Gwen Wagstrom. *Clergy, Retirement, and Wholeness*. Herndon, VA: Alban, 2005.

Kouzes, James M., and Barry Posner. *The Leadership Challenge*. San Francisco: Jossey-Bass, 1995.

Lehr, Fred. *Clergy Burnout*. Minneapolis: Augsburg Fortress, 2006.

Martin, Glen, and Gary McIntosh. *The Issachar Factor: Understanding Trends that Confront Your Church.* Nashville: Broadman & Holman, 1994.

Morgan, Tony, and Tim Stevens. *Simply Strategic Volunteers: Empowering People for Ministry.* Loveland, CO: Group, 2005.

Sisk, Ronald D. *The Competent Pastor.* Herndon, VA: Alban, 2005.

Steinke, Peter L. *Healthy Congregations: A Systems Approach.* Herdon, VA: Alban, 2006.

Wilson, Marlene. *How to Mobilize Church Volunteers.* Minneapolis: Augsburg, 1983.

Web sites

Alban Institute, Congregational Resource Guide:
www.congregationalresources.org

National Association of Church Business Administrators:
www.nacba.net

Resources for African American Congregations:
www.congregationalresources.org/AAR/Introduction.asp